Florida's Turtles, Lizards, and Crocodilians

UNIVERSITY PRESS OF FLORIDA

Florida A&M University, Tallahassee
Florida Atlantic University, Boca Raton
Florida Gulf Coast University, Ft. Myers
Florida International University, Miami
Florida State University, Tallahassee
New College of Florida, Sarasota
University of Central Florida, Orlando
University of Florida, Gainesville
University of North Florida, Jacksonville
University of South Florida, Tampa
University of West Florida, Pensacola

Florida's Turtles, Lizards, and Crocodilians

A Guide to Their Identification and Habits

R. D. BARTLETT AND PATRICIA P. BARTLETT

University Press of Florida
Gainesville · Tallahassee · Tampa · Boca Raton
Pensacola · Orlando · Miami · Jacksonville · Ft. Myers · Sarasota

Library of Congress Cataloging-in-Publication Data
Bartlett, Richard D., 1938–
Florida's turtles, lizards, and crocodilians : a guide to their identification and habits /
R. D. Bartlett and Patricia P. Bartlett.
p. cm.
Includes bibliographical references and index.
ISBN 978-0-8130-3668-7 (alk. paper)
1. Reptiles—Florida—Identification. I. Bartlett, Patricia Pope, 1949– II. Title.
QL653.F6B375 2011
597.9'09759—dc22   2011011281

The University Press of Florida is the scholarly publishing agency for the State
University System of Florida, comprising Florida A&M University, Florida Atlantic
University, Florida Gulf Coast University, Florida International University, Florida
State University, New College of Florida, University of Central Florida, University
of Florida, University of North Florida, University of South Florida, and University
of West Florida.

University Press of Florida
15 Northwest 15th Street
Gainesville, FL 32611-2079
http://www.upf.com

Contents

Preface xiii
Introduction 1
Questions Currently without Answers 5
Florida's Habitats 9
Laws and Regulations 37
How to Use This Book 39
Keys to Florida Turtles, Crocodilians, and Lizards 43
Digital Photography 47
Reptiles Defined 51
Basics of Captive Care 53
A Note on Toxicity 59
A Note on Taxonomy 61
Reptiles 63

1. Turtles and Tortoises: Order Chelonia 65

How to Find Turtles and Tortoises in Florida 66
Marine Turtles 67

Typical Sea Turtles: Family Cheloniidae 68

    1. Loggerhead, *Caretta caretta* 69
    2. Green Turtle, *Chelonia mydas mydas* 70
    3. Atlantic Hawksbill, *Eretmochelys imbricata imbricata* 71
    4. Atlantic Ridley, *Lepidochelys kempii* 72

Leatherback Sea Turtle: Family Dermochelyidae 73

    5. Atlantic Leatherback, *Dermochelys coriacea coriacea* 73
Fresh and Brackish Water Turtles 75

Snapping Turtles: Family Chelydridae 75

    6. Common Snapping Turtle, *Chelydra serpentina serpentina* 77

      7. Florida Snapping Turtle, *Chelydra serpentina osceola* 78

    8. Alligator Snapping Turtle, *Macrochelys temminckii* 78

Mud and Musk Turtles: Family Kinosternidae 79

    9. Striped Mud Turtle, *Kinosternon baurii* 82

    10. Eastern Mud Turtle, *Kinosternon subrubrum subrubrum* 83

      11. Florida Mud Turtle, *Kinosternon subrubrum steindachneri* 84

    12. Loggerhead Musk Turtle, *Sternotherus minor minor* 85

      13. Stripe-necked Musk Turtle, *Sternotherus minor peltifer* 86

    14. Common Musk Turtle, *Sternotherus odoratus* 86

Basking and Box Turtles: Family Emydidae 87

    Spotted Turtle: Genus *Clemmys* 87

    15. Spotted Turtle, *Clemmys guttata* 88

    Chicken Turtle: Genus *Deirochelys* 90

    16. Eastern Chicken Turtle, *Deirochelys reticularia reticularia* 91

      17. Florida Chicken Turtle, *Deirochelys reticularia chrysea* 92

    Map Turtles: Genus *Graptemys* 92

    18. Barbour's Map Turtle, *Graptemys barbouri* 93

    19. Escambia Map Turtle, *Graptemys ernsti* 94

    Diamondback Terrapin: Genus *Malaclemys* 95

    20. Carolina Diamondback Terrapin, *Malaclemys terrapin centrata* 95

      21. Ornate Diamondback Terrapin, *Malaclemys terrapin macrospilota* 96

      22. Mississippi Diamondback Terrapin, *Malaclemys terrapin pileata* 97

      23. Mangrove Terrapin, *Malaclemys terrapin rhizophorarum* 97

      24. Florida East Coast Terrapin, *Malaclemys terrapin tequesta* 97

    Cooters and Sliders: Genera *Pseudemys* and *Trachemys* 98

    25. Eastern River Cooter, *Pseudemys concinna concinna* 98

      26. Suwannee Cooter, *Pseudemys concinna suwanniensis* 100

    27. Florida Cooter, *Pseudemys floridana floridana* 100

      28. Peninsula Cooter, *Pseudemys floridana peninsularis* 101

    29. Florida Red-bellied Cooter, *Pseudemys nelsoni* 102

30. Yellow-bellied Slider, *Trachemys scripta scripta* 103
   31. Red-eared Slider, *Trachemys scripta elegans* 104
Box Turtle: Genus *Terrapene* 105
32. Eastern Box Turtle, *Terrapene carolina carolina* 106
   33. Florida Box Turtle, *Terrapene carolina bauri* 107
   34. Gulf Coast Box Turtle, *Terrapene carolina major* 108
   35. Three-toed Box Turtle, *Terrapene carolina triunguis* 108
Latin American Wood Turtles: Genus *Rhinoclemmys* 108
36. South American Wood Turtle, *Rhinoclemmys punctularia*
   punctularia 109

Afro-Neotropical Side-necked Turtles: Family Podocnemidae 110

Neotropical River Turtles: Genus *Podocnemis* 111
37. Yellow-spotted Amazon River Turtle, *Podocnemis unifilis* 111

Soft-shelled Turtles: Family Trionychidae 112

38. Florida Soft-shelled Turtle, *Apalone ferox* 114
39. Gulf Coast Smooth Soft-shelled Turtle, *Apalone mutica calvata*
   116
40. Gulf Coast Spiny Soft-shelled Turtle, *Apalone spinifera aspera*
   117

Tortoises: Family Testudinidae 118

Gopher Tortoise: Genus *Gopherus* 119
41. Gopher Tortoise, *Gopherus polyphemus* 120

2. Alligators, Caiman, and Crocodiles: Order Crocodylia 123

How to Find Alligators, Caiman, and Crocodiles in Florida 126

Alligators and Caiman: Family Alligatoridae 126

42. American Alligator, *Alligator mississippiensis* 126
43. Spectacled Caiman, *Caiman crocodilus crocodilus* 128

Crocodiles: Family Crocodylidae 129

44. American Crocodile, *Crocodylus acutus* 130

3. Worm Lizards, Lizards, and Snakes: Order Squamata 132

Worm Lizards: Family Amphisbaenidae 132
How to Find Worm Lizards in Florida 133
   45. Florida Worm Lizard, *Rhineura floridana* 134

4. Lizards: Suborder Sauria (Lacertilia) 136

How to Find Lizards in Florida 137
Agamids: Family Agamidae 138
   Old World Rock Lizards, Tree Lizards, Garden Lizards and Butterfly
   Lizards: Genera *Agama*, *Calotes*, and *Leiolepis* 138
   46. West African Red-headed Agama, *Agama agama africana* 140
   47. Asian Tree Agama, *Bronchocela mystaceus* 141
   48. Variable Agama, *Calotes versicolor* 142
   49. Butterfly Agama, *Leiolepis belliana* 143

Glass Lizards: Family Anguidae 144
   Glass Lizards: Genus *Ophisaurus* 145
   50. Eastern Slender Glass Lizard, *Ophisaurus attenuatus longicaudus*
      146
   51. Island Glass Lizard, *Ophisaurus compressus* 147
   52. Mimic Glass Lizard, *Ophisaurus mimicus* 148
   53. Eastern Glass Lizard, *Ophisaurus ventralis* 149

Old World Chameleons: Family Chamaeleonidae 150
   True Chameleons: Genera *Chamaeleo* and *Furcifer* 151
   54. Veiled Chameleon, *Chamaeleo calyptratus calyptratus* 151
     54A. Panther Chameleon, *Furcifer pardalis* 153

Geckos: Family Gekkonidae 153
   House, Day, and Wall Geckos: Genera *Gehyra*, *Gekko*, *Hemidactylus*,
   Lepidodactylus, *Pachydactylus*, *Phelsuma*, *Ptychozoon*, and *Tarentola*
   156
   55. Stump-toed Gecko, *Gehyra mutilata* 156
   56. Tokay Gecko, *Gekko gecko* 157
     56A. Golden Gecko, *Gekko ulikovskii* 159
   57. Common House Gecko, *Hemidactylus frenatus* 159

58. Indo-Pacific House Gecko, *Hemidactylus garnotii* 160
59. Tropical House Gecko, *Hemidactylus mabouia* 161
60. Asian Flat-tailed House Gecko, *Hemidactylus platyurus* 162
61. Mediterranean Gecko, *Hemidactylus turcicus* 163
62. Mourning Gecko, *Lepidodactylus lugubris* 164
63. Bibron's Gecko, *Pachydactylus bibroni* 165
   63A. Turner's Gecko, *Pachydactylus turneri* 166
64. Giant Day Gecko, *Phelsuma madagascariensis grandis* 167
65. Standing's Giant Day Gecko, *Phelsuma standingi* 168
66. Smooth-backed Flying Gecko, *Ptychozoon lionotum* 170
67. White-spotted Wall Gecko, *Tarentola annularis* 170
68. Moorish Wall Gecko, *Tarentola mauritanica* 171
Yellow-headed, Ocellated, Ashy, and Reef Geckos: Genera
Gonatodes, Sphaerodactylus 172
69. Yellow-headed Gecko, *Gonatodes albogularis fuscus* 172
70. Ocellated Gecko, *Sphaerodactylus argus argus* 174
71. Ashy Gecko, *Sphaerodactylus elegans elegans* 175
72. Reef Gecko, *Sphaerodactylus notatus notatus* 176

**Iguanian Lizards: Families Corytophanidae, Iguanidae, Leiocephalidae
Phrynosomatidae, Polychrotidae and Tropiduridae 177**

Basilisks: Family Corytophanidae 177

  73. Northern Brown Basilisk, *Basiliscus vittatus* 179
    73A. Green Basilisk, *Basiliscus plumifrons* 180

Iguanas: Family Iguanidae 180

  Iguanas: Genera *Ctenosaura* and *Iguana* 182
  74. Mexican Spiny-tailed Iguana, *Ctenosaura pectinata* 182
  75. Central American Spiny-tailed Iguana, *Ctenosaura similis* 184
  76. Green Iguana, *Iguana iguana* 185

Curly-tailed Lizards: Family Leiocephalidae 186

  Curly-tailed Lizards: Genus *Leiocephalus* 188
  77. Northern Curly-tailed Lizard, *Leiocephalus carinatus armouri*
    188
  78. Green-legged Curly-tailed Lizard, *Leiocephalus personatus
    scalaris* 189
  79. Red-sided Curly-tailed Lizard, *Leiocephalus schreibersi
    schreibersi* 190

Spiny Lizards and Relatives: Family Phrynosomatidae 191

Horned Lizards: Genus *Phrynosoma* 192
80. Texas Horned Lizard, *Phrynosoma cornutum* 193
Fence Lizards, Scrub Lizards: Genus *Sceloporus* 194
81. Eastern Fence Lizard, *Sceloporus undulatus* 194
82. Florida Scrub Lizard, *Sceloporus woodi* 195

Anoles: Family Polychrotidae 196

Anoles: Genus *Anolis* 198
83. Northern Green Anole, *Anolis carolinensis carolinensis* 198
84. Pale-throated Green Anole, *Anolis carolinensis seminolus* 199
85. Haitian Green Anole, *Anolis chlorocyanus* 199
86. Puerto Rican Crested Anole, *Anolis cristatellus cristatellus* 200
87. Large-headed Anole, *Anolis cybotes cybotes* 202
88. Bark Anole, *Anolis distichus* 203
89. Western Knight Anole, *Anolis equestris equestris* 204
90. Barbados Anole, *Anolis extremus* 206
91. Marie Galante Sail-tailed Anole, *Anolis ferreus* 206
92. Jamaican Giant Anole, *Anolis garmani* 207
93. Cuban Green Anole, *Anolis porcatus* 208
94. Cuban Brown Anole, *Anolis sagrei sagrei* 209

South American Collared Lizard: Family Tropiduridae 211

95. Guyana Collared Lizard, *Tropidurus hispidus* 211

Skinks: Family Scincidae 212

96. Ocellated Barrel Skink, *Chalcides ocellatus* 214
97. Brown Mabuya, *Mabuya multifasciata* 214
Typical Skinks: Genus *Plestiodon* 215
98. Southern Coal Skink, *Plestiodon anthracinus pluvialis* 215
99–103. Mole Skink, *Plestiodon egregius* ssp. 217
99. Florida Keys Mole Skink, *Plestiodon egregius egregius* 219
100. Cedar Key Mole Skink, *Plestiodon egregius insularis* 219
101. Blue-tailed Mole Skink, *Plestiodon egregius lividus* 219
102. Peninsula Mole Skink, *Plestiodon egregius onocrepis* 220
103. Northern Mole Skink, *Plestiodon egregius similis* 220
104–106. Florida's Three Five-lined Skinks 220
104. Common Five-lined Skink, *Plestiodon fasciatus* 221

105. Southeastern Five-lined Skink, *Plestiodon inexpectatus* 223
106. Broad-headed Skink, *Plestiodon laticeps* 224
107. Florida Sand Skink, *Plestiodon reynoldsi* 225
Ground Skink: Genus *Scincella* 226
108. Ground Skink, *Scincella laterale* 227
108A. African Five-lined Skink, *Trachylepis quinquetaeniata* 228

Racerunners, Whiptails, and Tegus: Family Teiidae 229

Ameivas: Genus *Ameiva* 231
109. Giant Ameiva, *Ameiva ameiva* 231
  109A. Green-rumped phase 231
  109B. Dusky phase 231
Whiptails and Racerunners: Genera *Aspidoscelis* and *Cnemidophorus* 232
110. Giant Whiptail, *Aspidoscelis motaguae* 232
111. Six-lined Racerunner, *Aspiodoscelis sexlineatus sexlineatus* 233
112. Rainbow Whiptail, *Cnemidophorus lemniscatus* 234
Tegus: Genus *Tupinambis* 235
113. Black-and-White Tegu, *Tupinambis merianae* 236
113A. Golden Tegu, *Tupinambis teguixin* 237

Monitors: Family Varanidae 237

114. Nile Monitor, *Varanus niloticus* 239
  114A. Savanna Monitor, *Varanus exanthematicus* 240
  114B. Asian Water Monitor, *Varanus salvator* 241

5. Peripheral Reptile Species 242

Basking Turtles: Family Emydidae 242

115. Southern Painted Turtle, *Chrysemys picta dorsalis* 242

Glossary 245
Acknowledgments 249
Bibliography and Additional Reading 250
Index 253

Preface

In the diversity of its indigenous herpetofauna—the reptiles and the amphibians—Florida is surpassed by very few other states. When the established alien species, unwanted though they may be, are factored in, the count becomes staggering. In Florida there are dozens of species each of anurans (frogs, toads, and treefrogs), caudatans (salamanders), snakes, lizards, and turtles; two crocodilians (three counting an introduced caiman); and a single amphisbaenian. We have discussed the amphibians and the snakes in other volumes and will here discuss the remaining taxa.

To herpetologists, herpetoculturists, field biologists, and field herpers, the turtles, crocodilians, and lizards of the state of Florida are easily identified, even if not always fully understood. To most nonspecialists, the identification and whys and wherefores of the creatures within these groups are a bit puzzling. Although most people recognize a turtle as a turtle, a lizard as a lizard, and an alligator as an alligator, beyond these, exact ID is a bit hazy.

Perhaps this is understandable, for, with a few exceptions, the reptiles are secretive creatures.

Of the 114 species and subspecies of turtles, crocodilians, and lizards now found in Florida, about one-half are established alien species. Most of these established aliens are lizards—geckos, anoles, and iguanas—and most are restricted to the southern part of the peninsula.

Larry David Wilson and Louis Porras's 1983 book *The Ecological Impact of Man on the South Florida Herpetofauna* analyzed the presence and effects (as determined by these authors) of the then-25 species of alien herpetofauna established in the state. As of 2009, the species count of established alien herpetofauna has more than doubled. Wilson and Porras discuss the population statistics of many of the native south

Florida herpetofauna and use the term "eco-collapse" to describe what they felt were ever-worsening environmental and ecological conditions in Florida, south of Lake Okeechobee. The result is a diminished herpetofauna native to south Florida and the establishment of 50 (plus or minus a few) exotic species.

As seriously beleaguered as Florida is, myriad diverse (though often fragmented) habitats remain. These may be as specialized as the sand pine and rosemary scrub habitats of the Lake Wales ridge or as general as flooded roadside ditches. In these and all the habitats between them, reptiles dwell. Some species, such as the sand skink and the mole skink, are specialized and of very local distribution. Others such as the red-bellied cooter, green anole, and six-lined racerunner are less specialized and can be found over the entire state.

Join us as we tour the habitats and look at each Florida species and subspecies of non-ophidian reptile, both native and introduced, in detail.

Introduction

In a mere nanosecond of geologic time (about 50 years, or two-thirds of a human lifespan, by our reckoning), Florida has changed dramatically in physical appearance. The changes are especially apparent to naturalists. Florida's great lake, Okeechobee, has been diked, tamed, and polluted. Vast expanses of the Everglades have been drained, and, where sawgrass once bowed before subtropical breezes, sugarcane and sodfields now reign supreme. Miami—once a small, friendly town with open windows, doors, and hearts—is now an impersonal, outwardly hostile megalopolis.

Nor is Miami the only of Florida's cities to change. Ft. Lauderdale, Tampa, Ft. Myers, Gainesville, Orlando, Pensacola, Jacksonville, Tallahassee—all are now sprawling cities, bursting at their seams, with little room or thought for things natural.

Changes have come to Florida's wildlife too. In our very reduced natural areas, more than 50 species of introduced and established exotic creatures compete with Florida's native wildlife.

In some wetland areas one may encounter introduced capybaras (an immense Neotropical rodent). On the southern peninsula, native painted buntings now compete with introduced and established common mynahs and flocks of parrots—including the occasional macaw—wheeling noisily overhead, settling eventually to feed on the fruits of exotic fig and palm trees. In Dade County, boa constrictors are known to breed regularly (but still in small numbers), Burmese pythons are found in the Everglades, and, with the accidental introduction of the spectacled caiman to our canals, our complement of crocodilians has risen to three species. Small native treefrog species are being outcompeted in some areas by the immense Cuban treefrog, and where once only two native species of anole lizard, the green anole and the Florida bark anole, foraged and displayed, an observer may see up to nine additional species of exotic anoles. Among these exotic anoles is the world's largest species, the knight anole, an interloper from Cuba. Basilisks and spiny-tailed iguanas, curly-tailed lizards, day geckos, and tegus—all are now here.

Escapees from the pet trade have created a night shift of lizards, with many nocturnal species of geckos. (Florida has only one native species of gecko, the tiny, crepuscular reef gecko, so secretive it is seldom seen except by dedicated observers.) But with the establishment of 15 less secretive species, most of them nocturnal dwellers in urban and suburban areas, it is now difficult *not* to see one or more species of geckos in much of Florida. This holds especially true for Florida's more subtropical areas.

Added to this amazing hodgepodge of alien species is the green iguana. These reptilian cows have become so abundant on the southern peninsula that in some areas it is nearly impossible to grow hibiscus, a primary component of the diet of the iguana in Florida.

The creatures we have mentioned are just the tip of the iceberg. As you will learn in the species accounts that follow, over a period of about 50 years, Florida's herpetofauna has increased and diversified with the addition of more than 50 exotic turtle, lizard, and crocodilian species. The presence of most alien species in the state can be traced to lackadaisical attitudes of employees or inadequate/insecure caging by reptile importers and wholesalers. An occasional deliberate release by a hobbyist or researcher has been documented, and escapees from a few storm-damaged cages have also contributed to the problems.

Two of the most recently established species in Florida are the omnivorous black-and-white tegu and the carnivorous Nile monitor, both large lizards. Other species will assuredly follow.

Of those present today in Florida, some have become firmly established and, barring cataclysmic climatic changes, will be here for a very long time—perhaps even longer than some of our beleaguered native species. Many of these exotics have become so commonplace that viewers do not realize they are non-native species.

Other species are less adaptable and less temperature tolerant, and it will probably take only one or two abnormally cold winters to extirpate their population. But now, in 2009, they are here, and since you just might see them in the wild, we have included them in these pages. Among these tenuously established species are lizards such as the

Marie Galante sail-tailed anole, the Barbados anole, and the Asian variable agama. At present, the Florida populations of all of these are very localized.

Some reptiles and amphibians have been collected or seen on one or two occasions, then not seen again. Many of these have been geckos and anoles seen on urban warehouse complexes and the surrounding vegetation. The presence of most have been traced to one or two escapees from a reptile dealership. We have not discussed these in this book.

In another category are those temperate species for which northern Florida is the southernmost extreme of their range. These species are usually localized and may be rare in Florida but common north or west of Florida. Examples are the southern coal skink and the Gulf Coast smooth soft-shelled turtle.

A final category is those species of herpetofauna found in either Georgia or Alabama within a very few miles of the Florida state line, actually possibly occurring in Florida. The sole reptile that qualifies for this category is the southern painted turtle. You will find a discussion about this pretty emydine in chapter 5, "Peripheral Reptile Species."

Reptiles and amphibians vary not only in size and shape but also in their activity patterns. Generally, they are categorized as diurnal, nocturnal, or crepuscular. While some lizards are actually restricted to daylight activity patterns, other lizards, as well as the turtles, crocodilians, and amphibians, may be active around the clock. This is especially true on overcast days and when the barometric pressure is low.

It is not always possible to generalize about the preferred activity patterns of our herpetofauna by family. For example, while most gecko species in Florida are crepuscular and nocturnal, the yellow-headed gecko and the day geckos are decidedly diurnal. Similarly, three of our four toads are crepuscular and nocturnal, but the tiny oak toad regularly indulges in diurnal activity.

Reptiles and amphibians live in a wide range of habitats, from the open ocean (sea turtles) and salt marshes (diamondback terrapins), to acidic hillside seeps (coal skinks), woodland river edges (river frogs), shaded, sphagnaceous ravines (various skinks), the yielding sands of dry, interior ridges (sand skinks and gopher tortoises), and human habitations (various geckos). Reptiles and amphibians can be arboreal (anoles and geckos), terrestrial (tegus and curly-tailed lizards), semiaquatic (basilisks and green iguanas), aquatic (softshell turtles and alligators), or subsurface burrowers (worm lizards and mole skinks).

Although populations of many of our native reptiles and amphibians do not persist long in areas of urban and suburban sprawl, populations of other species easily survive the changes wrought by humans, and populations of most introduced exotic species actually thrive in the proximity of human-altered habitats.

How stable are populations of Florida's herpetofauna? For most species, perceived relative abundance is speculative. Few long-term studies have been done on the population statistics of our herpetofauna, but some species seem harder to find today than only a decade ago.

Current state and/or federal laws offer some measure of protection to all marine and freshwater turtles, the gopher tortoise, two crocodilians, and three lizards. No exotics are protected.

Despite increasing tolerance of reptiles and amphibians, many pressures remain on Florida's herpetofauna. Among others are the following:

- continued habitat degradation
- carnage on canal edge, pondside, and highway
- collecting for the pet trade
- collecting for scientific research

Ensuring that all the native amphibians and reptiles of Florida are here for our descendants to view and appreciate in the wild will take a concerted effort on the parts of all persons. Whether we are researchers, herpetoculturists, or merely people with an interest in the creatures with which we share our world, it is time to join forces and promote the conservation of these interesting, beneficial, and highly evolved animals. We hope that our comments in this identification guide will help you better understand and appreciate the intricate lifestyles of Florida's reptiles and amphibians.

Questions Currently without Answers

Four questions are often asked about the status of non-native reptiles and amphibians in Florida. At present the answers to all are conjectural or conditional:

Q. *How did these creatures get here?*
A. Indications are that the introduced herpetofauna in Florida are mostly accidental escapees from the pet trade; however, deliberate introductions and releases (including the release of unwanted pets) are also suggested.

Q. *What actual harm do they do?*
A. The jury is still out on this. Feral populations of many smaller lizards (among them anoles, skinks, whiptails, geckos, and agamas) have existed for more than two decades and no provable harm to landscapes or native herpetofauna has occurred. On the other hand, noticeable and unwanted depredations by the green iguana on gardens and shrubs are well documented. It is feared that large carnivorous species such as the Nile monitor and the tegus may unsustainably pressure beleaguered native wildlife (such as burrowing owls or endangered rodents) by commandeering home burrows and/or preying on these creatures. Further studies are needed on all.

Q. *Will the herpetofauna now established in Florida continue to thrive?*
A. Our answer to this must be both guarded and qualified. Despite the fact that many populations of introduced exotic herpetofauna have been established for 30 or more years, the mortality caused to non-native herpetofauna (and to some native species such as the American crocodile)

by the very cold weather of January, February, and March 2010 unequivocally proved that at least some individuals in most locales were vulnerable to the vagaries of the weather. Cold-stressed, dying, and dead iguanas, knight anoles, and day geckos fell by the hundreds or perhaps even the thousands from freeze-damaged exotic trees.

As more normal weather patterns slowly returned to the Sunshine State, it was seen that despite obvious evidence of mortality, reasonable nuclei of many of the hardest hit but visible taxa survived; however, the status of the more secretive taxa (such as wall and house geckos) remains entirely unknown.

It is now June 2010. Memories of the uncomfortably cold weather are just that: memories. Although no actual studies have been done, many species of introduced herpetofauna seem less common than before the winter freezes. But for those that did survive, like the little Mediterranean geckos on our house and the brown anoles in our yard, it is still business as usual.

But a very real unknown persists: If Florida were to experience similar extremes of cold for two or three consecutive years, what would the outcome be?

Q. *What will be the next exotic reptile or amphibian species to become established in Florida?*
A. Although it could be a giant musk turtle of the genus *Staurotypus* (recently reported but not yet confirmed), it seems probable that Florida's next established non-native reptile or amphibian species will be a small to medium-sized lizard and that, like many other introduced species, it will probably first be seen in the proximity of an animal dealer. Two contenders, both anoles, first come to mind. Both species are agile, adept at escaping from holding cages, highly mobile, inexpensive, somewhat temperature tolerant, and periodically imported in substantial numbers by the pet industry.

Prior to the cold weather of early 2010, feral examples of one, the Hispaniolan white-lipped (or mustached) anole, *Anolis coelestinus*, a rather small and very pretty species, had been found in two locales in Broward County.

The second contender is *Anolis extremus* (often imported from Guyana as *Anolis roquet*). This is an olive green, yellow green, or bluish green species that may have anterior highlights of cobalt. Because of this it is often referred to as the "blue anole." The accepted common name is Barbados anole, and the population in Guyana is probably non-native to that country. This species was well known in Lee County in the late 1980s and early 1990s but seems to have since been extirpated by cold winter weather. During the 1980s feral examples were common in Miami-Dade County, but the trees in their rather circumscribed range were plowed down and replaced by a tri-rail station. They were also known in the 1990s in Broward County. The status of that population is currently unknown (see species account 90 for discussion).

Florida's Habitats

To find a particular species or subspecies of reptile in Florida, you must first look within its range, next in proper habitat, and then, in some cases, in a specific microhabitat.

Most Florida habitats are home to one or more species of reptiles.

Habitat Types

Xeric (dry) Uplands—standing water is uncommon

1. Scrub: Sandy, rapidly drained soils typify this habitat as does a plant community of sand pine, opuntia cactus, rosemary, wiregrass, and lichens. Reptiles such as the sand skink, mole skinks, scrub lizard, and gopher tortoise occur in this habitat.

2. Sandhills: Soils are sandy and fast draining. The typical plant community consists of turkey oak, longleaf pine, wiregrasses, and saw palmetto. This habitat supports such reptile species as the mole skinks, scrub lizard, fence lizard, worm lizard, and slender glass lizard.

3. Hammocks (oak, etc.): Red, bluejack, live, and laurel oaks are typical trees replacing the pines in these successional areas, but poor soils prevent succession to true woodlands. Wire and other grasses are present. Shallow, ephemeral ponds may be present.

This habitat supports such reptile species as various skinks and glass lizards and the gopher tortoise.

Mesic (damp) Uplands—ephemeral or permanent ponds or streams may be present

4. Hardwoods: An overstory community of oaks, beeches, magnolias, and other tall forest trees is present. Understory trees and shrubs, such as American holly and hophornbeam, are present. Catclawvine, grapes, ferns, and other vines and forest floor plants are usually evident. This habitat supports such reptile species as broad-headed skink, brown anole, green anole, fence lizard, and box turtle.

5. Pine: Longleaf pine is the dominant overstory tree in this community. A shrubby understory (such as palmetto) may or may not be present, but grasses and herbaceous growth grow thickly on the forest floor. Various skinks and glass lizards, fence lizards, and chicken turtles call this habitat home.

Mesic (damp) Flatlands—ephemeral or permanent ponds may be present

6. Pine flatwoods: With stands of natural or cultured longleaf pine as the dominant overstory tree, pine flatwoods are typified by poorly drained soils, a sparse understory at best, but profuse ground cover. Look for species such as the chicken turtle, eastern glass lizard, and mud turtle.

7. Prairie: A dense growth of herbaceous ground cover typifies this open, usually treeless habitat. Such understory plants as saw palmetto and willows may be abundant, especially around water holes and canals. Seek various turtles, anoles, skinks, eastern glass lizards, and alligators in and near water holes.

Hydric Flatlands—subject to periodic flooding

8. Wet marl prairie/Everglades: These poorly drained prairies are most common on the southern peninsula. They are open, often treeless expanses that may support stands of cypress and shrubs and a dense ground cover of sawgrass, wiregrass, rushes, spider lilies, and other flood-tolerant plants. Reptiles such as the chicken turtle, alligator, box turtle, and eastern glass lizard may be found here.

Marl (pinnacle rock) prairie, photo by Carl D. May

9. River swamp: Sweetgum, bay, and maples are among the more commonly seen larger trees in this habitat. Two species of titi, wax myrtle, and other shrubs and myriad low-light, ground-dwelling herbs occur on the forest floor. Expect to find skinks and anoles in this habitat.

10. Cypress swamp and cypress head: This habitat is flooded for much, if not all, of each year. Besides cypress, trees such as sweetgum and elder grow. Where conditions permit, shrubs and emergent herbs occur. Alligators, mud turtles, common musk turtles, soft-shelled turtles, and basking turtles may be encountered in this habitat.

11. Everglades hammock/swale: At one time this habitat, with shallow flowing waters and pinnacle rock excrescences, was found over much of southern peninsula Florida. Today it is restricted to outflows from Lake Okeechobee and the Big Cypress regions. Sawgrass and other plants that thrive with perpetually wet feet are typical of this habitat. Skinks, anoles, common musk turtles, mud turtles, basking turtles, soft-shelled turtles, and common snapping turtles occur in these swales.

Limestone Communities—canals have been dug through many of these habitats

12. Pine rocklands: Restricted to the southern peninsula and the Keys, this habitat supports sparse to moderate stands of slash pines beneath which grows a ground cover of drought-tolerant ferns, terrestrial orchids, cat-greenbrier, and harsh grasses. The eastern glass lizard, anoles, five-lined skinks, and many turtle species reside in this type of habitat.

13. Pinnacle rock hardwood hammock: Restricted to the southernmost areas of the state, these are elevated hammocks of densely growing tropical and temperate tree species such as live oak, gumbo-limbo, poisonwood, tamarind, and *Paurotis* and *Sabal* palms. The eastern glass lizard, anoles, five-lined skinks, and many turtle species frequent these hammocks.

Disturbed Habitats

14. Human habitations (including buildings, yards, urban parklands, roadside trash piles and recreation areas): Many introduced alien species of lizards are abundant within their respective ranges.

15. Modified habitats (pastures, fields, farmlands, agricultural areas): Look for box turtles, gopher tortoise, and skinks in these habitats.

Controlled burns

Artificially drained habitats

Mowed/plowed fields and pastures

Freshwater and Marine Habitats

16. Shady creeks streams (and adjacent mucklands and sphagnum bogs): Aquatic and stream-edge species such as soft-shelled turtles, mud turtles, musk turtles, box turtles, alligators, skinks, and anoles may be found in this habitat.

17. Ephemeral ponds and flooded ditches: These are poorly drained, low-lying (often manmade) areas that fill regularly during the rainy seasons but dry regularly between heavy rains. Drought-tolerant aquatic vegetation and submersion-tolerant semiterrestrial plants usually abound in these habitats. Chicken turtles and mud turtles are commonly found here.

18. Permanent ponds, lakes, swamps, and canals: Although water levels fluctuate with rainfall, permanent ponds, lakes, and canals usually retain water year-round. Shrubs often rim the perimeters, and emergent vegetation can grow thickly in the shallows. Submerged vegetation of many kinds grow where the water becomes too deep for emergents. Basking turtles, mud turtles, common musk turtle, alligators, and caiman may be encountered in this habitat.

19. Springs and spring runs: Various woodland trees grow to and in the shallows of these crystal-clear waters. Soft-shelled turtles, snapping turtles, musk turtles, and cooters may be seen here.

Spring and spring runs, photo by Carl D. May

20. Freshwater marshes: These are low-lying, poorly drained habitats that usually hold water. Cattail, pickerelweed, alligator flag, blue flag, and maidencane are commonly seen emergents, and shrubs such as wax myrtle and various willows often surround the area. Look for basking turtles, mud turtles, common musk turtle, alligators, and caiman in this habitat.

21. Seeps and steepheads: Acidic boggy hillside seepages are created by water percolating through porous, deep sandy soils until diverted by clay subsoil. Insectivorous plants, grasses, and dense herbaceous growth typify these habitats. Skinks and box turtles can be found in this habitat.

22. Streams, creeks, and rivers: These fluctuate in depth but are typified by year-round flowing water. Generally speaking, rivers are larger
than creeks and streams. Many originate from freshwater springheads
in densely wooded areas but meander near their mouths through tidal
marshlands or mangrove swamps. Dependent on water depth and soil
conditions, both emergent and submerged vegetation may be abundant.
Soft-shelled turtles, mud turtles, musk turtles, box turtles, alligators,
skinks, and anoles may be found in this habitat.

23. Coastal dunes and high beaches: These are above the high water mark in all but the most severe conditions: Sea oats, beach morning glory, saw palmetto and other shrubs are typical plants. Horned lizards, curly-tailed lizards, and anoles may be found here.

24. Mangrove swamps: These are low-lying, tidally influenced zones of transition between fresh and salt waters vegetated by red, black, and white mangroves and buttonwood. The Nile monitor, crocodile, and diamondback terrapin may occur in this habitat.

25. Salt marsh: Heavily vegetated, open regions of tidally influenced shoreline. The salinity is very variable. Cord and salt grasses and rushes are usually the dominant plants. Diamondback terrapins and the crocodile may be found here.

26. Open ocean (including shorelines and estuaries). This is the habitat for all sea turtles.

Laws and Regulations

Reptiles Protected in Florida

As of 20 July 2009 all native turtles and tortoises are protected in Florida. The following are also protected:

Alligator mississippiensis, American alligator
Crocodylus acutus, American crocodile
Plestiodon egregius egregius, Florida Keys mole skink
Plestiodon egregius lividus, blue-tailed mole skink
Plestiodon reynoldsi, sand skink

This list is subject to change at any time so is offered as only a guide.

Current information is always available through the headquarters of the Florida Fish and Wildlife Conservation Commission, at
620 South Meridian Street
Tallahassee, FL 32399–1600
myfwc.com
or through the U.S. Fish and Wildlife Service, at
Office for Human Relations
United Sates Fish and Wildlife Service
Department of Interior
Washington, D.C. 20240
www.fws.gov

In some cases it is legal to keep a regulated species; however, it cannot be sold or bartered. Check with the Florida Fish and Wildlife Conservation Commission for clarification.

How to Use This Book

In these pages we discuss 115 species and subspecies of turtles, crocodilians, and lizards, 114 of which are known to occur in Florida. The 115th species, the southern painted turtle, ranges to within a few miles of the Florida state line in Alabama and may eventually be found in the Sunshine State. While many of these species are of very dissimilar appearance, some are confusingly alike.

Many of these reptiles have two or more color phases, and some agamid and anoline lizards are capable of undergoing chameleon-like color or pattern changes. Because of this it would be difficult to categorize them by color or pattern; therefore, we opted to list and discuss all of them in a traditional manner, divided by family, genus, species, and subspecies.

We further believe that a guide of this sort is not the place to attempt to justify or decry "cutting-edge" taxonomy; we have tried to use names that are well accepted by the herpetological community. As our understanding of these creatures increases, future taxonomic changes will be made.

We have fully listed and numbered all species and subspecies in the table of contents. The numbers assigned there will coincide with the numbers assigned in both text and photographs. If you know or have a good idea of the identity of the species you are researching, begin with the table of contents.

We have listed each major group, genus, species, and subspecies alphabetically by scientific name; therefore, you may have to search some if you know only the common name of a species. Also check the photo and range map provided for each species.

Scientific names are of Latin or Greek derivation. They can be binomial (two names) or trinomial (three names), for example:

- Broad-headed skink, *Plestiodon* (pless-tee-oh-don) *laticeps* (lat-ih-seps). This large skink has not subspeciated; thus it is identified by only a binomial.
- Florida Keys mole skink, *Plestiodon* (pless-tee-oh-don) *egregius* (ee-gree-gee-us) *egregius*. This small skink has subspeciated and is identified by a trinomial.

Families	Species account numbers
Turtles	1–41, 114
Cheloniidae: Typical Sea Turtles	1–4
Chelydridae: Snapping Turtles	6–8
Dermochelyidae: Leatherbacks	5
Emydidae: Basking & Box Turtles	16–37, 114
Kinosternidae: Mud & Musk Turtles	9–14
Pelomedusidae: Afro-Neotropical Side-necked Turtles	15
Testudinidae: Tortoises	41
Trionychidae: Soft-shelled Turtles	38–40
Peripheral Turtle Species	110
Crocodilians	42–44
Alligatoridae: Alligators, Caiman	42–43A
Crocodylidae: Crocodiles	44
Amphisbaenians	45
Amphisbaenidae: Worm Lizards	45
Lizards	46–113B
Agamidae: Agamids	46–49
Anguids: Glass Lizards	50–53
Chamaeleonidae: Old World Chameleons	54–54A
Corytophanidae: Basilisks	73–73A
Gekkonidae: Geckos	55–72
Iguanidae: Iguanas	74–76
Leiocephalidae, Curly-tailed Lizards	92–94
Phrynosomatidae: Horned Lizards, Swifts	77–79
Polychrotidae: Anoles	80–91
Scincidae: Skinks	96–107
Teiidae: Racerunners, Whiptails	108–112A
Tropiduridae: South American Collared Lizard	95
Varanidae: Monitors	113–113B

If the specimen you are trying to identify is completely unknown to you, compare its external characteristics with those provided in the Key to Families. Once the family has been found, turn to that section of the book to compare pictures, range maps, and descriptions.

If you recognize the specimen as a member of a specific group, simply locate that group in the species list, find the appropriate pages in the text, and go from there.

Example: The turtle you see is walking in a woodland. You notice that it has a high-domed upper shell (carapace), and when you pick it up, it gives a weak hiss and draws the bottom shell (the plastron) tightly against the top. It has a dark brown or black carapace with yellow radiating markings and was found east of Tampa.

The key will first refer you to the emydine turtles, the basking and the box turtles, and then to the box turtles. Of the four subspecies of box turtles, only the picture of the Florida box turtle compares favorably with your example, and the range map will confirm the identification.

Some species such as the anoles may be a bit more difficult, but the same process as used for the box turtle will allow you to quickly winnow out many species and narrow the contenders.

Keys to Florida Turtles, Crocodilians, and Lizards

Turtles and Tortoises

1. Forelimbs flipperlike, marine habitats 2
   Forelimbs otherwise 3
2. Carapace hard and scute-covered (normal). . . . .
   . . . . **Family Cheloniidae, typical sea turtles**
   Carapace leathery and longitudinally ridged. . . . .
   . . . .**Family Dermochelyidae, leatherbacks**
3. Carapace hard and scute covered (normal). 4
   Carapace leathery, soft-edged, and lacking scutes . . . .
   . . . . **Family Trionychidae, softshell turtles**
4. Rear feet weakly to fully webbed, forelimbs normal. 5
   Front feet stout and spadelike, rear feet clublike, carapace high
   domed but flattened in center, terrestrial. . . . .
   . . . .**Family Testudinidae, tortoises**
5. Plastron reduced in size 6
   Plastron otherwise. 7
6. Posterior marginals strongly serrate. . . . .
   . . . . **Family Chelydridae, snapping turtles**
   Posterior marginals not strongly serrate . . . .
   . . . . **Family Kinosternidae (in part), musk turtles**
7. Plastron nearly full size, two functional hinges. . . . .
   . . . . **Family Kinosternidae (in part), mud turtles**
   Plastron lacking hinges or with only a single functional hinge. . . . . .
   . . . . **Family Emydidae, basking turtles and box turtles**

Crocodilians

1. Snout broadly rounded, 4th lower tooth from front not visible when mouth is closed ...... **Family Alligatoridae, alligator and caiman**
Snout slender, long, and tapering. Upper jaw notched near tip, 4th lower tooth from front visible in notch (prominent only on large examples) .... Family **Crocodylidae, crocodiles**

Lizards and Amphisbaenids

1. Scales arranged in prominent annuli, no functional eyes .... **Family Amphisbaenidae, Florida worm lizard** Scales otherwise, eyes functional. 2
2. Eyes turretlike and capable of independent motion; toes of each foot in two opposing bundles. .... **Family Chamaeleonidae, true chameleons** Eyes and toes otherwise 3
3. Eyelids not functional; eye covered by a transparent brille .... **Family Gekkonidae, geckos** Eyelids functional 4
4. Attenuate and lacking legs .... **Family Anguidae, glass lizards** Legs present and functional. 5
5. Ventral scales large, platelike, and arranged in 8, 10, 12, or 28+ longitudinal rows .... **Family Teiidae, whiptails and tegus** Ventral scales not large and platelike 6
6. Tongue greatly protrusible, tip deeply bifurcate .... **Family Varanidae, monitors** Tongue otherwise 7
7. Scales shiny and of similar size around entire body.............. .... **Family Scincidae, skinks** Scales not shiny 8
8. Crests present. 9
Crests not present 13
9. Finlike cranial crest present .... **Family Corytophanidae, Basilisks** Caudal, vertebral, and/or nuchal crest present 10
10. Low but distinct caudal, vertebral, and/or nuchal crest of serrate scales present 11

Caudal, vertebral, and/or nuchal crest of greatly lengthened individual scales 12

11. No tail curling or lateral skin folds. . . . .
. . . . **Family Agamidae (in part), agamas**
Tail curls upward or a lateral skin fold present. . . . .
. . . . **Family Tropiduridae, curly-tailed lizards**

12. Crest of greatly lengthened scales; adult size very large (more than 6 inches SVL) . . . . **Family Iguanidae, iguanas**
As above but adult size small (1½ to 5 inches) . . . .
. . . . **Agamidae (in part), agamas**

13. Size small to moderately large, snout long and tapering, scales small and unkeeled, toes tipped with elongate flattened pads, some species with notable color changing abilities, males with large distensible gular dewlap . . . . **Family Polychrotidae, anoles**
Size small, snout rather blunt, toe tips not flattened, scales strongly keeled to spinose, no distensible dewlap . . . .
. . . . **Family Phrynosomatidae, swifts and horned lizards**

Digital Photography

Photographing a turtle, tortoise, lizard, or crocodilian in the field or in a staged set-up can change your perspective of what's beautiful. A close-up shot of the head of a Florida cooter or the scales on a fence lizard has a tendency to make one stop and muse, "Y'know, that's really . . . pretty!" and soon you have 18 x 24-inch color prints of different kinds of turtles on every wall of your house. Looking around in our own home, we think there's absolutely nothing wrong with this—and have you seen this close-up of the iris of a Tokay gecko?

In a purely practical sense, photography can be the least intrusive way to document captive or wild behavior patterns, especially with the convenience of digital photography. The instant feedback of digital photography has taken a lot of the mystery out of getting a good shot. Even museums may now accept quality photos in lieu of a preserved voucher specimen.

Taking a good photograph of a lizard or turtle in the field requires knowledge of how soon that animal will react to the presence of a human, a bit of stealth, and a working knowledge of photography. Getting started is easy . . .

The equipment required will depend on a number of variables. What you're going to shoot—whether long-distance habitat shots, close-up field photography, or pictures of a turtle on a stage—is a factor you want to consider.

Photographing a reptile under controlled, staged conditions is infinitely easier than taking photos in the field, but figuring out how to position—or waiting until the creature positions itself—is still time consuming.

Basic Equipment Needs

A sturdy digital camera body with interchangeable lenses (single lens reflex [SLR] capabilities) is suggested, but with today's technology, not an absolute necessity. You may be able to get the results you want with a simple digital camera called a point-and-shoot camera, and such a camera is much easier to carry and set up.

Digital cameras offer a lot of options, and the Web is probably the most efficient way to see what's available. We like the LCD you can tilt so you can see what you're photographing even if the camera is flat on the ground, and we've found 7 megapixels a large enough capacity for details. If you want more, go for it, but you can get quite acceptable shots with 7 megapixels. Some quick online help on what to look for in a digital camera can be found at http://www.pcworld.com/article/125645/how_to_buy_a_digital_camera.html or http://solution.allthingsd.com/20070509/how-to-buy-your-next-digital-camera/

At one time, we would have suggested you look closely at good-quality secondhand equipment, but new digital equipment is much more affordable than the old film cameras, and "old" technology in digitals is not what you want.

Most of us buy our equipment from discount electronics stores, but this may not be your best choice. If you have access to a photo supply dealer who can accurately advise you about the equipment to buy and some features of that particular lens or body, treasure this person and buy from him/her.

Suggested lenses, for the non–point-and-shoot photographer:

28 mm wide angle for habitat photos
50 mm standard for habitat photos
100 mm macro for close-ups (suitable for almost every purpose)
75–205 mm zoom lens for variable field work
300 or 400 mm fixed focal length telephoto lens for field work (the 300 is by far the easiest to hand-hold)
Or a camera with both close-up capabilities and a high-quality 10X, 12X, or 20X zoom lens.

Flash units: one or more dedicated flash units (a dedicated flash interfaces with the camera's f-stop setting to furnish appropriate light levels).

Lens adapter: a 1.25x power magnifier or 2x doubler will help with many types of photos including telephotos.

Good equipment for anyone: A flashlight is a necessity for nighttime photography. We affix a small flashlight to the top of our camera using short loop-and-hook strips. Our flashlight operates on 1 AA battery. This self-contained arrangement allows a single person to focus on subjects at night in the field.

Although a sturdy tripod was once an absolute necessity for holding the larger magnification telephoto lenses steady, most digitals have an antishake or stabilization factor built in. A steady camera will ensure no blurring when you squeeze that "once in a lifetime" shot. Using a cable release can help.

If ever your camera will malfunction, it will be at that critical time when you are faced with an opportunity to take a "once in a lifetime" shot. It is always a good idea to have at least one spare camera body available.

Some Photographic Hints

For staged photography, create a small natural setting by placing rocks, mosses, leaves, or bark—whatever is most appropriate for the species you're photographing—on a stage. A stage can be as simple as an old cardboard box or a large lazy susan draped in black velvet, or it may be as sophisticated as you choose to make it. If you don't have a lazy susan or a similar contained area, just arrange the setting on a tabletop or tree stump, depending on where you are at the time. Ideally, once you have constructed your background, you will merely put the specimen in place, focus, and shoot; however, seldom are things ideal. Many herps are nervous, and it will take dedication, gentleness, and patience on your part to accomplish your goal. Having a photo assistant to help pose or repose, or catch or recatch the subject will help. Move slowly at all times when working with any amphibian or reptile.

Our stage for contrived shots is easily movable and always in the back of the car when we travel. It consists of the top half of a round trash can bolted to a large lazy susan. Black velvet clipped in place around the inside surface of the background gives a good unobtrusive background for our photographic efforts. We use one or more add-on flash units when light levels are low.

Again, remember to move very slowly when approaching a reptile in the field. Approach it slowly and obliquely. Avoid eye contact. If the reptile notices you or feels the vibrations from your footsteps (as it almost certainly will) freeze for a moment until it relaxes again, then resume the stalk. You may eventually be close enough to make the field shot for which you were hoping, or you may be led on a sort of tango, trying to get close enough to focus and shoot, or until the animal disappears from sight.

When done in the field, replace anything you've moved to find your subject. Lizards and turtles depend on the sunning perches in their home range, and it's unfair to rearrange perching sites and hiding spots and not replace them. Retrace your steps carefully, and leave nothing behind—nothing, that is, but your footprints and the specimen you just successfully photographed.

What about biting insects? Inure yourself. They'll be there. Field photography means contending with biting flies by day, with mosquitoes and no-see-ums by night, and with ticks and chiggers at both times. You can spare yourself a lot of grief by wearing socks, long pants, a long-sleeved shirt with a collar you can turn up, and a hat with a floppy brim. Tuck your pants into your socks, and your shirt inside your pants, to make it harder for ticks to find skin to latch onto. (You can rearrange your attire before you go into a diner or fast food site, or you can choose to ignore the looks you'll get.)

Spray your cuffs, collar, and hat brim with insect repellent to keep your hands clean. If you must use repellent on your skin, apply it before you need it and wash your hands carefully after applying it. Do not get any topical insecticide or repellent on your camera equipment. In addition to wreaking havoc on camera equipment, these materials left on your hands can be absorbed through the skin and are harmful to any reptiles you touch.

1. Loggerhead turtle, *Caretta caretta*, after nesting

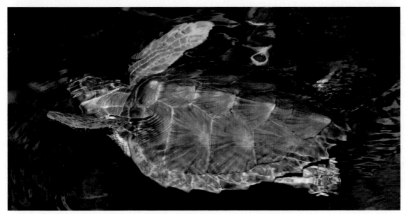

Loggerhead turtle, *Caretta caretta*, swimming

Loggerhead turtle, *Caretta caretta*, hatchling

2. Green turtle, *Chelonia mydas mydas*, taking breath

Green turtle, *Chelonia mydas mydas*, swimming

3. Atlantic hawksbill turtle, *Eretmochelys imbricata imbricata*

4. Atlantic ridley, *Lepidochelys kempii*

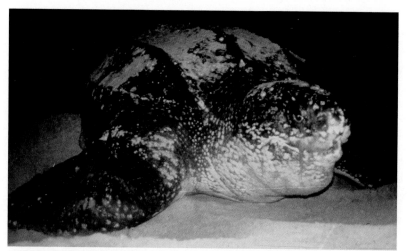

5. Atlantic leatherback, *Dermochelys coriacea coriacea*, adult, photo by Larry D. Wood

Atlantic leatherback, *Dermochelys coriacea coriacea*, hatchling

6. Common snapping turtle, *Chelydra serpentina serpentina*, adult

7. Florida snapping turtle, *Chelydra serpentina osceola*, adult

Alligator snapping turtle showing tongue structure

8. Alligator snapping turtle, *Macrochelys temminckii*, adult

Alligator snapping turtle, *Macrochelys temminckii*, hatchling

9. Striped mud turtle, *Kinosternon baurii*, normal pattern

Striped mud turtle, *Kinosternon baurii*, patternless phase

Striped mud turtle, *Kinosternon baurii*, blonde phase, photo by Carl D. May

10. Eastern mud turtle, *Kinosternon subrubrum subrubrum*

11. Florida mud turtle, *Kinosternon subrubrum steindachneri*, normal coloration

Florida mud turtle, *Kinosternon subrubrum steindachneri*, aberrant color, South Florida, photo by Carl D. May

12. Loggerhead musk turtle, *Sternotherus minor minor*, adult

Loggerhead musk turtle, *Sternotherus minor minor*, hatchling

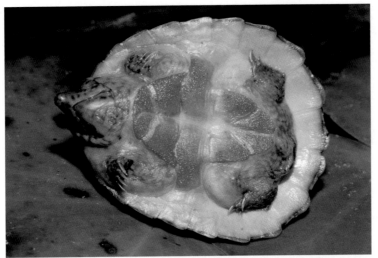

Loggerhead musk turtle, hatchling, *Sternotherus minor minor*, plastron

13. Stripe-necked musk turtle, *Sternotherus minor peltifer*, juvenile

14. Common musk turtle, *Sternotherus odoratus*, adult

15. Spotted turtle, *Clemmys guttata*, adult

16. Eastern chicken turtle, *Deirochelys reticularia reticularia*, adult

17. Florida chicken turtle, *Deirochelys reticularia chrysea*, adult

18. Barbour's map turtle, *Graptemys barbouri*, adult male

Barbour's map turtle, *Graptemys barbouri*, hatchling

19. Escambia map turtle, *Graptemys ernsti*, adult female

Escambia map turtle, *Graptemys ernsti*, adult male

20. Carolina diamondback terrapin, *Malaclemys terrapin centrata*

21. Ornate diamondback terrapin, *Malaclemys terrapin macrospilota*, adult swimming

Ornate diamondback terrapin, *Malaclemys terrapin macrospilota*, hatchling

22. Mississippi diamondback terrapin, *Malaclemys terrapin pileata*, adult

23. Mangrove terrapin, *Malaclemys terrapin rhizophorarum*, adult

24. Florida East Coast terrapin, *Malaclemys terrapin tequesta*, adult

25. River cooter, *Pseudemys concinna concinna*, adult

26. Suwannee cooter, *Pseudemys concinna suwanniensis*, adult

27. Florida cooter, *Pseudemys floridana floridana*, adult

28. Peninsula cooter, *Pseudemys floridana peninsularis*, adult

29. Florida red-bellied cooter, *Pseudemys nelsoni*, adult

Florida red-bellied cooter, *Pseudemys nelsoni*, hatchling

30. Yellow-bellied slider, *Trachemys scripta scripta*, juvenile

Yellow-bellied × red-eared slider, *Trachemys scripta scripta* × *T. s. elegans*, intergrade

31. Red-eared slider, *Trachemys scripta elegans*, adult

32. Eastern box turtle, *Terrapene carolina carolina*

33. Florida box turtle, *Terrapene carolina bauri*

34. Gulf Coast box turtle, *Terrapene carolina major*, old adult male

Gulf Coast box turtle, *Terrapene carolina major*, juvenile

35. Three-toed box turtle, *Terrapene carolina triunguis*

36. South American wood turtle, *Rhinoclemmys punctularia punctularia*

37. Yellow-spotted Amazon River turtle, *Podocnemis unifilis*, adult female

Yellow-spotted Amazon River turtle, *Podocnemis unifilis*, subadult male

38. Florida soft-shelled turtle, *Apalone ferox*, adult female

Florida soft-shelled turtle, *Apalone ferox*, hatchling

39. Gulf Coast smooth soft-shelled turtle, *Apalone mutica calvata*, adult female

40. Gulf Coast spiny soft-shelled turtle, *Apalone spinifera aspera*, juvenile

41A. African spurred tortoise, *Geochelone sulcata*, adult male

African spurred tortoise, *Geochelone sulcata*, hatchling

41. Gopher tortoise, *Gopherus polyphemus*, adult

Gopher tortoise, *Gopherus polyphemus*, hatchling

42. American alligator, *Alligator mississippiensis*, adult

American alligator, *Alligator mississippiensis*, hatchling

43. Spectacled caiman, *Caiman crocodilus*, juvenile

Crocodile, *Crocodylus* species, feral juvenile, species undetermined

43A. Smooth-fronted caiman, *Paleosuchus trigonatus*, juvenile

44. American crocodile, *Crocodylus acutus*, adult

American crocodile, *Crocodylus acutus*, dentition

American crocodile, *Crocodylus acutus*, hatchling

45. Florida worm lizard, *Rhineura floridana*

46. West African red-headed agama, *Agama agama africana*, dominant male, photo by
Jake Scott

47. Asian tree agama, *Bronchocela mystaceus*

48. Variable agama, *Calotes versicolor*

49. Butterfly agama, *Leiolepis belliana*

50. Eastern slender glass lizard, *Ophisaurus attenuatus longicaudus*

51. Island glass lizard, *Ophisaurus compressus*

52. Mimic glass lizard, *Ophisaurus mimicus*

53. Eastern glass lizard, *Ophisaurus ventralis*, adult

Eastern glass lizard, *Ophisaurus ventralis*, old male

54. Veiled chameleon, *Chamaeleo calyptratus calyptratus*, adult male

54A. Panther chameleon, *Furcifer pardalis*, adult male, blue phase

Panther chameleon, *Furcifer pardalis*, juvenile

55. Stump-toed gecko, *Gehyra mutilata*

56. Tokay gecko, *Gekko gecko*

56A. Golden gecko, *Gekko ulikovskii*

57. Common house gecko, *Hemidactylus frenatus*

58. Indo-Pacific house gecko, *Hemidactylus garnotii*

59. Tropical house gecko, *Hemidactylus mabouia*

60. Asian flat-tailed house gecko, *Hemidactylus platyurus*

61. Mediterranean gecko, *Hemidactylyus turcicus*

62. Mourning gecko, *Lepidodactylus lugubris*

63. Bibron's gecko, *Pachydactylus bibroni*

63A. Turner's gecko, *Pachydactylus turneri*

64. Giant day gecko, *Phelsuma madagascariensis grandis*, hatchling

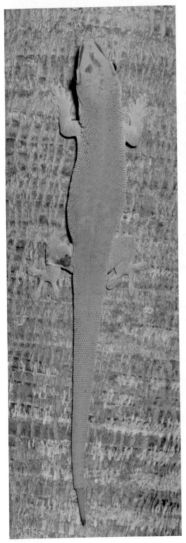

65. Standing's day gecko, *Phelsuma standingi*, hatchling

Giant day gecko, *Phelsuma madagascariensis grandis*, adult

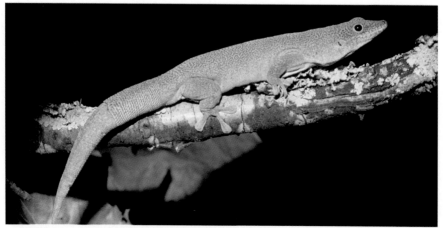

Standing's day gecko, *Phelsuma standingi*, adult

66. Smooth-backed flying gecko, *Ptychozoon lionotum*

67. White-spotted wall gecko, *Tarentola annularis*

68. Moorish wall gecko, *Tarentola mauritanica*

69. Yellow-headed gecko, *Gonatodes albogularis fuscus*, female

Yellow-headed gecko, *Gonatodes albogularis fuscus*, male

70. Ocellated gecko, *Sphaerodactylus argus argus*

71. Ashy gecko, *Sphaerodactylus elegans elegans*, adult

Ashy gecko, *Sphaerodactylus elegans elegans*, hatchling

72. Reef gecko, *Sphaerodactylus notatus notatus*, male

73. Northern brown basilisk, *Basiliscus vittatus*, young male

Northern brown basilisk, *Basiliscus vittatus*, juvenile

73A. Green basilisk, *Basiliscus plumifrons*, dominant male

74. Mexican spiny-tailed iguana, *Ctenosaura pectinata*

75. Central American spiny-tailed iguana. *Ctenosaura similis*

76. Green iguana, *Iguana iguana*, dominant male

Green iguana, *Iguana iguana*, juvenile

77. Northern curly-tailed lizard, *Leiocephalus carinatus armouri*

78. Green-legged curly-tailed lizard, *Leiocephalus personatus scalaris*, male

79. Red-sided curly-tailed lizard, *Leiocephalus schreibersi schreibersi*, male

80. Texas horned lizard, *Phrynosoma cornutum*

81. Eastern fence lizard, *Sceloporus undulatus*, female, photo by Daniel Dye

Eastern fence lizard, *Sceloporus undulatus*, male, photo by Daniel Dye

82. Florida scrub lizard, *Sceloporus woodi*, pair, female top

83. Northern green anole, *Anolis carolinensis carolinensis*, displaying male

84. Pale-throated green anole, *Anolis carolinensis seminolus*

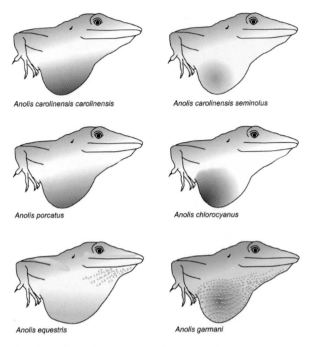

Anolis carolinensis carolinensis

Anolis carolinensis seminolus

Anolis porcatus

Anolis chlorocyanus

Anolis equestris

Anolis garmani

Dewlap colors of five species of green anoles

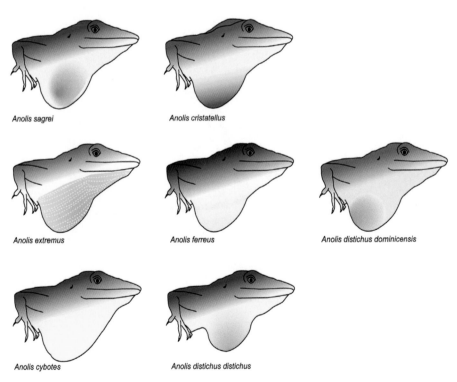

Anolis sagrei

Anolis cristatellus

Anolis extremus

Anolis ferreus

Anolis distichus dominicensis

Anolis cybotes

Anolis distichus distichus

Dewlap colors of six species of brown anoles

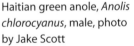

Haitian green anole, *Anolis chlorocyanus*, male, photo by Jake Scott

86. Puerto Rican crested anole, *Anolis cristatellus cristatellus*, male

85. Haitian green anole, *Anolis chlorocyanus*, female, photo by Jake Scott

87. Large-headed anole, *Anolis cybotes cybotes*, male

88. Bark anole, *Anolis distichus*, displaying male

89. Western knight anole, *Anolis equestris equestris*

Large-headed anole, *Anolis cybotes cybotes*

90. Barbados anole, male, *Anolis extremus*

91. Marie Galante sail-tailed anole, *Anolis ferreus*, male

92. Jamaican giant anole, *Anolis garmani*, male

93. Cuban green anole,
Anolis porcatus, male

94. Cuban brown anole, *Anolis sagrei sagrei*, displaying male

95. Guyana collared lizard, *Tropidurus hispidus*

96. Ocellated barrel skink, *Chalcides ocellatus*

97. Brown mabuya, *Mabuya multifasciata*

98. Southern coal skink, *Plestiodon anthracinus pluvialis*

99. Keys mole skink, *Plestiodon egregius egregius*

100. Cedar Key mole skink, *Plestiodon egregius insularis*

101. Blue-tailed mole skink, *Plestiodon egregius lividus,* subadult

Blue-tailed mole skink, *Plestiodon egregius lividus,* adult

102. Peninsula mole skink, *Plestiodon egregius onocrepis*

103. Northern mole skink, *Plestiodon egregius similis*

104. Common five-lined skink, *Plestiodon fasciatus*, adult male

Common five-lined skink, *Plestiodon fasciatus*, juvenile

105. Southeastern five-lined skink, *Plestiodon inexpectatus*, subadult

Southeastern five-lined skink, *Plestiodon inexpectatus*, adult male

106. Broad-headed skink, *Plestiodon laticeps*, adult female, photo by Daniel Dye

Broad-headed skink, *Plestiodon laticeps*, dominant male, photo by Daniel Dye

107. Florida sand skink *Plestiodon reynoldsi*

108. Ground skink, *Scincella laterale*

109A. Giant ameiva, *Ameiva ameiva*, green-rumped phase

109B. Giant ameiva, *Ameiva ameiva*, dusky phase

110. Giant whiptail, *Aspidoscelis motaguae*

111. Six-lined racerunner, *Aspidoscelis sexlineatus sexlineatus*

112. Rainbow whiptail, *Cnemidophorus lemniscatus*, adult male

Rainbow whiptail, *Cnemidophorus lemniscatus*, female

113. Black-and-white tegu, *Tupinambis merianae*

113A. Golden tegu, *Tupinambis teguixin*

Crocodile monitor, *Varanus salvadorii*

114. Nile monitor, *Varanus niloticus*, juvenile

Nile monitor, *Varanus niloticus*, adult

114A. Savanna monitor, *Varanus exanthematicus*, hatchling

114B. Asian water monitor,
Varanus salvator, juvenile

115. Southern painted
turtle, *Chrysemys
picta dorsalis*, juvenile

Reptiles Defined

Representatives of the groups marked with asterisks (***) occur in Florida

Kingdom	Animalia
Phylum	Chordata
Subphylum	Vertebrata
Class	Reptilia
Order	Rhynchocephalia (Tuataras)
	*** Crocodilia (Crocodiles, Alligators, & Gavials)
	*** Chelonia (Turtles & Tortoises)
	*** Squamata
	suborders
	*** Amphisbaenia (Worm Lizards)
	*** Sauria (Lizards)
	*** Serpentes (Snakes)

Beyond this, each order is divided into families, subfamilies, genera, species, and subspecies.

Basics of Captive Care

A Word of Caution

Before collecting or molesting reptiles in the wild, we urge you to check the list of protected or regulated species on page 37. In some instances, it is perfectly legal to collect a specimen (sometimes two) of state-regulated species of special concern for personal use (not for commercial purposes). You would be well advised to check with the regulatory division of the Florida Fish and Wildlife Conservation Commission for particulars. Violating the laws protecting reptiles and amphibians is a serious offense.

The keeping of reptiles in captivity is a mainstream hobby today. Millions of dollars are spent annually in the acquisition of reptiles and support equipment such as cages, cage furniture, and food items.

Many of Florida's reptiles are major components of the pet trade. Although hobbyists show most interest in snakes, some lizards and turtles also figure prominently.

General

Despite the fact that with each passing day there are fewer natural habitats in Florida and a correspondingly dwindling number of fauna, it remains entirely legal in Florida to volume collect and commercialize on any unprotected or unregulated native reptile. No established alien species are protected; however, with that said, many species of Florida reptiles and amphibians are now bred in captivity for commercial purposes. We advocate the purchase of domestically bred specimens whenever possible rather than continued collecting from the wild.

We have learned over the years that the long-term maintenance of reptiles and amphibians is not always as simple as it initially seems. Certainly a suitably sized terrarium and food and water will suffice for the short term for the specimen in question, but for long term, many species need more personalized, and in some cases, exacting care.

For example, many lizards, among them the anoles and geckos, do not recognize water in a ground-level dish. These species drink pendulous droplets of dew and mist from leaves, branches, and even the walls or eaves of buildings. To give these lizards water, it is necessary to mist their enclosure daily, or to otherwise provide water droplets. One technique is to elevate a water dish to perch level and continually roil the water surface with an aquarium air stone attached to the smallest available pump.

Ultraviolet rays, UV-A and UV-B, allow most heliothermic (sun basking) reptiles to synthesize vitamin D3 in their skin. The D3 then facilitates the normal metabolism of calcium from food. Without these rays, the natural production of calcium slows nearly to a halt. When calcium is not continually produced, the body takes calcium from the bones to maintain levels in the blood. Eventually the bones become soft, the face distorted and the backbone kinked. Calcium deficiency is completely preventable, but you do need to provide the correct diet and access to UV.

Although the best source of ultraviolet rays is natural, unfiltered sunlight, full-spectrum bulbs that provide some UV-A and UV-B rays are now available for both incandescent and fluorescent fixtures.

It was thought that diet augmentation with oral D3 and calcium was a suitable alternative to natural production by the reptiles. This is no longer thought to be so. Reptile nutritionists learned rather recently that very little calcium is actually metabolized properly from dietary additives. Again, it's sunlight you need.

Although calcium is imperative for survival, an overabundance of calcium can actually be harmful, for it can be drawn into the viscera, creating lesions and gout. Our recommendation is, whenever possible, go natural. Provide unfiltered sunlight, or use full-spectrum bulbs and allow your specimens to synthesize and metabolize their calcium needs naturally. When this is not possible, provide additives, but do so sparingly, and use mixtures with at least twice as much calcium as phosphorus.

Many lizards previously thought to be solely insectivorous or carnivorous will readily consume blossoms, leaves, and nectar. We suggest you provide your lizards (especially anoles, geckos, basilisks, and curly-tails) with a liquid honey-fruit mixture. The following formula is suitable:

1/3 small baby-food jar of pureed apricot or mango baby food
1/3 small baby-food jar of water
1/3 small baby-food jar of honey
1 level teaspoon of powdered D3-calcium additive.
Mix well, provide daily, keep unused portion in the refrigerator but
discard all not used weekly.

Fruit-flavored yogurt seems equally beneficial, is certainly less time consuming to prepare, and has a longer refrigerated shelf life.

Provide a suitably large and appointed terrarium. Research the basic needs of the species with which you're working, then improve those basics by at least 25%.

A terrarium can be built to simulate a number of habitats, woodland, arid land, semiaquatic, and aquatic among them. Terraria can be horizontally oriented for terrestrial species or vertically oriented for arboreal species.

In general, to be active and digest their food properly, reptiles need to be kept warm. The degree of warmth, and whether best provided by illumination (for heliothermic species) or radiantly (for thigmothermic species), will depend on the species being kept; however, by providing terraria having thermal gradients (warm on one end, cooler on the other), you will incorporate the comfort zones of many if not most Florida species. If providing heat by overhead bulbs, consider full-spectrum bulbs. The temperature of a selected basking area should be in the mid-90s to 105°F for Florida lizards and turtles and 10 to 15 degrees cooler at the cool end of the tank.

Above all, if you lose interest in your reptile or amphibian, either find it a new home with enthusiastic keepers, return it to the breeders, or release it in the exact spot it was collected.

Turtles and Tortoises

Since all the flippered marine species and the gopher tortoise are protected, we will limit our captive care comments to the brackish water diamondbacks and all freshwater forms.

For all semiaquatic turtle species, an aquarium with several inches of water and a brightly illuminated and warmed haul-out area is needed.

Diamondback terrapins feed on mollusks, crustaceans, worms, and other such fare in the wild. Females develop an enlarged head that helps them in crushing the shells of prey items. These turtles will thrive in captivity in a suitable terrarium with lightly salted water (one teaspoon of marine salt to a gallon of water is fine). They will also do well in freshwater, but if scratched or bruised are more apt to develop a fungal infection in a freshwater setup (and this type of infection is difficult to clear up).

Map turtles are the freshwater equivalents of the diamondbacks. The females of the two Florida species of map turtles both develop enormously enlarged heads with age and switch from eating worms and insects to eating shellfish. These turtles need very clean water to prevent bacterial shell diseases (again, a disease embedded in bone is very difficult to eradicate).

Babies of the sliders, cooters, and other freshwater turtles of Florida do very well in an aquarium. The cage can be as simple or as complex as you choose to make it. In the wild, babies of these turtles feed largely on insects, worms, and small gastropods. In captivity they will readily accept a commercial turtle diet as well as crickets, small worms, and other culinary delights.

Merely because of the large space you must provide for them, larger freshwater turtles can be difficult to keep indoors. They are more easily kept outdoors in a garden pool or similar setup. As the cooters, sliders, and red-bellied turtles grow, they become more herbivorous. Captive adults will do well on a diet of water plants, lettuces (no iceberg lettuce; it has very little nutritional value), other greens, and a little low-fat dog chow.

Chicken turtles are somewhat less adaptable, but some do well in setups like the ones described above. Chicken turtles seem to do best on a diet high in worms, crayfish, and minnows. Some will accept crickets and other invertebrates and low-fat dog foods.

Box turtles are also protected in Florida, but many are in captivity. This is a terrestrial turtle that does best in outside garden pens, with full access to Mother Nature.

Despite their reputation for herbivory, box turtles are actually very omnivorous. They enjoy succulent worms, crickets, and carrion, as well as mushrooms, berries, and some greens. Captives seem to do well on these items plus low-fat dog food with a few berries and bananas added.

Soft-shelled turtles are fully aquatic and will thrive for years in aquaria with a layer of fine sand on the bottom. It is necessary, of course, to maintain suitable water quality. Softshells readily accept minnows (long-term use of goldfish is not recommended), worms, and some prepared foods.

We have found hatchlings of the Florida softshell turtle difficult to maintain. These little turtles have a tendency to develop fungal problems no matter how clean their water. Perhaps highly acid water would overcome this problem.

It is a good idea to keep softshells singly. By doing so, you eliminate the possibility of them scratching one another and eliminate one potential for the development of fungus.

Crocodilians

The only one of Florida's crocodilians not protected in some manner by state or federal regulations is the introduced spectacled caiman, but a permit is needed to keep even this one in captivity.

Baby crocodilians of any type are irascible as babies, and they become more aggressive and problematic with increasing age and size.

Babies can be maintained in a large aquarium containing several inches of tepid water and a warmed, illuminated, smooth haul-out area where they can bask and dry. The cleanliness of the water must be maintained, of course.

Crocodilians are carnivores and will accept fish, worms, and suitably sized mice.

Lizards

The lizards of Florida run the full gamut of habitat preferences. There is much variety in habitat preference, even among lizards of a given family. For example, while the color-changing anoles are largely arboreal, most of the perpetually brown species live low on the trunks of trees or on the ground. Similarly, most geckos live rather high on the walls of buildings or, more rarely, trunks of trees; others, such as the reef and ocellated geckos, dwell in ground litter. Eastern glass lizards enjoy damper conditions in the wild than the other three Florida species of glass lizards, and broad-headed skinks are far more arboreal than a ground skink. Other skinks and worm lizards (amphisbaenians) are burrowers.

The message here is that, to provide suitable quarters for your captive lizard, you must be aware of its habitat preferences.

Provide dry quarters with climbing facilities for fence and scrub lizards, brown-colored anoles, and skinks with five lines (broad-heads, five-lines, southeastern five-lines). The substrate can be sand, newspapers, or paper towels, or flat dry leaves (such as those of the live oak). Glass lizards prefer a few inches of dry sand or sandy loam, topped with an inch or two of dry leaves or a flat board where they can seclude themselves.

Provide arboreal lizards, including the various color-changing anoles, basilisks, and baby iguanas, with a vertically oriented terrarium, or at least with a spacious, tall, horizontally oriented cage. Basilisks are nervous lizards prone to dashing into the glass of a terrarium when the cage is approached, damaging their noses as a result. A visual barrier such as a piece of cloth or newspaper can be taped to the front of the cage to prevent frightening these remarkable-appearing lizards.

Curly-tails appreciate a heated, illuminated rock or large-diameter log on the substrate for a vantage point.

Green and spiny-tailed iguanas do well as captives providing they are given sufficient space and a primarily vegetable diet. Despite the fact that the iguanas of both genera eagerly eat insects and meats, there is now irrefutable evidence that diets high in animal proteins are cumulatively deleterious to long-range health. A little animal protein may not hurt (especially the spiny-tails), but the major portion of the diet should be greens rich in vitamins and minerals and lacking oxalic acid (oxalic acid inhibits metabolism of calcium). It appears that neither green nor spiny-tailed iguanas metabolize oral calcium well. This is especially so when they are not provided with strong, full-spectrum lighting (unfiltered natural sunlight is best for this, but do not put a glass terrarium in the sun; you will literally cook your lizards). If you intend to use natural sunlight for any reptile, devise a cage from wire or wire over a wooden frame and be certain that adequate shade is provided.

A Note on Toxicity

Although it only makes sense to wash your hands after handling an amphibian or reptile, we felt a word of caution about possible toxicity and other potential dangers of a few species was needed.

No Florida lizard, crocodilian, or turtle has toxic potential, but there is a chance of contamination by salmonella or other pathogens from these and most other sources. Additionally, all can, and many will, bite.

Again we offer these admonitions: handle all reptiles carefully and wash your hands before and after handling any reptile!

A Note on Taxonomy

The science of classification is called taxonomy. With changing times have come changing, and often conflicting, methods of determining the long-time standing and validity of reptile family, genus, species, and subspecies determinations.

The long-standing method for determining a species was known as Linnaean taxonomy (biological classification). In this method the validity of a species was determined largely by its similarities to or differences from other taxa. Visible physical (structural) similarities and an ability to interbreed and produce viable young were important criteria. Subspecies were recognized on the basis of what was loosely termed the "75% rule": if 75% or more of a given population were different in some manner from other populations, that is, color, pattern, or scalation, but all were still able to interbreed successfully, the criteria for classification as a subspecies were satisfied. As an example, the Linnaean system of taxonomy identified *Kinosternon subrubrum subrubrum*, the eastern mud turtle, plus two additional subspecies, *K. s. steindachneri*, the Florida mud turtle, and *K. s. hippocrepis*, the Mississippi mud turtle.

Although the Linnaean system of taxonomy was inexact, the trinomial nomenclature of these mud turtles indicated a rather consistent difference in appearance between the three subspecies but a relationship, and the fact that they could (and do) intergrade and produce viable offspring.

The Linnaean system is still widely accepted, but today it is being widely challenged by phylogenetic (evolutionary) philosophies. Still in its infancy, the use of molecular data in species determination has already undergone several metamorphoses and will probably undergo several more before becoming universal practice. Hopefully a system of checks and balances, now sadly missing, as well as more attention to morphology, will be among the improvements.

Mitochondrial DNA (mtDNA) was among the first of the molecular technologies used. Although still used in some analyses it was quickly learned that because mtDNA is passed on matrilineally, even the most tedious analysis garnered only part of the answer.

Now nuclear DNA (nDNA), which is passed on sexually and discloses traits of both parents, provides more substantive data.

Because we feel that a field guide is not the proper forum for arguing taxonomic principles, we have continued using, in most cases, familiar, long used, conservative taxonomy.

Wherever we felt them suitable, both the common and scientific names used in this book are those listed in *Scientific and Standard English Names of Amphibians and Reptiles of North America North of Mexico, with Comments Regarding Confidence in our Understanding.* This effort at standardization of names resulted from the opinions of many eminent herpetologists and was compiled and edited for SSAR by Brian I. Crother of Southeastern Louisiana University in Hammond.

Reptiles

Reptiles in some obscure and poorly understood form evolved from amphibian stock more than 315 million years ago, during the early Upper Carboniferous Period. The lineage of modern reptiles can be traced back some 280 million years to the Permian Era.

Extant today are some 6,600+ species belonging to more than 900+ genera, 48+ families, and 4 orders.

Reptiles, of course, include species as diverse as 30-foot reticulated pythons, 20-foot saltwater crocodiles, 6-foot leatherback turtles, and 2-inch reef geckos.

Reptiles may be terrestrial, fossorial, arboreal, semiaquatic, or predominantly aquatic. In these latter two categories are some species so specialized that they cannot function well out of water.

Reptiles have scales (of some form) covering their skin, most have limbs, and if toes are present, claws are also usually present.

Of the four orders, three occur in Florida. One order, the Squamata, can be broken into three suborders, all of which have Florida representatives.

1

Turtles and Tortoises

Order Chelonia

These groups of shelled reptiles are all easily recognized as turtles, but specific identification can be more difficult.

Despite their similarities, turtles and tortoises are a diverse lot, with widely varying needs and lifestyles. Contained in the 13 families are some 75 genera and about 250 species.

Of these, 7 families and 27 species (41 subspecies) occur in Florida.

The family breakdown in Florida is as follows:

Family Cheloniidae, Typical Sea Turtles (4 species)
Family Chelydridae, Snapping Turtles (2 species)
Family Dermochelyidae, Leatherback Sea Turtle (1 species)
Family Emydidae, Basking and Box Turtles (11 species)
Family Kinosternidae, Musk and Mud Turtles (4 species)
Family Pelomedusidae, Advanced Sidenecks (1 species)
Family Testudinidae, Tortoises (1 species)
Family Trionychidae, Soft-shelled Turtles (3 species)

Although used differently in other parts of the world, in the United States the term *turtle* refers to both freshwater and marine species. The terms *cooter* (of African derivation) and *slider* are also used for some of the big basking emydines. In the United States, *terrapin* refers to the brackish and saltwater emydines known commonly as diamondbacks. The word *tortoise* is applied only to exclusively terrestrial species.

It is often thought that the shell makes turtles impervious to attacks and predation. Certainly the shell helps protect these creatures, but it does not always succeed.

Alligators routinely dine on their freshwater chelonian neighbors, and terrestrial box turtles and hatchlings still in nests are adversely impacted by an introduced scourge, the tiny tropical fire ant. Predation by raccoons, opossums, dogs, and cats occurs on eggs and hatchling specimens. The highest visible toll, though, is taken by cars and trucks as turtles cross roadways.

HOW TO FIND TURTLES AND TORTOISES IN FLORIDA

As with all other reptiles and amphibians, to find turtles (except by accident) you must travel to and carefully search their habitats.

Sea turtles, of course, are restricted to marine environments but are usually encountered only when females come ashore at night in the late spring, summer, and early autumn to lay eggs. Be aware, though, that all marine turtles of Florida are Endangered or Threatened, hence protected by both federal and state regulations. Their nesting activities are often monitored by watchdog groups that disallow close approach by observers. Sea turtles are most usually encountered on the southern three-fourths of Florida's Atlantic coast and on the beaches of Lee and Collier counties on the Gulf coast.

Box turtles are open-meadow and woodland animals that may be active by day during or following showers and are especially so in the spring and early summer months.

Gopher tortoises are creatures of the sandy ridges that support the grasses and herbs on which they feed. Their burrows are telltale signs of the tortoises' presence.

Diamondback terrapins are now uncommon throughout the state. They may occasionally be seen at low tide in brackish marshes as they swim or walk in water-retaining channels.

The big basking turtles—the sliders and cooters—are commonly seen in canals, ditches, lakes, and rivers throughout the state. They are wary where persecuted for food or other reasons but are often accustomed to rather close approach in state and federal parks where they are protected.

Marine Turtles

Sea turtles—Coastline Chelonians

The tide was low and the moon was new. The night was as dark as possible for a South Florida beachfront night. The waves were busily rearranging the sands, and we could dimly see sand crabs skittering up and down in the ever-changing ebb and flow. The hours moved slowly as we stood chatting, waiting, and hoping.

We had arrived as the last vestiges of daylight vanished and now, hours later, as the lights dimmed and winked out in the high-rises above us, we were about to despair. We had hoped against hope that a leatherback, the largest of the sea turtles, would choose this night to grace this nesting beach. But now we would gratefully accept the presence of any of the sea turtles, with our most likely chance being a loggerhead or a green.

We weren't alone in our hopes. There were others, waiting quietly in little groups—sea turtles have an amazingly large and diverse following of well-wishers and support groups.

Just as we began heading for our cars (already quietly discussing the best time for our next visit), a rounded shape, only a bit darker than the night itself, materialized in the shallows a few feet from the water's edge. We stopped and stared. A strong wave carried the shape a bit closer to shore. The shape lurched upward a few feet and rested. Then it moved a few feet more. Definitely a turtle, but what kind remained to be seen. Although we instinctively knew that what we were seeing was not the coveted leather-back, there was always a chance that rather than the relatively common log-gerhead sea turtle it could be the rarer green sea turtle.

Until they actually begin laying their eggs, a crawling or nesting sea turtle can be easily startled back to the sea. So we stood in silence in the dark as the creature crawled, lurched, and rested its way toward its destination, some-where near the dunes where sea grasses and sea oats grew, somewhere above the level of the high tides, somewhere determined suitable for nest-ing solely by the turtle's instincts.

But she never completed her journey. Down the beach came a running dog followed by a jogger. Although we tried to wave the runner down to alert him to the turtle's presence, dog and owner never slowed as they went between the turtle and her destination. The creature quickly reversed direc-tion and made a rapid return to the sea. We were able to identify her as a loggerhead, the most common of the three species that typically nest along that stretch of beach.

So, no nesting tonight. Maybe tomorrow night will be still and quiet enough for her to come ashore again to lay her eggs, and in a few months her hatchlings will emerge and make their spraddle-legged rush to the sea.

~~~~~~

TYPICAL SEA TURTLES: FAMILY CHELONIIDAE

There are four beleaguered members of this family that may be found in Florida's waters. Two, the loggerhead and the green turtle, nest here in some numbers, and two, the hawksbill and the Atlantic Ridley, are ac-cidental. Egg-bearing females return to their natal beach to lay their eggs.

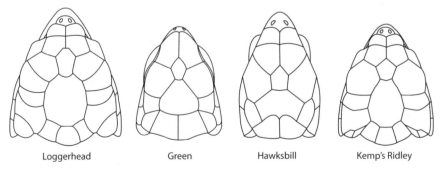

| Loggerhead | Green | Hawksbill | Kemp's Ridley |

Sea turtle head plates from top

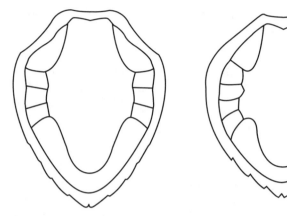

Comparison of bridge plates of loggerhead (*left*) and Atlantic ridley (*right*)

All these turtles have flipperlike limbs.

All, except the loggerhead, which is threatened, are federally endangered.

1. Loggerhead

Caretta caretta

Size: Third largest of the marine turtles, the loggerhead may attain a carapace length of more than 3½ feet and has been known to weigh more than 400 pounds. Hatchlings have a carapace length of 1¾ inches.

Identification: Once past the deep brown coloration of its hatchling stage, the turtle becomes reddish brown with tan highlights. On land the color is often obliterated by beach sand, and the true colors of this attractive turtle are easiest to note when the turtle is in the water. The following are additional clues to help you identify this species:

there are always 5 costal scutes on each side of the shell
the first costal scute always touches the nuchal scute
there are usually 3 non-pored scutes on the bridge
there are 2 pairs of prefrontal scales (between the eyes)

Habitat/Range: Tropical and subtropical oceans are home to the loggerhead. It may be seen anywhere along Florida's coastline.

Abundance: This marine species is relatively common but still considered a threatened species. It is the most commonly seen of the five marine species in Florida waters.

Behavior: Hatchlings emerging from the nest can become confused by bright lights on or behind the beach and crawl away from the water, explaining why beach lighting levels are set by law. Although their numbers are now depleted, comparatively speaking, loggerheads are the most commonly seen marine turtle in Florida. Loggerheads consume shellfish, crustaceans, coelenterates, fish, and myriad other marine creatures.

Reproduction: Females nest bi- or triennially, but in breeding years lay several clutches of (up to 100 or more) eggs at intervals through the summer. Prior to the actual nesting, a body pit is dug with the forelimbs. That done, the egg chamber is dug with the hind limbs. Incubation takes 2 to 3 months.

Similar species: No other marine turtle is a warm reddish brown. Hawksbills are darker brown or have calico carapacial scutes and have only 4 costal scutes. Green turtles have only a single pair of prefrontal scales and only 4 costals. Ridleys are comparatively small, olive gray or gray in color, and have 4 pored bridge scutes.

Comments: This turtle, considered threatened by both federal and state conservation agencies, is completely protected in the United States by provisions of the Endangered Species Act and by state law. Neither they nor their eggs should be bothered in any way.

2. Green Turtle

Chelonia mydas mydas

Size: This gigantic marine turtle is exceeded in maximum size only by the leatherback. Green turtles are adult at from 3 to 4½ feet in length and have been known to attain 5 feet. Weights of more than 500 pounds have been documented. Hatchlings average 2 inches in carapace length.

Identification: The carapace of adults is basically a light to dark brown. Radiating dark lines may be visible on some of the lighter specimens. There are 4 costal scutes on each side. The first costal is not in contact with the nuchal scale. The venter is light. Hatchlings are dark brown to nearly black with the flippers edged neatly in white.

This species has only a single pair of prefrontal scales (the scales between the eyes).

Habitat/Range: This is a species of open tropical and subtropical oceans that is often seen feeding on shallow eelgrass (turtle grass) flats. It may be encountered anywhere along Florida's coastline but is most common along the Atlantic coast.

Abundance: Fairly common in some tropical areas. This is the second most commonly encountered marine turtle species in Florida.

Behavior: This large turtle is often seen in shallow bays and estuaries where the various turtle grasses (its principal food) grow. Researchers now estimate that more than 200 females are nesting annually on Florida's beaches. This number is a bare remnant of the number that nested here in historic times; however, there are indications that the number that do nest here is once again increasing slowly.

Reproduction: Female green turtles nest only every two or three years. A body pit is first made with the front flippers, and then the nest is dug with the rear flippers. During her nesting year a female green turtle may lay from 1 to a half dozen times, depositing about 100 eggs at each nesting. The duration of incubation is about 2 months.

Similar species: All other sea turtles of this family found in Florida have two pairs of prefrontal scales.

Comments: In recent years green turtle populations have been plagued by rapidly developing viral fibropapillomas. It is thought that susceptibility to these viral growths may be enhanced by various pollutants. A great deal of research is now directed toward this problem. Florida populations are federally endangered.

3. Atlantic Hawksbill

Eretmochelys imbricata imbricata

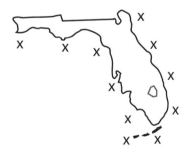

Size: This is a rather small sea turtle. Adults have a 28 to 32 inch carapace length. The record size is only 36 inches. Most hawksbills weigh from 100 to 175 pounds. Hatchlings are 1½ inches long.

Identification: The carapace of the hawksbill is brown(ish), often with a prominent tortoiseshell pattern. the carapacial scutes are imbricate (overlapping). The plastron is light yellow in color. Young are quite similar to the adults in color but usually have a more vividly contrasting pattern. Hatchlings are very dark brown and lack a carapacial pattern. This species has a narrow hawklike beak. Yellow interstitial skin is visible between the head scales.

Habitat/Range: A species of the open ocean, the hawksbill is more frequently seen in the Atlantic than in the Gulf.

Abundance: This is a rarely seen accidental in Florida.

Behavior: Thanks to the dedication of sea turtle researcher Larry Wood, data regarding the life of this turtle in Florida are now being accumulated. Hawksbills feed on algae and other vegetation as well as on sponges, mollusks, crustaceans, and myriad other marine creatures.

Reproduction: A body pit is dug, primarily with the foreflippers; the nest is then dug with the rear flippers. Females nest bi- or triennially. Several clutches are laid in nesting years. The clutch size varies from 50 to more than 150 eggs. Incubation takes about 60 days.

Similar species: This is the only sea turtle of Florida with 4 costal scutes on each side and 4 prefrontal scales.

Comments: Like most other sea turtles, the Atlantic hawksbill is considered endangered and is fully protected. The carapacial scutes are used for decorations, and young hawksbills are killed and stuffed as novelties.

Researcher Larry Wood (personal communication) has learned that a noteworthy population of hawksbills occurs in the waters just seaward from Palm Beach, Florida. His research has shown that they often remain in this protected locale for up to 15 years before journeying southward or eastward to their breeding beaches.

4. Atlantic Ridley

Lepidochelys kempii

Size: The Atlantic ridley is the smallest of Florida's sea turtles. It is adult at 20 to 25 inches. Its record size is only 29½ inches. Its average weight is about 90 pounds. Hatchlings are about 1½ inches long.

Identification: Hatchlings are a rather uniform gray with a lighter stripe on the trailing edge of each front flipper. Adults are olive green to gray above and yellowish ventrally. There are 5 costals, 2 pairs of prefrontal scales, and either 4 (usually) or 5 (rarely) pored scutes on the bridge.

Habitat/Range: This oceangoing species is accidental in Florida waters. It was once common in the Gulf of Mexico.

Abundance: Although very rare, this turtle may now be making a modest comeback.

Behavior: Although now often seen nesting singly (because there are so few of them), the Atlantic ridley is normally a communally breeding species. A headstart program is in place in Galveston, Texas, and ridleys now nest on Gulf beaches.

Reproduction: This species once appeared in vast nesting arribadas on the Gulf coast of northern Mexico. These congregations have been greatly reduced. Atlantic ridleys continue to breed in small numbers on the Mexican coast, on the Texas coast, and rarely on both coasts of Florida.

Females nest only every second or third year. First a body pit is dug, then the egg chamber. Seventy to 100 eggs are laid. Females may nest several times during each breeding season. Incubation lasts about 2 months.

Similar species: Green turtles have only one pair of prefrontal scales. The Atlantic hawksbill has 4 costals on each side. A loggerhead has only 3 scutes (non-pored) on the bridge.

Comments: This is the most seriously endangered of the Florida sea turtles. It is encouraging that a few females have been documented nesting on our beaches, but the number is far lower than needed to assure the species' survival.

LEATHERBACK SEA TURTLE: FAMILY DERMOCHELYIDAE

This oceangoing behemoth is the largest turtle still extant. A carapace length of more than 6 feet and a weight of more than a ton have been recorded. This family has been erected solely for this divergent turtle.

Like all marine turtles, the leatherback has flipperlike limbs.

5. Atlantic Leatherback

Dermochelys coriacea coriacea

Size: Most specimens seen have a carapace length of 3½ to 5 feet. 74¼ inches is the record carapace length. Hatchlings are about 2¾ inches long.

Identification: The carapace and skin are slate blue to black. There are no plates on the carapace. There are scattered white, yellowish, or pinkish markings. There are seven pronounced longitudinal keels on the carapace. The plastron is lighter than the carapace in color. Males have variably concave plastrons. Adult females tend to have pinkish markings on the top of the head; these may be present on males but often are not. The front flippers are proportionately immense. Hatchlings have a ground color much like the adults but have numerous small (often white) scales (later shed), white keels, and white outlining both front and rear flippers.

Voice: Leatherbacks are capable of emitting sounds reminiscent of a human belch.

Habitat/Range: This is a pelagic marine species about which very little is known. It is occasionally seen in Florida's Atlantic and Gulf coast waters.

Abundance: This is a rare and endangered turtle.

Behavior: This is a wide-ranging turtle that is capable, because of circulatory modifications, of sustaining a warm body temperature in very cold waters. The diet of this turtle consists almost entirely of jellyfish (including notably venomous species). When disturbed or injured, leatherbacks have been known to attack boats. They are immensely powerful, and extreme care should be used when observing them.

Reproduction: Above the tideline on open beaches, this immense turtle first digs a body pit with the foreflippers, then a nesting cavity with the rear flippers. Several clutches of up to 150 eggs are laid by a given female. A female lays only every second or third year. Incubation takes 2½ to 3½ months.

Similar species: None.

Comments: Encouraging news: In 2009 the greatest number of leatherback nestings in many decades—more than 300—was documented in the vicinity of Juno Beach, Florida.

Deaths of even large leatherbacks have occurred after the turtles have ingested floating clear plastic bags, apparently mistaking them for jellyfish.

Fresh and Brackish Water Turtles

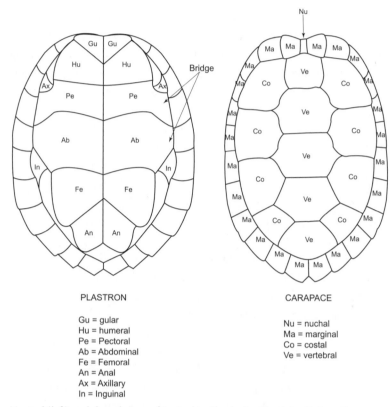

PLASTRON

Gu = gular
Hu = humeral
Pe = Pectoral
Ab = Abdominal
Fe = Femoral
An = Anal
Ax = Axillary
In = Inguinal

CARAPACE

Nu = nuchal
Ma = marginal
Co = costal
Ve = vertebral

Ventral (*left*) and dorsal view of typical turtle shell with plate designations

SNAPPING TURTLES: FAMILY CHELYDRIDAE

Adult males of the alligator snapping turtle are among the world's largest freshwater turtles. Several specimens of more than 200 pounds have been found, and believable anecdotal reports of at least one alligator snapper exceeding 300 pounds exist.

The common snappers are much smaller, but they still should be approached with extreme care on land. In the water they are much more benign. All the snapping turtles have long tails, and the two races of common snapper have very long necks. The brown carapaces of all are very rough and prominently keeled, at least when the turtles are young.

Snippets and Snappets about Snappers

The population of alligator snappers in the larger river systems of north Florida seems reasonably secure; certainly, when biologists from the State Fish and Wildlife Conservation Commission indulge in trapping attempts, they succeed in their quest. But concern for the long-term stability of the several populations of this, Florida's largest freshwater turtle species (some males exceed 200 pounds!), remains.

Every few years the finding of a hatchling alligator snapper, for no reason other than photography, becomes a seasonal herping priority. I think that all baby turtles are cute. I reserve "really cute" for hatchling alligator snappers, and if you ever hear me use the term "really, really, cute" when I'm out looking for one of these turtles, it means I've actually found one and that I'm very happily surprised, for I'm far more accustomed to failure in these searches than to success.

When the snapper-finding-bug bites, I look for a field herping companion such as Carl May or Kenny Wray, hop in the car, and head toward Florida's panhandle rivers. Once we are there, by day or by night, canoeing, wading, or walking the shoreline, marveling at the swallow-tailed and Mississippi kites overhead or the "plop" of a surprised river cooter or the caterwauling of barred owls, the search begins.

Sometimes the search will continue for more than a day before we concede failure and move on to a search for carnivorous plants or kingsnakes. But sometimes, albeit rarely, a blob of mud on the side of a submerged root will sprout legs, tail, and head and scuttle downward. We have then achieved our goal of finding one of those really, really, cute baby alligator snapping turtles. We leave, this time, elated.

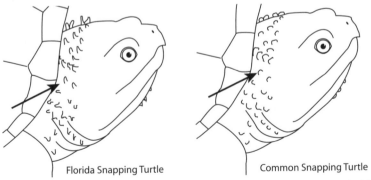

Florida Snapping Turtle   Common Snapping Turtle

Comparison of neck papillae of Florida (*left*) and common snapping turtle (*right*)

6. Common Snapping Turtle

Chelydra serpentina serpentina

common
Florida

Size: Of the two subspecies found in Florida, this is slightly the larger. It tops out at a carapace length of a bit more than 20 inches. The shell length with tail extended and neck only partially so would add up to a turtle with length of well over a yard! The weight of an adult wild specimen can be up to 40 pounds. Hatchlings have a carapace length of approximately 1 inch.

Identification: The color of the common snapping turtle's carapace is brownish tan, horn, or olive gray. Light-colored examples may have darker radiating markings on the costal scutes. The posterior edge of the carapace is strongly serrate. The papillae on the neck of this race are rounded, not pointed cones. Hatchlings are rugose and chestnut to dark brown. They have a light spot on the outer edge of each marginal. The plastron is very small and pliable. The tail is longer than the carapace, and the neck, when fully extended, is nearly as long. The tail has a strongly serrate dorsal crest.

Adults are proportioned like the juveniles but are less rugose. Specimens in water high in sulfur or iron may appear whitish or rusty. If algae are growing on the carapace, the turtle can appear green.

Habitat/Range: Nearly any quiet or slowly flowing and heavily vegetated body of freshwater, as well as weakly brackish water, is an acceptable home site for this adaptable turtle. It ranges throughout the Florida panhandle and in Nassau County.

Abundance: This is a common turtle.

Behavior: The snapper eats all manner of aquatic life, either living or as carrion, as well as a substantial amount of plant material. When safe in its aquatic element, this turtle is usually quiet and relatively benign. When on land, it can be savagely defensive. Do not approach this turtle carelessly. It might elevate its hind quarters prior to snapping, or it might stand high on all four legs, but neither behavior is an invariable sign of an impending snap.

Reproduction: These are fecund turtles that usually construct a body pit before digging the nest. More than 50 eggs can be laid. Females nest annually. Depending on nest temperature and soil conditions, hatchlings can emerge after incubating slightly less than 2 months or more than 4 months.

Similar species: The alligator snapper has a more massive head, a strongly down-hooked beak, and a shorter neck, and it lacks a strongly serrated dorsal tail crest.

Comments: Snapping turtles continue to be a food source for many people. They are often indiscriminately killed by fishermen who erroneously blame the beasts for depleted stocks of game fish.

7. Florida Snapping Turtle, *Chelydra serpentina osceola,* replaces the common snapper on the Florida peninsula. It is found from Columbia, Baker, and southern Nassau counties to the southern tip of the peninsula. Hatchlings are rugose and chestnut to dark brown. They have a light spot on the outer edge of each marginal. Adults are somewhat smoother and olive brown to dark brown. The plastron is very small and pliable. The tail is longer than the carapace, and the neck, when fully extended in a snap, is nearly as long. The tail has a strongly serrate dorsal crest.

Adults are less rugose than the juveniles. This subspecies has conical papillae on the head and neck.

Specimens in water high in sulfur or iron may appear whitish or rusty. If algae are growing on the carapace, the turtle can appear green.

8. Alligator Snapping Turtle

Macrochelys temminckii

Size: Males are by far the larger sex. They occasionally exceed 175 pounds and rarely attain 250 pounds (or more). Carapace length of a big male is 20–24 inches! Adult females usually weigh less than 55 pounds. Hatchlings have a carapace length of about 1½ inches.

Identification: This is a brown turtle at all stages of its life. Hatchlings are mud brown, dorsally and ventrally. Adults may darken or pale. On pale specimens there may be an indication of radiating dark lines on the costal scutes. Hatchlings are extremely rugose. With growth the carapace smooths somewhat and the rugosities of the proportionately large head and neck become less accentuated. The plastron is very small. Although they are not easily seen, an extra row of scutes, the supramarginals, lie between the costals and the marginal scutes. The head cannot be withdrawn entirely within the shell. The dorsal surface of the tail is weakly serrate.

This turtle has a white (when at rest) to red (when in use) tongue appendage that resembles a worm. When angling, the mouth is opened widely, and the appendage is flicked and twisted. When a passing fish swims into the mouth to investigate, the jaws snap shut, and dinner is served.

Habitat/Range: This is a turtle of big rivers, big creeks, backwaters, and reservoirs. It is found from Gilchrist and Alachua counties westward throughout the panhandle.

Abundance: This gigantic turtle is moderately common to uncommon throughout its Florida range.

Behavior: Rather placid in the water, this turtle can be aggressively defensive on land. Since its neck is not as long, it cannot snap for as great a distance as a common snapper. Alligator snappers are persistently aquatic and seldom wander onto land. Among other items, fish, frogs, and other turtles are eaten.

Reproduction: Breeding occurs in the early spring, and egg laying begins a month or so later. In a site above the high-water line, the female alligator snapper digs first a body pit and then the nest. An accessible bank, extensive sandbar, or island is often chosen. Up to 50 eggs are laid. Incubation duration is somewhat more than 3 months.

Similar species: Common snappers have proportionately smaller heads, very long necks, and strongly serrate tails.

Comments: Larger specimens are eaten by humans. The hatchlings, perennial favorites in the pet trade, can no longer be commercialized in Florida.

MUD AND MUSK TURTLES: FAMILY KINOSTERNIDAE

Collectively, the Florida representatives of this family are small turtles, and all have a rather highly domed carapace. Although basically aquatic, they often occur in shallow water situations, and some may wander far afield in search of new habitats.

Our musk turtles have pointed conical noses, and their single-hinged plastrons are so reduced in size that they offer little protection to the turtle's soft parts. (In contrast, the plastron of the mud turtle is larger and has 2 hinges. The nose is not as pointed as the nose of the musk turtle.)

Adult male musk and mud turtles have a heavy, enlarged tail that in some species is tipped with a curved spur.

These turtles all have strong jaws and will bite if carelessly handled.

If a carapacial pattern is present it is often most visible when the turtle is wet.

An odorous exudate (the musk) is produced in glands situated where the skin meets the bridge of the shell. Generally speaking, most people need only one sniff of the musk turtle bridge area to agree the turtles do indeed smell.

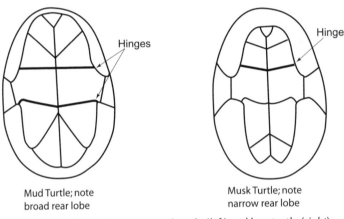

Mud Turtle; note
broad rear lobe

Musk Turtle; note
narrow rear lobe

Comparison of hinged plastra: mud turtle (*left*) and box turtle (*right*)

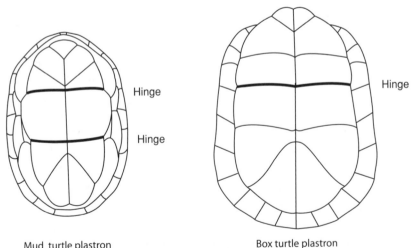

Mud turtle plastron

Box turtle plastron

Comparison of plastra: mud turtle (*left*) and musk turtle (*right*)

Muds/Musks—A Query about the Florida Mud Turtle

Where have all the Florida mud turtles gone?

Please understand that I'm not asking about all the mud turtles in Florida. Many kinds are still here and in relative profusion; rather, I am asking in particular about the Florida mud turtle, *Kinosternon subrubrum steindachneri*—that little (usually) black mud turtle with the horn-colored plastron and the big head.

Although I never considered Florida muds particularly common, today (late 2009), they seem actually uncommon to me. Is this a true reflection of their numbers, or merely a reflection of my inability to find the species?

In the 1980s there was a little grassy retention pond next to a little church in Ft. Myers where I could always depend on finding a couple of Florida mud turtles (in the pond—not the church). Adults were most common, but every year I would find a hatchling or two.

Then, although the pond and the turtles stayed, the church became a big church. The paved parking lot grew and almost surrounded the pond. The church expanded again, and the parking lot grew, completely surrounding the pond. Apparently parking space was still insufficient, for between two of my visits the pond was filled, tamped, and paved. The only locale I knew in Lee County where I could be assured of finding a Florida mud turtle was no more.

Despite my wanderings throughout Florida, I have found no more Florida muds. Striped muds are abundant, eastern muds are common, intergrades between eastern and Florida muds occur in expected habitats. But full-blooded Florida muds appear to be absent.

Although I conducted no dedicated searches for them, over a span of 15 years I found only one of these turtles. And during that same time frame, during his perambulations in South Florida, Carl May found only two or three. His were of such different appearance that they almost went unrecognized. Hailing from a region of pinnacle rock prairie flooded periodically by shallow algae and phytoplankton-covered water, the turtles Carl found were yellow, not black, in overall coloration! I saw a few of normal coloration on a collector's Web site, but compared with the hundreds of other mud turtles seen in Florida in the same time period, the number of Florida muds is painfully few. Which brings us back to the original question: do the comparative numbers we have seen reflect actuality, or are they merely an artifact of biased field practices?

Only time and dedicated studies will tell.

9. Striped Mud Turtle

Kinosternon baurii

Size: Most striped mud turtles are adult at 3½ to 4¼ inches in carapace length. An occasional example will approach a full 5 inches in length. Hatchlings have a carapace length of 1 inch or slightly less.

Identification: Carapace color can vary geographically. In most areas striped mud turtles have a black, brown, or duskily translucent carapace. There are usually three longitudinal yellowish lines on the carapace; however, carapacial stripes are typically lacking in Gulf Hammock, Okefenokee, and some Keys populations. Individuals from the seasonally flooded pinnacle rock prairies in extreme southern Florida may have a weakly striped blonde carapace. The large plastron is olive yellow to orange with dark pigment outlining each scute. The head is usually dark but may be predominantly yellow. Two variably prominent stripes on each side of the mottled face and a yellowish chin stripe are often present. The facial stripes may be lacking in some individuals and populations.

Habitat/Range: Ponds, lakes, swamps, marshes, canals, ditches, and most other freshwater situations are all utilized by this small turtle. It occasionally enters estuaries and other weakly brackish habitats as well. At times it may be found far from water, hunkered down under boards, leaf mats, or other terrestrial debris.

This mud turtle is found throughout the Keys and the peninsula but is absent on the panhandle west of the Chipola River.

Abundance: This turtle is abundant in most freshwater and some brackish water situations throughout southern peninsular Florida and the Keys, but it is uncommon to rare in north Florida.

Behavior: The striped mud turtle may be active by day, but actively forages in water-edge situations after nightfall. It may bury deeply into the mud when its water source dries, or it may strike out across country in search of more hospitable conditions. Populations often concentrate in puddles that form as their home waters dry.

Reproduction: Adult females lay several clutches of 1 to 4 eggs. The nesting site may be in water-edge soil or in decaying aquatic vegetation, either at water's edge or more rarely in thick floating mats. Incubation takes 3 to 4 months.

Similar species: The common musk turtle also has facial stripes but lacks carapacial stripes and has a reduced plastron. Florida mud turtle has a short rear plastral lobe that leaves much flesh exposed.

Comments: The Lower Key populations are considered endangered and are protected.

10. Eastern Mud Turtle

Kinosternon subrubrum subrubrum

eastern

Florida

Size: This small mud turtle is adult at a length of 4 to 4¾ inches. Hatchlings are about an inch in length.

Identification: The carapace of the eastern mud turtle is a warm to dark olive brown. The posterior edge of each carapacial scute, including the marginals, may be outlined by dark pigment. There may be whitish spots on the cheeks, and the jaws of many specimens are lighter than the head. The plastron is orangish. Hatchlings have a roughened carapace and pinkish plastron.

Male eastern mud turtles do not seem to develop the enlarged head often seen on males of the Florida race.

Habitat/Range: Ponds, cypress heads, flooded flatwood situations, river edges, and estuarine situations are among the habitats utilized. The eastern mud turtle is found in Florida in a narrow band from the Georgia border southward to Taylor, Columbia, and Duval counties and westward throughout the panhandle.

Abundance: Common, but not often seen in large concentrations.

Behavior: Seldom seen by day, this reclusive turtle enters shallows to forage at night.

Reproduction: Adult females produce several clutches of 3 to 5 eggs during the spring and summer months. The nests may be dug in sand, soil, or decaying vegetation. The hatchlings emerge after a 3-month incubation.

Similar species: The striped mud turtle is darker and usually has carapacial stripes. Where the ranges of the eastern and the Florida mud turtles abut, the two subspecies interbreed, and differentiating the two is a problem.

Comments: Eastern mud turtles often wander far from water and may be found beneath terrestrial debris.

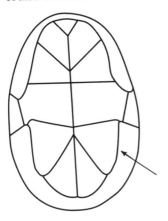
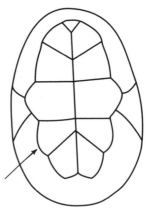

Eastern Mud Turtle   Florida Mud Turtle

Comparison of plastra: eastern (*left*) and Florida (*right*) mud turtle

11. Florida Mud Turtle, *Kinosternon subrubrum steindachneri*. Throughout most of its range, the Florida mud turtle is very similar in coloration to the eastern mud turtle. However, on the seasonally flooded pinnacle rock prairies in extreme southern Florida this turtle may have an olive carapace and extensive blonde reticulations on the head (very prominent on the face) and upper limbs. The Florida mud turtle has a proportionately narrower bridge than the eastern mud turtle as well as a short rear plastral lobe that leaves much flesh exposed. This subspecies occurs throughout the southern three-quarters of the peninsula. Although the Florida mud turtle is often found sympatrically with the striped mud turtle, it is never as common as the latter.

This highly aquatic turtle seems less prone to long overland journeys than the striped mud; however, the Florida mud turtle does wander and may occasionally be found far from water.

12. Loggerhead Musk Turtle

Sternotherus minor minor

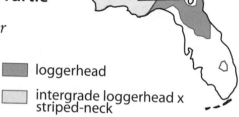

loggerhead

intergrade loggerhead x striped-neck

Size: An adult size of 5 inches is attained by this species. Hatchlings average 1 inch in carapace length.

Identification: The high three-keeled carapace can vary through several shades of brown and has downward radiating dark lines most prominent on the costal scutes. The head is grayish and liberally peppered with black dots. The small plastron is yellowish. Old adults are very dark in overall color, develop an enormous head, and may have light mandibles. Males have considerable expanses of skin showing between the scutes of the tan to olive tan plastral scutes; females have almost no skin showing. Hatchlings have a light olive tan carapace and a bright pink plastron.

Habitat/Range: This turtle is associated with flowing, freshwater habitats and their associated overflows and drainages. Look for it in the clear springs and rivers of the northern half of the Florida peninsula and the eastern panhandle.

Abundance: The loggerhead musk turtle is a common turtle.

Behavior: Although loggerhead musks are highly aquatic, they do occasionally move about on land. They may bask by ascending protruding snags or cypress knees or exposed, sloping tree trunks. They are active day and night but are more apt to enter shallow water situations after dark.

Reproduction: Adult females usually lay several clutches of 2 to 5 eggs early each summer. Little effort is made to conceal the nests, which may be situated against a tree, stump, rock, or other prominence, or merely scratched into the ground litter. Incubation takes about 3 months.

Similar species: Mud turtles have proportionately larger plastrons. The common musk turtle is darker and usually has well-defined yellow facial stripes.

Comments: At night these musk turtles walk, rather than swim, along the bottom of the river in search of worms or insects. These turtles can and will bite hard if carelessly restrained.

13. Stripe-necked Musk Turtle, *Sternotherus minor peltifer.* From Walton County westward on the panhandle, loggerhead musk turtles begin to show the influence of the more westerly race, the stripe-necked musk turtle. The carapace of the stripe-necked musk turtle is proportionately flatter, and the two dorsolateral keels are less prominent. The overall color may be darker, and the head and neck spots coalesce into stripes. This race also prefers creeks and streams but may inhabit nearby lakes and reservoirs and can be particularly common in impoundments.

14. Common Musk Turtle

Sternotherus odoratus

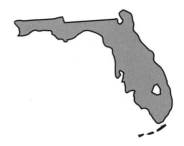

Size: The carapace length of adults of this common turtle ranges from 3 to 4½ inches. Hatchlings are 1 inch long.

Identification: Old adults have an olive black (rarely olive) to black stippled to solid black rather high but smoothly domed carapace. The small plastron is horn color. Males have considerable expanses of skin showing between the plastral scutes; females have almost none. The skin of the head and limbs is dark, and there are two variably prominent yellow lines on the side of the head. The carapace of the hatchlings is usually black in color and rough, with a strong medial keel and a weak dorsolateral keel on each side.

Habitat/Range: The common musk turtle may be found throughout the state in virtually any still or slowly flowing water source.

Abundance: Although very secretive, this species is abundant throughout the state.

Behavior: Despite its aquatic propensities, the common musk turtle often wanders extensively on land. After sundown during the spring breeding season, it occasionally enters shallow water in great numbers.

Reproduction: In Florida, female common musk turtles begin nesting early in the spring. Each female may nest two or more times, and the usual clutch size varies from 1 to 5 eggs. Hatchlings emerge after about 2½ months of incubation.

Similar species: Striped mud turtles have striped faces but also usually have carapacial stripes and a large hinged plastron.

Comments: This is one of the most abundant turtles in Florida (and the eastern United States). At night individuals often walk, rather than swim, along the bottom of ponds or lakes in search of worms or insects. These turtles can and will bite hard if carelessly restrained.

BASKING AND BOX TURTLES: FAMILY EMYDIDAE

The emydine turtles are well represented in Florida. There are a total of 11 species containing 21 subspecies. With the exception of 4 subspecies of box turtles and the introduced South American wood turtle, all Florida emydines are primarily aquatic.

Some, such as the spotted turtle, are rarely encountered in Florida. Others such as the various cooters and sliders are so common that it is sometimes difficult to complete a day in the field without seeing one or several. Most of the basking turtles are freshwater species; however, the diamondback terrapins (one species with 5 Florida races) are creatures of brackish and saltwater habitats.

Spotted Turtle: Genus *Clemmys*

Once thought to encompass many diverse New World and Old World turtles, in later years the genus *Clemmys* was restricted to the 4 North American "pond turtles," the wood turtle, bog turtle, Pacific pond turtle, and spotted turtle; however, this genus has again been redefined and now contains only the little spotted turtle, a species of woodland and pasture ponds and marshes.

The life history of the spotted turtle in the northeastern United States is rather well understood; the life history of this turtle in the southeast, and especially in Florida, remains enigmatic.

Unlike many other basking turtles, most of which seek sunny warmth during their periods of activity, the spotted turtle is a creature that is active during times when temperatures are moderate. It seems most active at temperatures between 60 and 75 °F, becoming inactive when temperatures drop into the low 50s or rise above the high 80s.

Emydines—A Spotted Lesson *Not* Learned

It seems that one or two spotted turtles are found in Florida every year, although I haven't managed to be one of those lucky few who find them. But my failure to find this pretty little turtle in Florida doesn't surprise me at all, because, for the most part, the spotted turtle is a cool-weather turtle, and Florida doesn't offer a whole lot of cool weather. Farther north, where spotted turtles are more common, they seem most active and quite ambulatory, weather permitting, from late winter to early summer and again in autumn.

This is a tale of the last spotted turtle, as far as I know, found in northeastern Florida—and sadly, it is a short tale.

In late January 2008 Paul Moler called to say that if I wished to photograph a real dyed-in-the-wool Florida spotted turtle, they had one, turned in by a motorist, at the Fish and Wildlife Commission office. Since the office is within a quarter-mile of our house, it took me less than 5 minutes to be standing on premises, camera in hand.

Pictures taken, within a half-hour I had learned the exact origin of the turtle and that within a few days "Old Spotty" was going to be fitted with a transmitter and turned loose almost precisely where he had been found. I thought that was great news for herpetologists, who still know precious little about the life cycle of *Clemmys guttata* in Florida. This was, I hoped, at least the start of an information trail.

After several weeks had passed without mention of the turtle, I queried Paul about its status. Sadly, Paul divulged that the turtle had been released on schedule, but before any information had been accumulated, Spotty had again wandered onto the same road where he had been found and met his demise beneath the wheels of a passing vehicle.

Despite all efforts, we know no more now about the life of the spotted turtle in Florida now than we did before Spotty came along.

15. Spotted Turtle

Clemmys guttata

Size: This is the smallest of Florida's turtles. Adults of both sexes attain from 3½ to 4½ inches and rarely may grow to 4¾ inches. Hatchlings are just over 1 inch in length.

Identification: The black head of both sexes is spotted with yellow dorsally. The mandibular area, nose, and chin of females are yellowish or orange. The corresponding facial areas of adult males are suffused with dark pigment. Spots on the sides of the head, neck, and legs are usually distinctly orange. The skin at the apices of all limbs and the neck is orange. Males usually have brown eyes; females have yellow or orange irises (irides). The plastron is a dark-smudged orange. The carapace is very deep brownish black to black with from one (hatchlings) to one or several (adults) yellow(ish) spots on each of the scutes (plates), including the marginals.

Habitat/Range: Spotted turtles have been found from Polk County northward throughout the peninsula and beyond. Many of the southernmost records in Florida lack voucher specimens or confirmation. Most spotted turtles found were crossing roadways in the vicinity of periodically flooded pine flatwoods or sphagnum swamps. In some areas of their range, spotted turtles periodically wander far from their water sources. It is unknown to what extent this occurs in Florida. This species is not known west of Wakulla County.

Abundance: Although very little is known about the population statistics of the spotted turtle in Florida, it seems uncommon to rare.

Behavior: The spotted turtle is most common in heavily vegetated (often sphagnaceous) ponds with occasional small to extensive open swimming areas. Unless hard pressed, spotted turtles as often as not walk and burrow through and into the herbaceous aquatic vegetation. Northern populations of spotted turtles are most active in cool weather (spring and autumn) and primarily diurnal in their activity patterns. By virtue of existing ambient temperatures in their Florida range, these southernmost spotted turtles may be more tolerant of heat than their northern counterparts; however, it is possible that in Florida spotted turtles are active primarily during the comparative coolness of late autumn, spring, and possibly winter.

Reproduction: Nothing is known with certainty about the breeding biology of the Florida populations of the spotted turtle. Specimens from north of Florida breed in the rather early spring, and females lay their small clutch of eggs (as few as 2, often 3 to 5, rarely 6 or 7) in the early summer. Captive spotted turtles can double clutch. Because of their normal period of summer inactivity, multiple clutches may not occur in the wild.

Similar species: None. There are no other Florida turtles with the yellow-spotted black carapace of the spotted turtle.

Comments: Every aspect of the life history of the spotted turtle in Florida is badly in need of study. Virtually everything stated about the behavior, needs, and even the range of the spotted turtle in Florida is conjectural. Most definitive comments are based on the knowledge gathered from observations of more northerly populations.

This species is often kept as a "pet" turtle, and it is now being bred in some numbers in captivity.

Chicken Turtle: Genus *Deirochelys*

The single species in this genus contains 3 subspecies, the Florida, the eastern, and the western chicken turtles. Of these, the Florida and the eastern can be found in Florida.

Compared with the water-bound sliders and cooters, the chicken turtle has an almost nomadic lifestyle. Chicken turtles are entirely at home in ephemeral water-filled ditches and ponds, and as these dry up, the turtles seem almost equally at home plodding through woodlands and savannas in search of new ponds.

The chicken turtle feeds on minnows, worms, and tadpoles but seems inordinately fond of crayfish.

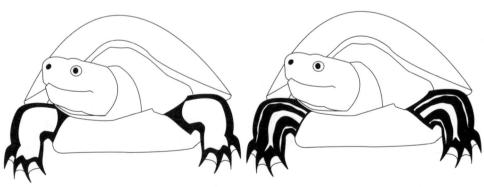

Comparison of leg striping: chicken turtle (*left*) and yellow-bellied slider (*right*)

16. Eastern Chicken Turtle

Deirochelys reticularia reticularia

Eastern

Florida

intergrade zone

Size: Although most specimens are adult at 5 to 7 inches, occasional examples may slightly exceed 9 inches in length. Hatchlings are about 1⅛ inches in length.

Identification: The ovoid carapace of the eastern chicken turtle is dark olive green to brownish and patterned with a netlike reticulum of narrow pale yellow lines. Darker circles and lines may also be present, but these do not contrast strongly with the ground color. Fine linear rugosities exist on all carapacial scutes and to a lesser degree near the midline of the plastral scutes. These rugosities are roughly longitudinal on the marginals and costals but arranged in a radiating manner on the vertebrals. The slightest coating of algae will obscure these features. If viewed from above, the carapace is seen to be edged in yellow. The neck of the chicken turtle is long, and the head is narrow. Both are green(ish) and striped with yellow. The anterior of each forelimb bears a *broad* yellow stripe. The skin posterior to the shoulder and on each side of the tail bears vertical yellow markings. The plastron is a rather bright unmarked yellow. Hatchlings and juveniles are more brightly colored and strongly patterned than adults.

Habitat/Range: Chicken turtles are typically associated with quiet, heavily vegetated bodies of water. Such habitats as grassy ditches, ephemeral ponds, shallow canals, weedy permanent ponds, and equally weedy lake edges are among the preferred habitats of this turtle. This subspecies ranges from central Alachua County northward and westward throughout the panhandle.

Abundance: This is a fairly common turtle, but it is less frequently seen than many other aquatic species.

Behavior: Chicken turtles bask extensively atop water-surface vegetation and exposed snags. They occasionally bask on the bank but are very wary and dive at the slightest disturbance. They wander far afield during the spring and summer months. If conditions become too dry, this turtle may dig down into the dirt or litter to await a rainy-day continuation of its journey. This turtle may be active on all but the coldest winter days. Chicken turtles will bite readily if molested. Crayfish are very high on the list of preferred prey.

Reproduction: The chicken turtle is a fecund species that breeds from late winter to autumn. Clutch sizes of as many as 15 eggs have been reported; however, most clutches number from 5 to 10 eggs. Females are known to multi-clutch. The eggs of the chicken turtle undergo a short to lengthy diapause (a temporary cessation of development) at some point. Diapause may be caused by reduced ground humidity, cooling ground temperatures, or other such changes.

Similar species: No other turtle in Florida has an ovoid carapace, very long neck, and narrow head.

Comments: Because it favors ephemeral wetlands, during drought, populations of this turtle may experience dehydration and high mortality.

17. Florida Chicken Turtle, *Deirochelys reticularia chrysea,* can be found from coast to coast from Alachua County southward to the tip of the peninsula.

It is brighter in color and has a more contrasting pattern than the eastern subspecies. Hatchlings are particularly brightly colored. A patina of mud or dried algae can obscure all indications of the pattern. The head, neck, limbs, and tail of this subspecies are striped with bright yellow.

Map Turtles: Genus *Graptemys*

As a group, the map turtles are riverine species with fully webbed hind feet. They are among the wariest of turtles and best watched and identified with binoculars.

There are two groups: the narrow-headed insect eaters and the group in which the adult females develop immensely enlarged heads and prey on gastropods and mollusks as well as insects. There are no representatives of the first group in Florida, but two taxa from the second group can be found in the state's panhandle waters.

Females of the larger species are slow maturing, apparently requiring 10 or more years to attain sexual maturity. On the other hand, the comparatively diminutive males reach sexual maturity in about 4 years.

An elaborate courtship involving head nods and/or forelimb vibrations occurs.

18. Barbour's Map Turtle

Graptemys barbouri

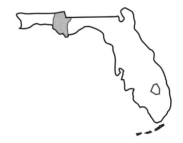

Size: This species is noticeably dimorphic. Females routinely attain 9 inches in carapace length. Some may attain 12 inches in length. Males are rarely larger than 4½ inches. Hatchlings are 1¼ inches long.

Identification: The carapacial ground color is gray to olive brown. A prominent black vertebral keel is present on Barbour's map turtles of all ages, but it is particularly prominent and saw-toothed on juveniles and males. Old females may lack any darkened highlights. Juveniles of both sexes and males of all ages have numerous yellow maplike lines in each carapacial scute, including the marginals. The plastron is cream to yellow olive, with each scute outlined in dark pigment. The skin of the head and limbs has a ground color of olive or olive gray. A very broad yellow-green blotch occurs posterior to each eye. This may curve up onto the snout between the eyes or break behind the eyes, leaving the interorbital marking a discrete blotch. A broad curving bar on the chin parallels the lower jawline. A series of thin dark and light lines outline the posterior edge of the postocular blotches. The neck and limbs bear many thin greenish yellow lines. Adult females have a much enlarged head and massive, crushing jaws. Take care not to be bitten by one. Males have a normal-sized head.

Habitat/Range: The Barbour's map turtle is a riverine species that is not known to migrate over land. In Florida this species occurs in the Apalachicola and Chipola rivers, and it also ascends some of the feeder creeks of these rivers.

Abundance: This impressive turtle is locally common. It is most abundant where the current is relatively strong, where mollusks and crustaceans are common, and where limestone substrate is exposed.

Behavior: This very wary turtle is both difficult to approach in the field and a very powerful swimmer. Barbour's map turtle basks extensively. It is often seen on exposed snags but only occasionally on river-edge sandbars.

Reproduction: Barbour's map turtles breed in the spring of the year, and females lay the first of two or more clutches two or three weeks later. Each clutch usually contains a dozen or fewer eggs, and a large, healthy female may nest four or more times annually. Permanently exposed sandbars and other sandy river-edge situations are the preferred nesting sites. Incubation is lengthy, often taking 70 or more days.

Similar species: Range, coupled with the sawlike vertebral keel, should identify this turtle in the field. Also see account 19 for a discussion of the Escambia map turtle.

Comments: This taxon is now fully protected in Florida. Without a permit it may not be collected for any purpose.

19. Escambia Map Turtle

Graptemys ernsti

Size: Females with carapace up to 11 inches have been found. Males are adult at about 4½ inches. Hatchlings are 1¼ inches long.

Identification: Carapace color is olive gray, gray, or olive brown. A map-like pattern of dark-edged, light lines is present on all carapacial scutes, including marginals. The pattern is best defined on juveniles and males and may be almost completely obscured on old adult females. A black vertebral keel is present. This is most prominent on juvenile and male examples. The plastron is yellow, but dark pigment is present along the seams of the scutes. The yellow-olive postocular and interorbital blotches are discrete. There are light lines on the neck and limbs. There is a light chin blotch at each outermost edge of the lower mandible.

Habitat/Range: This riverine species occurs in swiftly flowing waters of fairly large rivers and creeks. It prefers areas with many exposed snags and logs upon which it can bask. In Florida the range of this rather newly described species is defined by the waters of the Escambia River.

Abundance: Suitable stretches of river can hold considerable populations of this turtle. Because of its limited distribution it is considered a vulnerable species.

Behavior: Like all map turtles, *G. ernsti* is wary and very difficult to approach. It suns extensively on protruding snags and branches and seldom comes fully ashore except for the purpose of egg-laying.

Reproduction: Several clutches of as many as 10 eggs are laid annually. The nesting site is usually on a sandbar or more rarely a sandy shore. Incubation duration is about 75 days.

Similar species: Barbour's map turtle has a broad, curved bar on the chin paralleling the lower jawline. Barbour's map turtle does not occur in the Escambia River drainage.

Comments: Until rather recently this turtle was considered conspecific with the Alabama map turtle, *G. pulchra*. It and a more westerly species were recognized as distinct in 1992.

Diamondback Terrapin: Genus *Malaclemys*

As currently understood, five confusing subspecies of the diamondback terrapin occur along the Florida coastline. Two additional subspecies, the northern and the Texas, are extralimital. All the subspecies have gray(ish) (rarely brownish) carapaces and spots or streaks of black on a gray skin. The carapace usually shows prominent growth annuli. Dark pigmentation may follow the ridges of these annuli. The ornate diamondback of Florida's west coast race has an orange center in each carapacial scute. Adult female diamondback terrapins are mollusk and crustacean eaters. The smaller males eat small crustaceans, aquatic worms, and insects.

The various subspecies are difficult to identify. If trying to determine a subspecies, knowing the origin of a specimen is almost mandatory. Where ranges abut, some degree of intergradation is almost inevitable. Viewing the relative shape of the carapace from above may also help.

These turtles of brackish and saltwater habitats are now much reduced in numbers.

20. Carolina Diamondback Terrapin

Malaclemys terrapin centrata

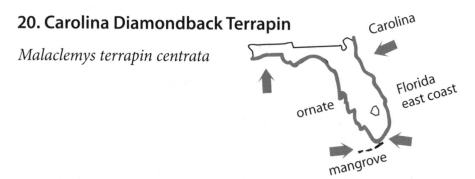

Size: Females of the Carolina diamondback terrapin attain a carapace length of 6 to 7½ inches. Males are smaller, often being only 4½ to 5½ inches long. Hatchlings are 1 to 1½ inches in length.

Identification: This is a variable and pretty turtle. At one extreme it may have a very dark, unicolored carapace with prominent growth annuli, while other examples might be light gray or light brown with black annuli. The sides of the carapace are nearly parallel when viewed from above. This race does not have a prominent dark middorsal line and keel, but if the carapace is light in color, the vertebral tubercles are usually darker than the surrounding shell. The plastron may vary from yellowish orange to greenish gray. The head and limbs are light gray spotted with black.

Habitat/Range: This subspecies ranges along the coastline southward from the Albemarle region of North Carolina to southern Flagler County on Florida's east coast.

Abundance: Although still occurring in many suitable areas, this turtle can be considered common in only a choice few.

Reproduction: As might be expected, larger female diamondbacks lay larger clutches than smaller ones. But with that said, clutches of most diamondbacks are not large to begin with. Between 4 and 8 eggs are normally laid in each clutch. Females often nest several times annually. Incubation duration is variable, apparently according to both soil temperature and nest depth. Incubation can vary from 60 to 85 days.

Behavior: These are wary turtles, quick to take fright and difficult to observe. They may be seen (with binoculars) basking on or walking between mangrove stilts, oyster beds, and mudflats. Diamondbacks may be active year-round in Florida.

Similar species: The various diamondbacks are the only turtles in Florida that are gray(ish) in color, that have normal feet (not flippers), that have a grayish skin speckled or marked with black, and that inhabit salty or brackish water. Any of the other emydine turtles that may enter salt water will have yellow-striped heads and necks.

Comments: Only 40 years ago diamondback terrapins were relatively common in Florida. Even 25 years ago, chats with crabbers disclosed that many diamondbacks of various subspecies were caught (and often inadvertently drowned) in crab traps. By 20 years ago, many fewer diamondbacks were seen, and today it takes a concerted search, or more than a modicum of luck, to find one.

21. Ornate Diamondback Terrapin, *M. t. macrospilota,* is another very variable race and arguably, at least in some of its variations, the most colorful. It has a gray(ish) (rarely brownish) carapace with orange scute cen-

ters and a gray skin that may be profusely or sparsely dotted with black. A dark vertebral line (actually a very low keel) is present. The keel of some specimens is more prominent than that of others, and there may be a bulbous protuberance at the rear of each central scute. Females usually have a proportionately larger head than males. The plastron is dark and may be smudged with dark pigment. The center keel of some hatchlings may be so bulbous that the babies look deformed. This subspecies is a resident of brackish and saltwater marshes, estuarine areas, coastlines, and similar habitats from the panhandle's Choctawatchee Bay to Key Largo.

22. Mississippi Diamondback Terrapin, *M. t. pileata.* At the far side of Florida, from the panhandle area of Choctawatchee Bay westward to (and beyond) the state line, we may encounter the very dark-colored Mississippi diamondback terrapin. The carapace is grayish black to charcoal. The vertebral tubercles are often at least slightly darker than the surrounding shell color, producing a variably dark vertebral stripe. Except for the black cranial area, the skin of the head, neck, and limbs is light to dark gray and may be spotted or almost monochromatic. The upper mandible is dark, giving the appearance of a mustache.

23. Mangrove Terrapin, *M. t. rhizophorarum.* South of Key Largo in the Florida Keys, we enter the realm of the very pretty, poorly known, and seldom seen mangrove terrapin. It is a rather dark race. The carapace is blackish and there is a vertebral keel. The plastral seams are variably (but often broadly) edged with black pigment. The top of the head is black, the head and neck spots are coalesced into irregular black stripes and the upper mandible is dark. The sides of the face and the neck are light gray. The overall appearance is very pleasing.

24. Florida East Coast Terrapin, *M. t. tequesta.* The fourth race of diamondback in Florida, the Florida east coast terrapin, usually has a grayish carapace. There are no dark rings outlining the prominent annuli. The center of each carapacial scute may be lighter than the rest of the shell. A weak vertebral keel is present. The raised tubercles may be darker than the surrounding shell. The sides of the head, neck, and limbs are light gray, and the spots of the face are big (but usually not stripes) and boldly black. The center of the head is dark, and a variably dark mustache is usually present.

Cooters and Sliders: Genera *Pseudemys* and *Trachemys*

Taxonomic comments: Taxonomic uncertainty is rampant in this genus. Please see the comments in the accounts of river cooter, Suwannee cooter, Florida cooter, and peninsula cooter (species accounts 25, 26, 27, and 28) for current thoughts.

One species or another of these big pond and river turtles can be found somewhere in the state of Florida. The sliders, now in the genus *Trachemys*, were long contained in the genus *Pseudemys*.

The sliders and cooters are persistent baskers, but they slide into the water at the first sign of disturbance. The females are often larger than the males. The males of many have elongated front claws, used during aquatic courtship rituals.

Babies are brightly colored (usually green with darker markings dorsally), adults usually less so. Old adult males of some species become suffused with pattern-obliterating melanin and may look virtually black or olive black. The heads and necks of most are strongly striped.

Location of the highest point on the carapace may be as important for positive identification as shell and head patterns. Also take note of the pattern on the second costal scute.

Because of the release of specimens no longer wanted by their owners, the popular pet turtle, the red-eared slider has become the most widely distributed turtle in the world. Besides the Mississippi drainage (to which it was native), it occurs virtually throughout the United States (including Florida, of course) and in France, Japan, Australia, parts of South America, and other countries as well.

Hatchling and young cooters and sliders are largely insectivorous, but larger specimens of many species are primarily herbivorous.

All may be difficult to identify, especially if dry. Wet shells show age-obscured or algae-covered patterns the best. The field marks mentioned will usually allow a positive identification, but these marks can vary on some specimens.

25. Eastern River Cooter

Pseudemys concinna concinna

Eastern river
Suwanee

Size: This is a large species of freshwater turtle. Females regularly attain 11 and occasionally 12 inches in carapace length. Males are usually somewhat smaller. Hatchlings are about 1½ inches long.

Identification: Hatchlings are a pretty, busily patterned green. Adults are equally busily patterned, and dark brown to nearly black. The carapacial markings of old adults are difficult to discern. The second costal scute contains a stylized C in the upper rear corner. The arms of this C can continue into and close in the next scute, forming an O. Consider *only* the part of the marking in the second scute. The plastron is yellow with dark pigment following the scute seams. Ocelli occur on the underside of each marginal. Each ocellus involves the rear of one marginal scute and the anterior of the next. The head and legs are very dark with well-defined orangish striping. There is a rather broad orangish interorbital stripe. Males have greatly elongated foreclaws.

Habitat/Range: This is a turtle of springs, spring runs, rivers and large creeks. River cooters may also be occasionally encountered in brackish and saltwater estuaries. They are restricted in distribution to the panhandle of Florida, from Wakulla and Leon counties westward.

Abundance: Eastern river cooters remain common throughout their range.

Similar species: Chicken turtles have a single broad stripe on the forelimb, a narrow head, a very long neck, and an unmarked plastron. The Florida cooter has an unmarked plastron and no C on the second costal scute. The yellow-bellied slider has a prominent yellow cheek patch. The red-eared slider has a red postorbital bar. The Florida red-bellied cooter has an arrow between the eyes and a single broad (usually orange) vertical bar in the second costal scute.

Behavior: This is a very wary turtle that usually does not allow close approach. Binoculars will help with long-distance identification. Eliminate as many similar species as possible, taking the range into account, and go from there.

Reproduction: River cooters typically construct three nests, a principal center nest into which most of the clutch is laid, and a satellite nest on each side which usually contain only a few eggs each. Following the deposition, the central nest is usually covered carefully and largely obliterated but less care is shown in covering the subordinate nests. Predators, such as raccoons, often find and pillage the subordinate nests but may be less apt to locate the main nest. As with most turtles, clutch size (and, perhaps, egg size) varies with the size of the female; the largest females produce most eggs, larger eggs, and nest most often during each season. From 8 to 24+ eggs are laid in each clutch, and healthy females have been found to nest up to six times in a season. Females may need to wander far from the water to find a suitably exposed nesting spot. Incubation takes from 2½ to 3 months.

Comments: Once thought to contain as many as 5 subspecies over its broad range, this common turtle is now considered monotypic by some researchers. We have elected to continue treating the Suwannee cooter (next account) as a subspecies of *P. concinna*.

26. Suwannee Cooter, *P. c. suwanniensis*. The taxonomic status and range of the Suwanee cooter are also in question. Some authorities consider it allopatric, interpreting the range as Florida's western peninsula from Hillsborough to Dixie counties. Such interpretation is in error. The impression of allopatrism is the result of inconclusive sampling rather than reality. Actually, Wakulla County, in the eastern panhandle, is the dividing line between the two contiguous races.

The Suwannee cooter is very similar to the common river cooter in most respects; however, it is larger, with females regularly attaining a carapace length of 16+ inches, and the head stripes are paler. Striping is often white, pale yellow, or greenish yellow. The ground color is very dark. Unless the point of origin is known for any given specimen, positive identification can be problematic.

27. Florida Cooter

Pseudemys floridana floridana

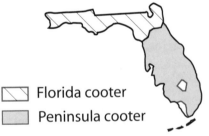

Florida cooter
Peninsula cooter

Size: Although the largest females can exceed 15 inches in carapace length, most are smaller. From 8 to 12 inches is the usual size for both sexes. Hatchlings vary from 1 to 1¼ inches in size.

Identification: This big, dark, olive green to olive brown cooter has a busy carapacial pattern of light (often pale green) markings, but lacks the C that identifies the river cooters. There is usually a broad light vertical bar on the second costal. This may be forked at its extremities. The marginals bear oval ocelli. The yellow to pale orange plastron is unmarked. Hatchlings are a much brighter green than the adults.

Habitat/Range: This turtle is pretty much a generalist in its choice of aquatic habitats. It is found in sloughs, marshes, slow areas of rivers, ponds, lakes, and most other water bodies. It is distributed widely in northern peninsular Florida and throughout the panhandle.

Abundance: This is a common turtle over most of its range.

Behavior: On sunny days during most of the year, this turtle basks extensively on exposed snags or nonvegetated areas of the shoreline. Florida cooters often bask with sympatric species, but they may be inactive during the coldest days of winter.

Reproduction: As do the river and Suwannee cooters, the Florida cooter digs a main nest and (usually two) subordinate nests. The main complement of eggs is placed in the main chamber, with a few in each of the subordinates. The main nest is carefully concealed when deposition is completed. Often less care is shown in obliterating the telltale signs of the satellite nests. Clutch size varies from 8 to 20+, and large, healthy females routinely nest several times annually. Depending on soil temperature and nest depth, hatching may occur in as little as 60 or as many as 90 days.

Similar species: Chicken turtles have a narrow head, long neck, nonserrate rear marginals, and single broad stripe on the forelimbs. River and Suwannee cooters have a light letter C on the second costal. The yellow-bellied slider has a large yellow cheek patch, and the red-eared slider has a broad reddish postorbital stripe. The Florida red-bellied cooter has a yellow arrow extending to the snout from between the eyes.

Comments: In some areas Florida cooters are known to hybridize with river cooters, producing specimens difficult to identify. Sometimes the best an observer can do is to say that a questionable specimen most closely resembles one or the other species. Some researchers consider this turtle conspecific with the river cooter, *Pseudemys concinna*.

28. Peninsula Cooter, *P. f. peninsularis*, the southern representative of this species, has a distinctive head and neck pattern of 2 "hairpins." The open ends of the hairpins continue well onto the neck. It ranges northward from the tip of the Florida peninsula to Levy, Alachua, and Duval counties.

It, too, is big (to 14+ inches) and dark, and the highest point of its shell is anterior to midpoint. Besides the pair of hairpins, the head is patterned with numerous stripes. The peninsula cooter is considered a full species by some researchers.

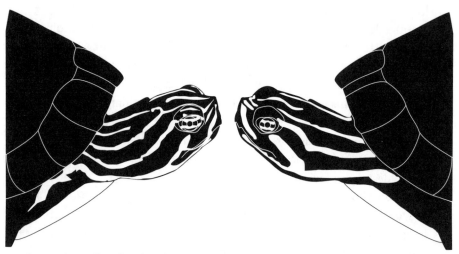

Comparison of head and neck patterns: peninsula cooter (*left*), Florida red-bellied cooter (*right*)

29. Florida Red-bellied Cooter

Pseudemys nelsoni

Size: This is a big, thick-shelled turtle that occasionally exceeds 12 inches in length. Females are the larger sex. Hatchlings are about 1¼ inches long.
Identification: Hatchlings are green with a busy dark carapacial pattern. The plastron may be yellowish but is most often a bright orange to red orange with large but discrete dark spots along the seams of some scutes. Adults are olive brown to nearly black with vertical orange bars in each costal. The plastral pattern and color fade. The plastron is often an unrelieved orange yellow or yellow. Submarginal markings are entirely dark rather than only ocelli. Males are often more brightly colored than females. A suffusion of melanin sometimes largely obscures the colors of old red-bellies of both sexes. There are few yellow lines on the dark head.

The most constant identifying mark is the arrow. The shaft is between the eyes, and the point contours the snout. The jaw style is also diagnostic for this species in Florida. A medial notch in the upper jaw is edged on each side by a downward projecting cusp. Males have long foreclaws.

Habitat/Range: The Florida red-bellied cooter occurs in nearly any permanent body of freshwater. Among others, ponds, lakes, ditches, canals, rivers, and streams are all utilized. It may be found over the entire peninsula and occurs in an apparently disjunct population in the Apalachicola region of the panhandle.

Abundance: This beautifully colored turtle is a common sight throughout its range.

Behavior: Although wary, the Florida red-bellied cooter may allow closer approach than congenerics. It may be especially approachable in state, federal, and privately owned parks. These are among Florida's most beautiful turtles.

Reproduction: From 8 to 25+ eggs are laid in each clutch. Females may nest several times annually. A female *P. nelsoni* may dig her nest either into the soil or into an alligator's nest. Incubation can vary from 50 to 80 days.

Similar species: When this turtle is in hand or within suitable binocular distance, the arrow between the eyes is a good diagnostic tool. The orange (juvenile specimens) to yellow (larger specimens) plastron and vertical orange costal bars should further assist in a positive identification.

Comments: This is a wary turtle that is usually best observed with binoculars; however, in parks and other areas where it is protected, it may be acclimated to the presence of people.

30. Yellow-bellied Slider

Trachemys scripta scripta

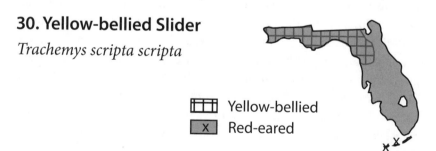

<table>
<tr><td>▦</td><td>Yellow-bellied</td></tr>
<tr><td>X</td><td>Red-eared</td></tr>
</table>

Size: This pretty turtle attains an adult length of 5 to 8 inches, and a few may exceed 10 inches. Adult males are usually somewhat smaller than females. Hatchlings are about 1¼ inches long.

Identification: The coloration of this slider varies with age. Hatchlings have a dark green carapace with many darker and lighter markings. The head is greenish, with extensive areas of yellow on the sides of the face and diagonal yellow lines from the snout to the chin. The limbs are also greenish and bear several stripes (forelimbs) or spots (hind limbs) of yellow. The skin on each side of the tail is vertically striped with green and yellow.

With growth the green in the ground color first dulls, then darkens. The carapace, limbs, and head become olive drab or olive black. The yellow markings of the carapace broaden but dull to an olive yellow or a pale olive green. The yellow of the cheeks and snout are the last of the markings to dull (if they ever do).

Old specimens may be almost uniformly black (with the oldest males the darkest), but at least vestiges of the yellow cheeks may remain visible.

Juveniles, subadults, and young adults have prominent dark rounded markings on the lower surface of the marginals and on the anterior plastron. These obscure with age. Most sexually mature males have elongated front claws.

Habitat/Range: The yellow-bellied slider may be seen in heavily vegetated ponds, lakes, canals, ditches, and other such bodies of water. It ranges northward from Alachua County to (and beyond) the Georgia state line and throughout the panhandle.

Abundance: This is a common pond slider throughout its range.

Behavior: Yellow-bellied sliders bask extensively on exposed snags and banks or on mats of surface vegetation. They are usually wary and difficult to approach. They are best observed from a vehicle with binoculars. Babies may often be found foraging atop floating mats of *Hydrilla* or other such vegetation.

Reproduction: Mating occurs in the spring and early summer, and egg-laying follows shortly thereafter. Females can lay from two to several nests of 8–17 eggs at roughly monthly intervals. They may wander well away from the water in search of a nesting site. Depending on temperature and ground moisture levels, incubation can vary from 55 to 90+ days.

Similar species: This is the only turtle of Florida with prominent yellow cheeks. The chicken turtle has an extraordinarily long neck and only a single yellow stripe on the front of its forelimbs.

Comments: This turtle is a mainstay of the pet industry.

31. Red-eared Slider, *T. s. elegans*, is native to Mississippi River drainages. Because of releases of unwanted pet red-ears, this non-native turtle can

now be found through much of Florida, including the Keys. Intergrades between this and the native yellow-bellied slider are often seen.

For seven (or more) decades, the red-eared slider has been prominent in the pet trade of the world. It is the little "green" or "painted" turtle once seen in the pet departments of nearly every five-and-dime and pet shop in the United States. Federal health regulations have now curtailed its availability somewhat, but it is still readily available.

Hatchlings of the red-eared slider have carapaces of green patterned with numerous *narrow* lighter and darker lines. The submarginal and plastral scutes are patterned with irregular dark ocelli. The face and limbs are green with numerous yellow stripes. The very broad red temporal stripe, from which this turtle takes its name, is usually prominently evident.

Colors and pattern dull with age. Males are often duller than females of a similar age. Old males can be entirely devoid of pattern and nearly a uniform dark olive to olive black in color. This species attains a carapace length of 7 to 12 inches. Sexually mature males have elongate front claws.

The presence of the red-eared slider in Florida's waters (indeed, throughout much of the world) presents an unequaled but unwanted story of success. It seems that wherever the turtle is released, it takes hold and thrives. Unwanted pet specimens should be placed in caring foster homes, never released into the wild.

Box Turtle: Genus *Terrapene*

The 4 subspecies of the eastern box turtle are the most divergent of Florida's emydine turtles. All are primarily terrestrial in habits, with only one, the Gulf Coast box turtle, seeming to readily enter deep water. In fact, most box turtles are distressed in the water and bob on the surface like corks as they paddle clumsily to land.

The forefeet are stubby and short; the rear feet are rather typical but unwebbed. These turtles all have comparatively highly domed carapaces, although the carapace of the Gulf Coast box turtle is often flattened centrally.

The plastron of adult box turtles is prominently hinged crossways and is closable. It is attached at the bridge by tough cartilage. The hinge is nonfunctional at hatching but is fully so by the time the box turtle is half-grown.

There is some indication that populations of box turtles are being ad-

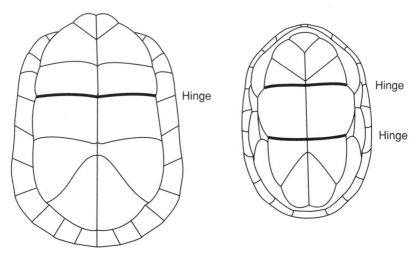

Comparison of hinged plastra: box turtle (*left*), mud turtle (*right*)

versely affected (in some areas of the country, seriously so) by predation by the introduced tropical fire ant.

32. Eastern Box Turtle

Terrapene carolina carolina

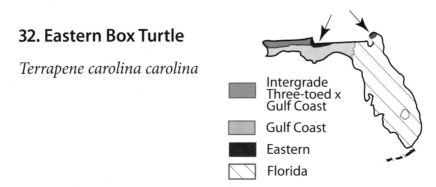

Intergrade Three-toed x Gulf Coast

Gulf Coast

Eastern

Florida

Size: Adult males attain a length of between 5¾ and 7⅝ inches. Females are seldom more than 5½ inches long. Hatchlings are 1 to 1¼ inches in length.

Identification: The variably colored oval carapace of the eastern box turtle is high domed. The plastron may be colored similarly to the carapace or be somewhat different. Either the dark or the light color may predominate. The carapace, head, neck, and limbs of this turtle are usually brown or brownish with irregular olive, orange, or yellow markings. Males often have bright red irides; those of females are buff or brown. Occasional individuals may have white irides. Males, which are the larger sex and which have a variable degree of flaring of the rear marginals, have a prominent concavity in the rear lobe of the plastron. This race usually has 4 toes on the hind feet.

Habitat/Range: The eastern box turtle enters Florida only in Nassau County and possibly in extreme northwestern Jackson County. Some examples from Baker County look much like eastern box turtles, but most appear intermediate between the eastern and Gulf Coast races.

Abundance: Despite a terrible mortality from vehicles as the turtles cross roadways and from collection for the pet trade, this species remains relatively common over much of its range. It does not appear to be common in its very limited Florida range.

Behavior: Box turtles are primarily terrestrial but will readily enter the shallow water of a sloped ditch or rain puddle to drink and soak.

Reproduction: Breeding occurs in the spring and early summer. The usual clutch consists of 2 to 5 (rarely to 7) eggs, laid in a freshly dug hole that may be so shallow that it barely contains them. Incubation duration varies from 55 to about 68 days.

Similar species: Box turtles are the only high-domed terrestrial turtles found in Florida with a single plastral hinge. The aquatic mud turtles are less colorful, smaller, more elongate, and lower domed and have two plastral hinges.

Comments: Because the subspecies readily interbreed, where ranges abut or overlap, the box turtles in Florida may be almost impossible to assign to a subspecies.

33. Florida Box Turtle, *T. c. bauri*, has a narrow, high-domed carapace with the highest point posterior to midpoint. Its color is deep brownish black to black with radiating yellow lines and a yellow vertebral keel. There are two yellow stripes (these may be broken into irregular spots on aged individuals) on the sides of the face, which is otherwise rather light in color. The skin of the leg apices and neck is also light. The plastron is yellow with variable dark markings.

Hatchlings are colored like the adults, but the yellow carapacial radiations are irregular spots. The vertebral keel is yellow, and dual yellow cheek lines are present. The eyes of both sexes are dark.

Males attain a carapace length of about 6¼ inches. Females are adult at between 4 and 5 inches.

Most Florida box turtles have only 3 toes on each hind foot. Over much of its range the Florida box turtle is now reduced in number. This race ranges from Key West northward nearly to the Georgia state line. It seems to retain its subspecific integrity better than the other three races.

34. Gulf Coast Box Turtle, *T. c. major*, is the largest of Florida's box turtles. Adult males attain a carapace length of 7½ to 8½ inches. It is also the most aquatic of the box turtles and occasionally can be seen walking or foraging on the bottoms of ponds, puddles, or canals. It also forages terrestrially. This subspecies is found in the woodlands, stream and canal edges, pinewoods, and marshes of the southern Florida panhandle.

The Gulf Coast race is a dark box turtle. The ground color is brown or black, and the variable carapacial markings are yellowish or olive. Males often have red irides; those of the females are dark. The high-domed carapace is flattened centrally. The plastron is usually darkest anteriorly. Gulf Coast box turtles have 4 toes on each hind foot. Old adult Gulf Coast box turtles (especially males) have a prominent flaring of the posterior marginals. Old males often have a variable amount of white on their faces. This may be restricted to the anterior chin and mandibles or so extensive that it involves the whole head.

35. Three-toed Box Turtle, *T. c. triunguis*. The more westerly three-toed box turtle does not actually enter Florida; however, since its influence can be seen in the Gulf Coast box turtles found on the Florida panhandle along the Alabama and Georgia borders, we mention it here.

In its nonintergraded form the three-toed box turtle is usually quite dull in coloration. The carapace ground color is horn, olive, tan, or buff with or without lighter radiations or teardrop-shaped markings. Eye color does not differ significantly by sex. The plastron is yellowish or olive and devoid of markings. Males often lack the rear-lobe plastral concavity so prominent in other races. Variable red and/or white markings may be present on the dark cheeks. This is a small race. It is often fully adult at 4 to 5 inches in carapace length. This race usually has 3 toes on each hind foot.

Latin American Wood Turtles: Genus *Rhinoclemmys*

Several of the turtles in this genus are primarily aquatic in habits, but others are at least partially terrestrial. These latter may be found far from water, foraging in dry thornscrub or soaking in available ephemeral ponds. Representatives of this genus are found from northern Mexico to northern South America. The single species now found in Florida is a pet trade species often imported to America from the Guyanas and Suriname.

36. South American Wood Turtle (also called Guyana Wood Turtle)

Rhinoclemmys punctularia punctularia

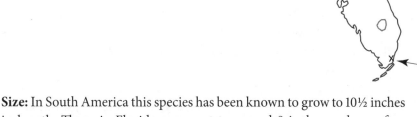

Size: In South America this species has been known to grow to 10½ inches in length. Those in Florida seem not to exceed 8 inches and are often smaller. Hatchlings are about 2 inches long.

Identification: The domed black carapace of this turtle bears a vertebral keel. The plastron is mostly dark but may have yellow pigment along the scute seams and the outer perimeter. The front of the forelimbs are clad in overlapping, black-spotted yellow and/or red scales. The head is dark but patterned with 3 pairs of red stripes, of which the uppermost is the thickest and most prominent.

Habitat/Range: In Florida this South American turtle is associated with canal and wetland (Everglades) habitats in Miami-Dade County.

Abundance: Unknown. This is not a commonly found turtle.

Behavior: Although it swims well, it is often seen walking slowly through shallow water or wet grasses. Most Florida examples have been found near parking lots and on dirt roads on Miccosukee Indian land.

Reproduction: The breeding biology of this species is unknown in Florida. In South America this turtle lays up to 3 (normally only 1 or 2) very large eggs. It is not known whether this species multi-clutches but it is suspected to do so.

Similar species: No other Florida turtle has 3 pairs of narrow red stripes on the face.

Comments: Since there are no reptile dealers in the area where these turtles are now found, it must be surmised that their introduction to the state was due to deliberate release.

AFRO-NEOTROPICAL SIDE-NECKED TURTLES: FAMILY PODOCNEMIDAE

Sidenecks—Recent Return to Days of Old

Two of the three children stood on the bank of the Kendall canal, a big bucket between them. The third was up to his chest (his overall height must have been all of four feet!) in a patch overgrown with grasses, hyacinths, and water lettuce. I had been passing by on my way to check the status of a population of introduced whiptail lizards, but, unable to bypass such a scene, I hurriedly pulled over, eased over the curb, and parked on the grassy verge.

The children stopped what they were doing, looked warily at me for a moment, then grabbed the bucket and started to move away. I called out, asking what kind of fish they had been finding (in this area there are dozens of species of escaped tropical fish). The kids stopped, looked shyly at each other and then answered quietly that they had been looking for turtles, not fish.

Now my interest was really piqued. "What kind?" I asked.

"Yellow spots" was the reply.

Well, I thought, there were red-bellies, peninsula cooter, and musk turtles in the canal. I would have referred to all as "yellow stripes" (the color of the facial markings), but none as "yellow spots." Could someone have dropped baby spotted turtles into the canal?

I described a spotted turtle to the kids.

"No" was their collective response. They added that the spots were only on the head, not on the shell.

Now I was confused.

"Could I see one?" I asked.

It seemed the answer was no, that they had already taken those they had found home. I pleaded. Then I added two of the few Spanish words I knew—"Por favor."

Again the children murmured quietly to each other, and one ran off toward the nearest houses. A few minutes later he was returning with another bucket.

I don't know exactly what I expected to see, but it certainly wasn't what was in the bucket. Under the plucked grass were five tiny gray turtles, and, sure enough, they had spotted heads—yellow spotted heads. The turtles were yellow-spotted Amazon River turtles, a species that hadn't been seen in Miami for several decades!

In the 1960s and 1970s this South American turtle was an important component of the American pet trade, and escapees and releasees were commonly seen in the maze of canals from Hialeah to Homestead. Over the years the populations dwindled—possibly to collecting or possibly to suboptimal winter temperatures. Had these turn-of-the-twenty-first-century babies hatched from eggs from adults that had somehow survived, or were they from a newer attempt to establish the species in South Florida?

I would guess that it was probably the latter. But next time I'm in Miami, I'm going to drive by that canal and hope . . .

This is a family of predominantly aquatic turtles distributed in Africa, Madagascar, and South America. Only a single species occurs in the Florida, and it is, at best, very rare. It may have been extirpated.

Neotropical River Turtles: Genus *Podocnemis*

This is a genus of 6 river turtles of northern South America. Four of the taxa are adult at 12 inches or less in length, but adult females of the other two attain an adult length of 24 to 36 inches. Males are smaller.

37. Yellow-spotted Amazon River Turtle

Podocnemis unifilis

Size: Hatchlings are about 1¾ inches in shell length. In South America adult males reach 12 inches in length, and adult females attain a carapace length of about 24 inches. Maximum size in Florida has not been ascertained.

Identification: This is a pretty, smooth-shelled, olive gray to olive brown turtle. Hatchlings of both sexes have a series of clownlike yellow spots on the head. These spots are retained into adulthood by males. Adult females lose the brilliant facial adornment, but vestiges of the markings can still usually be seen. Limbs, neck, and tail are gray. The narrow plastron is yellowish but may be suffused or smudged with dark pigment on adults.

Habitat/Range: It is very local and rare in one or more canals in Miami. It is endangered in its native northern South American range. Although it basks occasionally, this turtle is predominantly aquatic.

Abundance: Unknown in Florida.

Behavior: This is a wary turtle that is able to agilely negotiate considerable currents. It basks occasionally but seldom strays far from the water. Nesting is usually accomplished on a sandbar or sandy bank.

Reproduction: Virtually nothing is known about this turtle in its Florida range. In South America a female will lay 2 clutches of up to 25 eggs each annually.

Similar species: None. The clownlike facial markings of the juveniles and males will differentiate them from all other Florida turtles. The large size and smooth gray oval carapace will identify adult females.

Comments: Tens of thousands of babies of this turtle were imported annually from Colombia by the pet trade In the 1960s and early 1970s. During these years hatchlings were occasionally released or escaped. This species was seen swimming in Miami-Dade County canals well into the 1980s, but reports gradually died out. That this turtle is still breeding in southern Miami-Dade County was confirmed again in 1999 and 2000.

SOFT-SHELLED TURTLES: FAMILY TRIONYCHIDAE

Three species of soft-shelled turtles occur in Florida; only one, however, ranges widely. With a weight of more than 80 pounds, this, the Florida softshell, is also the largest native softshell species in North America.

Soft-shelled turtles are almost fully aquatic. They are powerful and agile swimmers with fully webbed feet. Two of the three species often bask while in the water (the Florida softshell often comes ashore to bask), choosing shallows where the sun's warmth can easily penetrate. Collectively, softshells have a long neck and a Pinocchio nose.

The Florida softshell diverges from the norm by selecting ponds, lakes, swamps, canals, and other quiet, rather than flowing, waters as its preferred habitat.

Softshells have a rounded or oval carapace (when viewed from above) covered with a thick, leathery skin rather than keratinized scutes. Although the center of the shell is comparatively rigid, the edges of the carapace are flexible. There are only 3 claws on each of the fully webbed feet. Males have a greatly enlarged tail extending well beyond the edge of the carapace.

Softshells—A Visit with the Western Panhandle Pancakes

Field-herping is a lot like field-birding (bird watching, if you will), except that the former is often a bit more up-front and personal. Whereas the birds are highly mobile and illegal to touch and truly disturb, in many cases the herps, if found, can actually be captured and carefully handled if the searcher so chooses. Of course, some of the speedy snakes and lizards will make you work for the honor (and some can kill you), but many herps are quite approachable, and it is always wonderful—even if you fail to find the designated herps—to get out in the field.

So one morning when Barry Mansell called and suggested that he, Brad Stith (who was willing to trailer his boat), and I might, on such a pretty day, want to go looking for Gulf Coast smooth soft-shelled turtles, there was not a moment's hesitation on my part.

Barry and I rendezvoused at Brad's, and Brad, who graciously made more room in his vehicle by carefully stowing materials in the boat to be towed, soon had us all uneventfully under way. At least the way was uneventful for a while. Very soon after accessing the Interstate, we noticed a broken trail of materials behind us; only a moment later we determined the origin of that trail, and it was actually our towed boat. Whoops! Time to repack.

Within minutes we were on our way again—next stop (barring rest stops and gas stations): the smooth softshell turtle river.

Finally, we bumped and clunked our way to the boat launch, happily found the river low and the water moderately clear, clambered from the land-based vehicle to a water-based one, and sped off in search of barely submerged sandbars.

Barry and I searched the edges of a bar about a quarter-mile long. No softshells. Barry and I opted for another sandbar. Brad, a manatee researcher who swims like a seal, decided to chase down a baby map turtle (he succeeded!).

Ah ha. In the shallows of a small bar I quickly lucked out and found a pair of adult smooth softshells—the first of this taxon I had seen in Florida. I was just about to holler, "success!" when Barry hollered, "Dick. Got one!"

Brad was also happy with the map turtles he had seen. The trip was a total success.

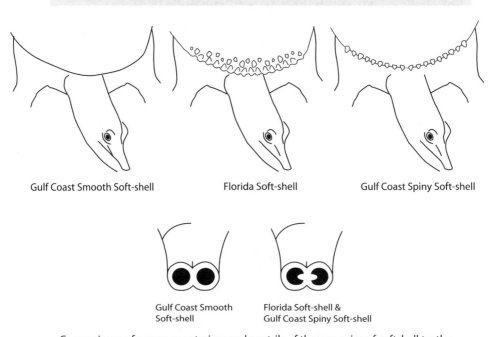

| Gulf Coast Smooth Soft-shell | Florida Soft-shell | Gulf Coast Spiny Soft-shell |

Gulf Coast Smooth Soft-shell

Florida Soft-shell & Gulf Coast Spiny Soft-shell

Comparisons of carapace anteriors and nostrils of three species of softshell turtles

38. Florida Soft-shelled Turtle

Apalone ferox

Size: There is often tremendous disparity in the adult sizes of the two sexes of this species. Females regularly exceed 12 inches in carapace length, and the largest female specimen confirmed to date measured 24¾ inches. Males most often measure between 6 and 10 inches in length at maturity, but many have been confirmed at nearly twice that size. The hatchlings measure about 1½ inches in carapace length.

Identification: Because of the many large dark spots on the carapace, at first glance, hatchling Florida softshells seem to be a solid olive green to olive black. In fact, there is a narrow, light olive-tan reticulum separating the carapacial spots. A yellow to olive yellow band edges the carapace. The plastron is dark olive gray, and the dark head is busily spotted and striped with yellow.

With growth, both sexes fade to an olive tan to olive brown, but males are more apt than females to retain some of the juvenile pattern. Facial markings are in the form of longitudinal spots rather than stripes. Bright yellow ochre on hatchlings, the facial markings darken and obscure with age.

When viewed from above, the carapace of this species is strongly oval. The anterior edge of the carapace is studded with somewhat flattened (low hemispherical) tubercles. There is a horizontally oriented ridge on the nasal septum.

Habitat/Range: Of the three soft-shelled turtles in Florida, this species is the only one that rather consistently chooses nonflowing waters for its home. The Florida soft-shelled turtle is common to abundant in ponds, lakes, canals, ditches, swamps, marshes, cypress heads, and other such habitats. It occurs in every county in the state.

Abundance: Common in quiet waters throughout the state.

Behavior: Usually sedate while in the water, when on shore a fair-sized Florida soft-shelled turtle can become a formidable adversary. The long neck and strong jaws must be carefully reckoned with. Besides the jaws, the raking claws of a carelessly handled specimen can leave deep scratches.

This species basks far more extensively than either of the other soft-shells of Florida. Banks, exposed snags, mats of floating vegetation, and tangles of subsurface sticks are used for basking sites. Florida softshells occasionally wander far afield and may be seen crossing water-edge roadways.

Reproduction: An average-sized female Florida soft-shelled turtle lays from 10 to 25 eggs per clutch. As far as is currently known, the record clutch contained 38 eggs. Several clutches are laid each summer. The nest is constructed in a sandy location but may be obscured from the water. The nest may sometimes be only a few feet from the water line, but is often much more distant. Incubation takes somewhat more than 2 months. **Similar species:** The other species of softshells are more rounded when viewed from above, have a light carapace with dark spots, and well defined light lines on the sides of the face.

Comments: There is considerable human pressure on these softshells. A thriving fishery catches and prepares them for human consumption, and the babies are popular in the pet trade.

39. Gulf Coast Smooth Soft-shelled Turtle

Apalone mutica calvata

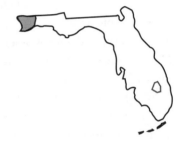

Size: Females of this small soft-shelled turtle reach 10½ inches (rarely a little more); the smaller males vary from 4 to 6 inches in carapace length. Hatchlings are about 1½ inches in length.

Identification: The carapace of this softshell has a ground color of olive tan to light olive brown with numerous, well-separated, large dark spots. A single, often faded, black line follows the carapace near the edge. The plastron is *lighter in color* than the brownish underside of the carapace. A dark-edged yellow stripe extends diagonally downward from the rear of each eye to the rear of the head. The forelegs are not strongly patterned, there are no bumps of any description on the anterior edge of the carapace (hence the common name of smooth), and there is no horizontal ridge on the nasal septum. Males tend to retain the carapacial spots of babyhood. The carapacial spots and the dark perimeter line become obscured on large female specimens.

Habitat/Range: This turtle is most common where extensive, open sandbars occur. Although having a wide range in the southeastern United States, this species is known to occur in Florida only in the northern reaches of the Escambia River, Escambia County.

Abundance: The Gulf Coast smooth softshell is common in the state within its very restricted range.

Behavior: This wary species is difficult to approach. If carelessly grasped, it will scratch with vigor. It is perfectly capable of delivering strong bites but seems less apt to do so than the spiny and Florida softshells. Following hatching and prior to dispersal, hatchlings may be found in the shallow waters at the edge of sandbars. This species is adept at burying itself in the sand in water shallow enough to allow its snout to break the surface when the turtle's long neck is extended.

Reproduction: In Florida, as elsewhere, this turtle nests on open sandbars. It seems that this species always nests where the water is visible from the nest. Nests have been found with 6 to 31 eggs but normally contain 8 to 20. Florida females lay fewer and larger eggs than specimens from farther north. Following an incubation period of somewhat more than 2 months, the hatchlings emerge. A female lays several clutches a summer.

Similar species: The Florida softshell is big, dark, and strongly oval when viewed from above. The Gulf Coast spiny softshell has small ocelli, not large dark spots, on the carapace and two or more dark lines delineating the edge of the carapace. Both of these species have either tubercles or spines on the anterior edge of the carapace.

Comments: This softshell has the most restricted range of Florida's three species.

40. Gulf Coast Spiny Soft-shelled Turtle

Apalone spinifera aspera

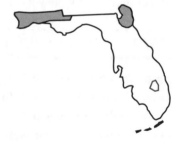

Size: Like other softshells, the Gulf Coast spiny is dimorphic. Females commonly attain a carapace length of 7 to 12 inches and occasionally grow to 16 inches. Adult males are about half that size. Hatchlings are 1¼ inches long.

Identification: The carapace color of the Gulf Coast spiny softshell is tan to olive brown. There are dark ocelli in the central area of the carapace and dark spots closer to the edge. The plastron is *about the same color* as the underside of the carapace. There are at least two dark lines bordering the edge of the carapace. There are two dark-edged yellow lines on each side of the face that converge and meet on the neck. The feet are heavily spotted and streaked. A horizontal ridge is present on the nasal septum. The anterior of the carapace bears conical spines.

Habitat/Range: Besides rivers, this soft-shelled turtle also occurs in lakes and large ponds. It is found from Gadsden County westward and in the St. Mary's River in Nassau, Duval, and eastern Baker counties.

Abundance: This softshell is quite common in North Florida.

Behavior: This is an active, agile, turtle that is entirely at home in the water. It easily negotiates considerable current. It is wary and difficult to approach.

Reproduction: This softshell lays several clutches that average about 16 eggs. Occasionally 25 (or more) eggs are laid by large females. Incubation takes about 2½ months.

Similar species: The shell of this species is round when viewed from above. The Florida softshell is oval and darker when viewed from above. The carapace of the Gulf Coast smooth softshell is marked with solid dark spots, not ocelli. This latter species lacks anterior spinous processes on the carapace and horizontal extensions on the septum.

Comments: Like all softshells, this species is an agile swimmer and fully capable of chasing down and consuming small fish. At least as often, however, the turtle secludes itself in river-bottom silt and sand to ambush fish and crayfish that stray within reach of its long neck and strong jaws.

TORTOISES: FAMILY TESTUDINIDAE

This, the only native tortoise of all of eastern North America, now has occasional company in Florida in the form of feral African spurred tortoises.

Typically, tortoises are restricted to upland areas with sharp drainage. The gopher tortoise is no exception. It occurs virtually throughout the state but is absent from wetlands, swamps, and marshes. It can be common on high, dry, offshore islands but has in general been seriously reduced in number in the last half-decade. The elevated, rapidly drained habitats required by the gopher tortoise are also coveted by developers. There can be no question about which of the two is winning the contest.

These terrestrial vegetarians dig extensive home (and occasionally satellite) burrows.

An upper respiratory ailment is afflicting many gopher tortoise populations. Research into this malady continues.

Comment: Many feral examples of the African (Sub-Saharan) Spurred Tortoise, *Geochelone sulcata*, have been found in Florida. This inexpensive, fecund, fast-growing, very large tortoise (males to 200 pounds, females less than half that) is very popular with novice herpetoculturists. Although the strongly sculpted, sand-colored carapace is highly domed, it is flattened centrally. Few hobbyists who purchase the hatchlings realize that the adults of this bulldozer of a tortoise will require a very strong, room-sized (or larger), escape-proof cage. Some tortoises escape from their facility, but others are eventually released. This is an illegal act in Florida. Although found with some regularity throughout Florida, this species has not yet been documented breeding in the state.

Gopher Tortoise: Genus *Gopherus*

For centuries the gopher tortoise has been a food staple for many southern families.

The home burrow of this tortoise provides refuge for more than 300 sympatric creatures, some of which occur in no other habitat.

Tortoises—A Gopher by Any Other Name

Although feral examples of the African spurred tortoise are now being seen in Florida with increasing regularity, our only native tortoise species is the gopher tortoise. In fact, the three species of gopher tortoises (there is a fourth species in northern Mexico) are the only tortoises native to the entire United States.

The gopher (the popular contraction for the gopher tortoise) is a fairsized tortoise (to 16 inches) that inhabits sandy highlands and digs long burrows—some to more than 30 feet in length, and may be more than 10 feet below the surface in the yielding soils it chooses. More than 350 species of other creatures—insects, spiders, rats, mice, rabbits, skunks, amphibians, and other reptiles among them—utilize the tortoises' burrows. While to some creatures the burrow is just a temporary home, a fair number (the commensals) are found nowhere else.

Gophers often lay their eggs in the sandy apron at their burrow entrance. Hatchlings are much more brightly colored than the adults. Except that hatchling gophers may be eaten by some predatory co-residents, the burrow-sharers are usually no great problem to a gopher tortoise. It is the threat from above—the developers, whether building homes, shopping centers, or roads or laying out citrus groves—that negatively affects these chelonians the most. The quickly drained sandy soil habitats of the gopher tortoise happen to be just what the developers are looking for. Even though gophers are provided a modicum of state protection, adverse anthropogenic changes (the effect of humans on the natural world) are rampant and usually irreversible.

An upper respiratory ailment affects the gophers in many populations. The disease was once thought fatal to the tortoises contracting it, but it now seems that this is not always so. Researchers making periodic checks on gopher tortoise populations have found that tortoises that test positive this year may test negative in a year or two. Despite this good news, it is still illegal to handle or move tortoises between colonies.

While gopher populations are reduced over much of their range, they are nearly extirpated from the heavily developed corridor of sandy soil along Florida's east coast between Miami and Merritt Island.

Despite the fact that they are reduced in number, gopher tortoises can still be seen over much of Florida, excluding the Everglades and Big Cypress regions. The tortoises can be seen foraging along the verges of busy highways (including interstates and turnpikes), in many open scrub woodlands, and in a great many of the state's parks, preserves, wildlife management areas, and wildlife refuges.

If you approach hastily you may only see the tail end of the tortoise as it dashes down its burrow. But if you approach the creature stealthily you may be able to observe it feeding on wire grass, cacti, or other rough vegetation, or merely lazing, stretched out as only a shell-encumbered tortoise can stretch, in the warming sunshine of a cool Florida morning.

41. Gopher Tortoise

Gopherus polyphemus

Size: This is a large tortoise made to look even larger by the height of its high-domed but flat-topped carapace. Although 10 to 13 inches is the normal size, occasional individuals up to 16 inches long have been found. Hatchlings are 1½ to 2 inches long.

Identification: Adult gopher tortoises are merely large tan or brown (sometimes almost black) turtles that, when young, show prominent growth annuli. The plastron is somewhat lighter than the carapace in color. The head is rounded, the neck is fairly short, the digging forefeet are broad, flattened, and spadelike with stout claws, and the rear feet are clublike. Hatchlings are quite brightly colored. Their carapace has peach or yellowish colored centers to the dark-edged carapacial scutes, and the head and limbs are yellowish.

Habitat/Range: Sandy open scrub habitats; turkey oak–longleaf pine associations; sandy, vegetated coastal dunes; and other well-drained habitats with ample low herbaceous growth are utilized by the gopher tortoise. It may be found throughout the state, save for the Everglades and associated swamps and marshes.

Abundance: The gopher tortoise is still widely distributed in Florida but is now of spotty distribution. Some populations have been largely (or entirely) extirpated, and many of those that remain are in decline.

Behavior: These tortoises dwell in (sometimes extensive) colonies and dig burrows that may exceed 15 feet in length. The burrows are often 6 or more feet deep and sufficiently wide to allow the turtle to reverse direction at any given point. Hatchlings may construct a burrow of their own or temporarily stay with an adult. Numerous other reptile, amphibian, insect, and mammal species also use gopher tortoise burrows for refuge. Breeding male gopher tortoises produce a clucking sound.

Reproduction: Gopher tortoises are slow to reproduce and have high hatchling mortality. The nest is dug in the late spring or early summer in or near the apron of sand at the mouth of the burrow. Although up to 12 eggs may be laid by old, healthy females, most clutches number between 5 and 9 eggs. Incubation takes about 3 months. Only one clutch is laid annually.

Similar species: None native but see comments about the African spurred tortoise (page 119). Box turtles, the only other native terrestrial turtles with highly domed carapaces, have a hinged plastron.

Comments: Because of habitat degradation, including fragmentation, the continued presence of the gopher tortoise over much of its range on the southern peninsula and in other areas with burgeoning human populations is far from assured. This is one of the most thoroughly studied reptiles in Florida, and we know what is necessary to ensure the continued success of the species. The question now is, are we willing to provide the basic necessities?

Alligators, Caiman, and Crocodiles

Order Crocodylia

The crocodilians are among the best known and most readily recognized of the reptiles. All, even the smallest, are comparatively immense, semi-aquatic creatures with osteoderm-protected backs and bony, broadly flattened, rounded (alligators and caiman) or variably pointed (crocodiles) snouts.

All are primarily predatory, but many will eat carrion. American alligators and spectacled caiman are capable of overcoming and consuming sizable prey. American crocodiles prefer prey the size of a water bird or smaller. The males of alligators and caiman are quite cannibalistic; females provide care and protection of nests and hatchlings. Vegetation is gathered by female American alligators and spectacled caiman into nest mounds; female American crocodiles dig a nest above the vegetation line in a low mound of scraped-together sand and beach debris or merely in the beach sand. The female American crocodile provides less overall nest and hatchling protection but does assist in release of hatchlings from the nest.

Alligators and caiman are more strongly dimorphic than crocodiles, with females the smaller sex.

Comparatively huge American alligators may survive in relatively small freshwater waterholes they sometimes widen and deepen by thrashing around. American crocodiles are creatures of tidally influenced estuarine areas. All crocodilians bask extensively in the sunlight. They are active both by day and after nightfall.

All have a strongly developed homing instinct. Relocated "problem" specimens will return time and again to their home territories.

Both the American alligator and the American crocodile are protected in Florida; the introduced spectacled caiman is not. American alligators have caused human fatalities in Florida. Extreme care should be taken when near large specimens.

Although it is thought not yet established in Florida, from one to several specimens (accounts vary) of released/escaped South American smooth-fronted caiman, *Paleosuchus trigonatus*, have been found in and near canals in Miami-Dade County since 2000. Because it is comparatively small (to 7 feet but usually smaller) and has a strange, heavily armored appearance, this species is popular in the pet trade and frequently imported.

These reptiles all have voices. During the nesting season adults may be more irascible than at other times.

Representatives of two families occur in Florida:

Family Alligatoridae (Alligators and Caiman)
Family Crocodylidae (Crocodiles)

Gators, Caiman, and Crocs—Native and Introduced

As I stand on Paynes Prairie Preserve State Park and look at 200 to 300 alligators, 3 feet to 12 feet in length, basking all catawampus along La Chua Trail, I can't help but muse about the scarcity of these creatures only five decades ago. In the mid-20th century, gators had been hunted to "near extinction" or were at very best very severely depleted. The generally accepted count was that more than 10 million had been harvested.

By that time it was also realized that the alligator was a keystone species in the Everglades and other ecosystems and that we needed to do every-thing possible to protect the species. The term *keystone* simply refers to a creature, in this case the alligator, whose day-to-day activities help to cre-ate and maintain a healthy ecosystem. One of the most common and well understood of these activities is the alligator's creation of "gator holes." Al-ligators select a pond for residence, and by pushing and shoving the bottom muck and mulm with tail and snout, as the water recedes during a drought, they create water-retaining depressions in which they and other creatures survive until water levels rise once more.

But saving the alligator was not an easy task. Even after the big creatures were protected (first by state decree in 1967 and then by federal designation as endangered species in 1973), the laws were often overlooked by gator hunters. But eventually gators began to increase, and today the official es-timate is about 1 million in Florida. The unofficial estimate argues that the actual number may be twice that. The number may certainly seem that high when you count the alligators killed crossing highways or if you wake up to one or more swimming in your backyard pool. Whatever the actual current number of alligators, the conservation effort that allowed their increase is a true success story.

Although on a far smaller scale, the conservation effort for the American crocodile seems equally successful. In contrast to the freshwater-dwelling alligator, the slender-snouted, olive green crocodile is restricted to saltwater habitats around the southern tip of the peninsula and the Keys. Just a half-century ago, crocodile numbers were in the low hundreds, perilously close to the "too few to make it" count that spells doom for too many endangered species. Recent counts have estimated the population in Florida to be near 2,000 (give or take a few). That is a pretty significant increase for a creature with a restricted home range.

But our crocodilian populations are being bolstered by a new species, the spectacled caiman. Originally from the Neotropics, the spectacled is the only crocodilian known to have established in Florida. It is restricted to freshwa-ter habitats on the southern peninsula (it seems most common near Home-stead), and its numbers are unknown.

Since the turn of the century in 2000, from one to a few (depending on who is relating the facts) smooth-fronted caiman have been found in Ever-glades canals. This impressively armored little crocodilian is not yet thought to be breeding in Florida.

HOW TO FIND ALLIGATORS, CAIMAN, AND CROCODILES IN FLORIDA

All crocodilians are normally restricted to the vicinity of permanent water. Alligators are abundant in most state and federal parks in Florida. On sunny days they can also be seen basking on the sides of most sizable canals running parallel to roads, along rivers, and near favored fishing holes. They can be dangerous. Do not molest or even approach any alligator. Females may be unseen but in attendance of babies. Feeding or catching an alligator is in violation of state and/or federal laws.

Caiman are secretive and difficult to find. They are established only along a few canals in Dade and Broward counties Florida but reportedly expanding their range.

American crocodiles can be regularly seen in Everglades National Park, Florida Bay, and Crocodile Lake National Wildlife Refuge, on northern Key Largo. Specimens are occasionally seen 100 (or more) miles farther northward.

Crocodilians can be found by their eyeshine at night. Look into swamps and rivers at night while holding a flashlight at eye level. You may be pleased to see red reflections from their eyes shining back at you.

ALLIGATORS AND CAIMAN: FAMILY ALLIGATORIDAE

These are the broad-snouted representatives of the order. The American alligator, once made uncommon by hunting for the skin trade, is now abundant again in Florida.

42. American Alligator
Alligator mississippiensis

Size: Females seldom exceed 8 feet; males regularly attain 12 feet. The reported record size is 19 feet 2 inches (but this is now suspect)! A male measuring 14 feet ⅝ inch was recently found in central Florida. Hatchlings are about 9½ inches long.

Identification: This is the darkest colored of our crocodilians. Babies are black with yellow crossbands. Adults are dull in color and contrast and often largely or entirely a dusky olive black. If yellow markings are retained, they will be most prominent on the sides. The snout is bluntly rounded.

Voice: Babies produce a high-pitched grunt. Adults voice muffled, spluttering roars.

Habitat/Range: Although this is primarily a freshwater species, alligators are occasionally encountered in estuarine or saltwater habitats. They may be seen in and along ponds, canals, lakes, rivers, large streams, borrow pits, swamps, and marshes or virtually any other water-retaining habitat.

Abundance: The American alligator is now abundant throughout Florida except for the southern Keys.

Behavior: Shy when unfamiliar with humans, alligators accustomed to the presence of humans can become dangerous nuisances. During the breeding and nesting seasons, alligators of both sexes can be more adversarial than normal. Females may protect both the eggs and young. Normal prudence dictates steering clear of any large crocodilian. Household pets and small children are more at risk than an adult human.

Despite their huge size, even adult alligators are capable of raising themselves high on their sturdy legs and running for short distances.

Reproduction: This is a mound-nesting crocodilian. From 20 to 50+ eggs are laid annually. Breeding males and nesting females can both be irascible and dangerous to approach. Hatching occurs after 65–75 days of incubation.

Similar species: Both the spectacled caiman and the American crocodile are olive green or olive gray with dark (not yellow) crossbands, have narrower snouts, and are likely to be seen only in extreme southern Florida. American crocodiles are most apt to be encountered in brackish or saltwater habitats.

Comments: Do not feed or otherwise "tame" these potentially dangerous creatures. To do so not only is illegal but also could prove fatal. Call the closest office of the Florida Fish and Wildlife Conservation Commission to report nuisance alligators.

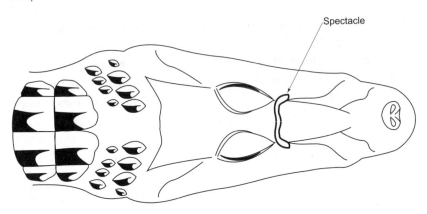

Spectacle

Spectacled caiman head showing spectacle

43. Spectacled Caiman

Caiman crocodilus crocodilus

Size: Although in tropical America the spectacled caiman occasionally attains a length of 8 feet, Florida specimens seldom exceed 6 feet. Hatchlings are about 8½ inches in total length.

Identification: Hatchlings of this "small" crocodilian are banded with very dark brown on a dark olive ground. The overall color darkens and the pattern obscures with advancing age and size. A curved ridge extends across the snout connecting the anterior extreme of both eyelids. The snout of the spectacled caiman is moderately sharp.

Voice: Hatchlings produce a high-pitched grunt. This deepens in tone as the size of the caiman increases. Adult males produce a muffled, grunting roar.

Habitat/Range: This is a secretive crocodilian of freshwater marshes and heavily vegetated pond, lake, and canal edges in extreme southern Florida. This race of the spectacled caiman is native to much of northern South America.

Abundance: Rare and of very localized distribution in Florida. Breeding populations occur in Dade County and possibly in Monroe County. Feral, nonbreeding specimens may occasionally be encountered anywhere in South Florida.

Behavior: Although comparatively small and secretive, spectacled caiman are feisty if cornered. Even babies will bite sharply if molested.

Reproduction: From 10 to about 40 eggs are laid in summer in a temperature-stabilizing mound nest. Large females produce the largest clutches. Incubation is of variable duration but in south Florida seems in the range of 75–95 days. Hatchlings are more contrastingly patterned than the adults.

Similar species: American alligators are black with yellow banding. American crocodiles are colored similarly to the caiman but have a sharper nose and are usually in estuarine habitats.

Comments: Spectacled caiman have been imported in considerable numbers for the pet trade for more than 50 years.

"Specs" are temperature-sensitive creatures that if caught away from relatively warm water can be immobilized or killed by even a short freeze.

Many "pet" specimens have escaped, and more have been deliberately released into Florida's canal systems. Some of these have acclimated and thrived.

CROCODILES: FAMILY CROCODYLIDAE

In general, these are the most narrow-snouted of the crocodilians. Although some of the world's crocodilians are confirmed man-eaters (Africa's Nile and Australia's saltwater crocodiles for example), the American crocodile in Florida is a shy fish-eating creature usually difficult to find. Until the very severe winter of 2010, when more than 100 crocodiles died in Florida, their numbers had been increasing annually. The population in the state had reportedly increased to more than 2,000 adults. This species is protected by both state and federal legislation.

Except for caiman, escaped or released exotic crocodiles are almost never reported from the wilds of Florida; however, three years ago a juvenile crocodile was found in the Big Cypress area of southwest Florida. Although crocodiles can be "testy," this one proved exceptionally so. More than irascible, it was almost sinister in its behavior. Genetic testing has failed to disclose the parentage of this feral waif. Rather than confirming that this is an American crocodile, genetics indicate that it is a hybrid between a New World species and an Old World—perhaps American × Siamese.

44. American Crocodile

Crocodylus acutus

Size: Hatchlings are about 10 inches in total length. Adults in Florida, the northernmost area of their range, attain 8–12 feet in total length. In South America, the American crocodile may attain a larger size than in Florida.
Identification: The ground coloration of this crocodilian is olive brown to dark olive green. The crossbands are darker (not lighter). Small specimens are more contrastingly patterned than large ones. The snout is slender and tapering. The upper jaw is notched anteriorly, causing the fourth tooth of the lower jaw to be permanently visible.
Voice: Hatchlings produce a high-pitched croaking grunt, but specimens of more than a few weeks of age seldom vocalize.
Habitat/Range: This is a species primarily of estuarine situations, brackish canals, mangrove flats, and saltwater habitats. Look for this crocodile in Miami-Dade County, Monroe County (including the Keys), and northward to Charlotte County on the Gulf coast. This species can also be found in the West Indies, Mexico, Central America, and northwestern South America.
Abundance: Local but increasingly common on the southern tip of Florida. It is now estimated that the population of the American crocodile has reached 2,000 individuals in Florida.
Behavior: This a shy, quiet, and normally inoffensive crocodile. It seems less potentially aggressive toward humans than a similarly sized American alligator, but with that said, it is still prudent to avoid close contact with large crocodiles. This is a federally endangered reptile. Do not molest it.
Reproduction: Female American crocodiles scrape together a nest mound of beach debris and sand or simply nest in a hole dug in the beach-sand. From 20 to 50+ eggs are laid. Incubation takes about 3 months. Females assist in the escape of the young from the nest and may carry the young to the water, but offer no further maternal assistance.

Similar species: The American alligator is black with yellow crossbands and has a bluntly rounded snout. The spectacled caiman is colored somewhat like the crocodile but occurs in freshwater habitats and has a more bluntly rounded snout with a ridge across it.

Comments: Studies of nesting successes and population stability in the state of Florida continue. Recently, one or more large crocodiles have been seen with regularity on Sanibel and Pine islands in Lee County.

3

Worm Lizards, Lizards, and Snakes

Order Squamata

WORM LIZARDS: FAMILY AMPHISBAENIDAE

Despite the fact that they are not true lizards, the amphisbaenians have long been referred to as such. These are specialized burrowers with the scales arranged in rings (annuli) that make the creatures look annulated like an earthworm. There are many representatives in the subtropical and tropical parts of the world, but despite long-existing rumors of a second species present in the United States, only a single taxon has been confirmed here.

Except for three Mexican species with forelimbs, the amphisbaenians are limbless. None have functional eyes.

HOW TO FIND WORM LIZARDS IN FLORIDA

Unless driven from their burrows by heavy rains, worm lizards almost never come to the surface. They can be found when raking fallen leaves from a sandy substrate and by brushing sand and debris from near the base of sand-scrub plants. Worm lizards often construct their burrows less than 1 inch beneath the surface of the soil.

Amphisbaenids—Look Ma, No Hands, No Feet, and No Eyes

Amphisbaenids—worm lizards, if you prefer—are creatures of the soil. I've rooted them out of flower beds while gardening in Tampa, from isolated sandy dunes along the Lake Wales Ridge, and from under a mat of leaves in Gainesville. Being fossorial creatures, worm lizards are always on or in the ground. Except for one . . .

I always enjoy happening across a Florida worm lizard. It is such a rare occasion, and I just plain like the attenuated, annulated creatures. Their stubby tuberculated tail-tip, underslung lower jaw, lack of external eyes, and pink coloration all somehow add to their allure. Denizens of the dark, damp earth, those I find exposed are usually dead, and I am disheartened by their demise.

I was walking along a little wooded trail in a city park near my home in Gainesville. I seldom see much at the park, but once in a while the sighting of a broad-headed skink or the singing of a white-eyed vireo makes the walk worthwhile. This time I was looking for a shrub, *Euonymus americanus*, known locally as "heart's a-bustin' with love" because of the appearance of its fruiting structures.

It was a pretty day, and I was halfway around the mile-long loop, walking under the limbs of some venerable old live oak trees. Gray squirrels were churring overhead, and right above me I heard an animated rustling in the leaves. A squirrel squabble? Maybe a raccoon rumble? I slowed and looked up. I could see nothing, and the rustling had stopped. I took a step, and something landed on my shoulder. Not thinking much about it, I brushed it away and it landed heavily at my feet.

I stared in disbelief. It was a freshly dead Florida worm lizard (a species incapable of climbing) with no external signs of trauma. There was nary a beak or tooth mark on the little pink reptile. But dead is dead, with or without an obvious reason. What creature had caught the lizard? (and how? where?)

This is a question about which I still wonder!

45. Florida Worm Lizard

Rhineura floridana

Size: Most specimens found are 6–12 inches in length. Very occasional specimens of more than 14 inches have been reported. Hatchlings are about 3¾ inches long.

Identification: The worm lizard varies from pale sandy pink to a very bright pink. The nose, throat, and tail often appear the brightest. This species has no limbs and no functional eyes. The head is wedge-shaped, and the short tail is studded dorsally with conical tubercles. The lower jaw is countersunk, preventing sand from getting into the mouth.

Habitat/Range: Sandy, easily burrowed soils are preferred by this interesting species. Worm lizards occur in sandy habitats throughout much of the Florida peninsula north of Lake Okeechobee. They have adapted well to urban and suburban life, where they are often found while gardening. A single specimen has been found in southern Georgia.

Abundance: Because of its burrowing habits, the population statistics of this little creature are difficult to assess with accuracy. Except when flooded out, it is seldom seen but it would seem to be a common reptile.

Behavior: The lifestyle and behavior of the worm lizard can be summed up in one short phrase: "it is a persistent and obligate burrower."

Reproduction: Little is known about the breeding biology of the worm lizard. Females with 1–3 fully formed oviductal eggs have been found in the summer. It is thought (but not confirmed) that 60–90 days are required for incubation.

Similar species: This is the only annulated reptile in Florida.

Comments: During the spring of the year, worm lizards are frequently found beneath leaf litter during gardening operations. They may be plowed to the surface during commercial planting activities. They also seem to near the surface when the weather begins to cool in the autumn. Burrow-inundating rains can force amphisbaenians to surface at any time of year.

Rumors that the Baja two-footed worm lizard, *Bipes biporus,* has been released in Florida have long existed. Gardeners and others have recounted finding two-legged worm lizards occasionally in central Florida. Thus far no two-legged Florida specimens have reached museum collections or herpetologists for confirmation.

4

Lizards

Suborder Sauria (Lacertilia)

Worldwide, the suborder Sauria contains more than 3,800 species in about 400 genera and 24+ families.

They are all scaled, most have functional limbs with clawed feet (but some have limbs reduced in size or are legless), and many have functional eyes with lids. Others have functional eyes protected by a transparent, spectacle-like brille rather than by lids; yet others lack functional eyes.

Lizards vary in size from the slender 12-foot crocodile monitor to minute, delicate 1½-inch geckos dwelling in the litter of forest floors in the Neotropics.

In Florida we have 67 confirmed species in 13 families, as follows:

Family Agamidae, Agamids (4 confirmed species)
Family Anguidae, Glass Lizards (4 species)
Family Chamaeleonidae, Chameleons (2 confirmed species)
Family Corytophanidae, Basilisks (1 confirmed species)
Family Gekkonidae, Geckos (18 confirmed species)
Family Iguanidae, Iguanas (3 species)
Family Leiocephalidae, Curly-tailed Lizards (3 species)
Family Phrynosomatidae, Spiny and Horned Lizards (3 species)
Family Polychrotidae, Anoles (11 confirmed)
Family Scincidae, Skinks (10 species)
Family Teiidae, Racerunners and Whiptails (6 species)
Family Tropiduridae, South American Collared Lizards (1 species)
Family Varanidae, Monitors (1 confirmed species)

Of this number more than two-thirds are introduced alien species. Most of the aliens are restricted to the southern peninsula, with Miami-Dade County the epicenter. The native species range far more widely, with many found over the entire peninsula and some found over the entire state. As an escape mechanism, the tail of most Florida lizards is easily broken. The tails of some actually have fracture planes in the caudal vertebrae to facilitate the breaking (termed autotomizing). In most cases the tails quickly regrow, but the bone is replaced by cartilage, and the shape and scalation differ from the original. Our native lizards are all diurnal to crepuscular. Several of the introduced gecko species are nocturnal.

HOW TO FIND LIZARDS IN FLORIDA

The lizard fauna of Florida may be conveniently divided into six non-technical groups. There are diurnal lizards, nocturnal lizards, arboreal lizards, and terrestrial lizards, and among each group are some that inhabit natural areas and others that are more or less restricted to the vicinity of human habitations.

The introduced geckos are all associated with dwellings or warehouse complexes. They can be found at night with the aid of a flashlight (get permission to prowl!). The introduced anoles are usually found in similar settings but are active on sunny days and more apt than the geckos to colonize roadside trees. In most cases, permission should again be sought to prowl suburban neighborhoods. Most of the introduced geckos and anoles are restricted in distribution to Dade, Monroe, and Lee counties.

All three species of introduced iguanas and the brown basilisk are also most common in Dade and Monroe counties, but are most often found in parks, fields, and along canals. Look for them on nonbreezy, sunny days.

Most glass lizards and skinks are burrowers in open woodlands and sandhills. Raking the sand from around shrubs and turning debris may divulge some specimens. Our spiny lizards and racerunners also occur in these areas but will be seen either running on the surface of the sand or climbing in shrubs or trees.

Check piles of construction rubble in Dade County for curly-tails, brown anoles, and many geckos.

AGAMIDS: FAMILY AGAMIDAE

The family Agamidae contains a multitude of diverse Old World lizards that roughly parallel the former family Iguanidae in habits and habitats; however, none of the agamids attain the large size of the true iguanas.

The three (possibly four) agamas now present in Florida are pet trade species. One, the red-headed agama, dwells amid rocky aridland habitats in Africa. The butterfly agama is a burrowing Malaysian species, the variable agama is persistently arboreal, and if the fourth species, the Asian tree agama, is still present in Florida, its habitat is reflected in its common name.

When suitably warmed and if healthy, these species are very alert, very active, very fast, and very difficult to approach.

A fifth species, the little spiny agama, *Agama hispida*, from South Africa, was known from a single vacant lot in Miami-Dade County. It has not been reported in more than a decade.

Old World Rock Lizards, Tree Lizards, Garden Lizards and Butterfly Lizards: Genera *Agama*, *Calotes*, and *Leiolepis*

There are four agamid lizards contained in four genera now established in Florida. All are of moderate size (usually 16 inches or less), and one-half

Agamas—Red Heads on the Rocks

As I drove slowly by an overgrown field in Hollywood, Florida, a lizard darted from the weeds and stopped on the curbstone. Since there were no vehicles behind me, I stopped quickly and backed up. The lizard saw this act as a threat and darted back into the vegetation. But I had seen enough to know I was in the right place, for that lizard had an orange head—not pale orange, but fiery orange—a color impossible to miss. It was a male red-headed agama, native to eastern Africa.

So why was I not surprised to see this lizard? I knew that a very large reptile dealer was located nearby, and that the red-headed agama was a fast, agile, and accomplished escape artist, and it was a prominent and frequently imported pet trade species.

The agamas are of exclusively Old World distribution. Besides the red-headed agama, many additional species of agamas are regularly imported by the American pet trade. Although some species are rather slow and methodical in their method of movement, the red-headed agama is not among that group. Because of its speed and agility, the presence of the red-headed agama in Florida might be more readily attributed to accidental escape than to deliberate introduction.

But as they say, the times, they do change, and the presence of the East African red-headed agama, *Agama agama agama*, in Florida seems a thing of the past. Despite the escape of many, the East African form of this lizard has not seemed to survive in Florida long enough to reproduce.

But there are still agamas in Miami. Another imported species, the West African agama, *Agama agama africana*, is every bit as adept at escaping, and it seems more forgiving (read that as "tolerant") of our supersaturated summer weather. To date this interloper has been found in at least a dozen diverse areas on the southern peninsula, with perhaps the largest population at Fairchild Tropical Botanic Gardens in Miami. There, among the hordes of tropical plantings and landscaping boulders, the "new" red-headed agama has set up housekeeping and is successfully breeding. Blue of body and red of head, sun-warmed dominant males are as brightly hued as the plantings that surround them.

to two-thirds of this length is tail length. Two are arboreal, one is preferentially saxicolous but can climb trees well, and one is terrestrial. All show some degree of dimorphism, and all are wary speedsters. All of those in Florida are deliberate introductions or escapees from the pet trade.

46. West African Red-headed Agama (African Rainbow Lizard)

Agama agama africana

Size: Males attain a 12 inches in length; females are somewhat smaller. Hatchlings are about 3 inches long.

Identification: This lizard is both geographically and populationally variable and dimorphic. At an optimum temperature, nonstressed males in nuptial coloring have brilliant orange heads, a bluish gray to charcoal dorsum, an orange vertebral stripe, a light venter, and a tail that is light at the base, orange medially, and black distally. Nonbreeding, stressed, or cool males are paler and may lack the orange on the head. Females and juveniles are clad in yellows or earthen tones dorsally, are lighter beneath, and have at least traces of dorsal barring. Breeding females may have an orangish or bluish blush to the head and a bluish blush on the limbs. A low vertebral keel is always present.

Red-headed agamas are slightly flattened, and heavily gravid females become enormously enlarged.

Habitat/Range: These lizards may be seen climbing trees, on the cinder block walls of houses and property barriers, on bridge abutments, amid rubble piles, and in similar habitats in Broward, Miami-Dade, Charlotte, Seminole, Duval, and Martin counties.

Abundance: Although still of local distribution, this lizard is well established in several locales.

Behavior: Red-headed agamas often thermoregulate while facing the sun. These lizards are active, agile, and wary. Dominant males and sun-warmed lizards are more brightly colored than cool ones. These lizards are less active on cloudy days but seem able to thermoregulate sufficiently to allow a normal lifestyle on cool but sunny days.

Reproduction: This lizard routinely produces 2 or 3 clutches of up to 20 eggs each. Normal clutch size varies from 8 to 15. Hatchlings are only rarely seen in Florida.

Similar species: There are no lizards of similar color in Florida.

Comments: Most of the populations of the red-headed agama are in close proximity to reptile dealerships, strongly suggesting the lizard's gateway to Florida.

When the red-headed agama was initially described as being established in Florida, the ones then seen were of the East African subspecies, *A. a. agama*. These are very similar to the West African subspecies but have an all-blue (often blue green) tail.

47. Asian Tree Agama

Bronchocela mystaceus

Comments: Once (and possibly still) present in Okeechobee County, feral examples of this slender arboreal Asian lizard have apparently not been seen since 2002. Since there is a chance that this lack of sightings is merely an oversight, we provide a description and photograph for identification purposes.

Males in Florida have a grayish body and a variably blue head. During the breeding season the throat may become orangish. Females tend to be brownish with both darker crossbars and longitudinal dorsolateral stripes. A black shoulder spot is present as is a prominent crest, strongest anteriorly. Because of their slenderness, these lizards tend to look smaller than their 15-inch overall length.

48. Variable Agama (also called Bloodsucker)

Calotes versicolor

Size: Adult males may attain 17 inches in length. Females grow to about 14 inches long. The tail is twice as long as the SVL. Hatchlings are a bit over 3 inches in total length.

Identification: Nonbreeding individuals (including hatchlings) are brown, olive brown, or grayish with darker markings. Breeding males are suffused with yellow and usually have a bright orange head and shoulders and a pair of prominent black spots between the throat and shoulders. Chameleon-like, the colors may enrich, dull, or change in only a few moment's time. A prominent vertebral crest is present, and the gular area is weakly distensible. The limbs are long, and in keeping with the lizard's arboreal habits, the claws are sharp and recurved.

Habitat/Range: Known in Florida only from a small area of St. Lucie County, this is a pet trade species from southern Asia.

Abundance: This lizard is very secretive and well camouflaged but does not seem rare.

Behavior: Hatchlings are most often found in low herbaceous vegetation. Adults are more arboreal, at times ascending more than 25 feet in trees. This is an alert and nervous lizard that is quick to climb and put the trunk of a tree between it and an approaching person. This agama often assumes a head-down position on the trunk of a tree while foraging.

Reproduction: Adult females lay up to 25 eggs. It is probable that this species lays 2 to 4 clutches annually during the late spring and summer months. Hatchlings emerge after about 65 days of incubation.

Similar species: There are no other lizards in this area of Florida with this suite of characteristics.

Comments: As is often the case with newly established alien species, the existence of this interesting lizard in Florida was known to pet trade collectors for almost a decade before it was known to researchers.

49. Butterfly Agama

Leiolepis belliana

Size: Males attain a length of 16 inches; females are smaller. Hatchlings are about 4 inches long.

Identification: This beautiful lizard is somewhat flattened in appearance. Its dorsum is a warm olive brown and marked by 3 prominent stripes formed of discrete ocelli (a dorsolateral stripe on each side and a vertebral stripe) between which are a varying number of randomly placed ocelli. The darker sides bear about 7 vertically oriented bright orange bars. The belly is usually light but may have bluish spots or bars. Females are less brightly colored than the males. Hatchlings are dark brown to olive black dorsally with 5 light stripes. Between each pair of stripes is a row of light spots.

Habitat/Range: This Malaysian taxon is known in Florida from a single residential area in Miami-Dade County.

Abundance: Butterfly agamas are common in their single known population.

Behavior: These alert and nervous lizards dig long home burrows in manicured lawns or gardens to which they immediately retire when startled. The burrows may be 36 inches long and 12 inches deep at the terminus.

The ribs are long and free-ended and flexed forward to stretch and display the orange bars during both territorial displays and thermoregulation. This species is believed to be monogamous, and during the breeding season a pair often shares the same burrow then temporarily shares the refuge with hatchlings.

Reproduction: This lizard lays about 6 large eggs, but almost nothing else is known about its breeding biology in Florida.

Similar species: None in Florida.

Comments: Even though the lizard constructs its home burrows in lawns and gardens, affected homeowners do not seem to object to its presence. This lizard has been present in Florida since the 1980s.

GLASS LIZARDS: FAMILY ANGUIDAE

Anguids—A Glass Lizard Kind of Day

The miles rolled by, the hours also, but less quickly. I was driving northwestward to the Apalachicola National Forest (ANF) on the Florida panhandle. I was on a glass lizard search. I had no idea what had brought this search about, but upon awaking that morning, I had simply known it should be a glass lizard day. I took this to be an omen. I seldom question omens. To do so is bad juju.

I drove up I-75, turned west on I-10, and watched the gas gauge signal time for a fill-up. A day's drive of herping was no longer a day of relaxation. Somehow it had become a path to financial ruin.

Finally the lady who lives in my GPS told me, "turn here." Hardly a mile up the road I encountered a young adult eastern glass lizard. A half mile farther, and another one was crossing. But then came a long "dry spell." I encountered nothing for the several miles I drove before deciding to retrace my route.

Back to the starting point. Nothing. Back to the turning point. Still nothing. Then as I was passing by and marveling at a big field of pitcher plants, a glass lizard emerged onto the road, and dashed back onto the verge. I parked and walked the right-of-way. About the third time I turned and retraced my steps, the lizard emerged. No plain eastern glass lizard, this one; rather, it was an adult eastern slender glass lizard with a perfect (nonregenerated) tail.

It wound up being a good night for crossing snakes and amphibians. I was glad I hadn't questioned the omen.

The lizard family Anguidae is represented in Florida by four confusingly similar legless species called glass lizards. It may be necessary to have the lizard in hand to check the positioning of the dark lateral stripes to assure identification of the lizard. Three of the four species are rather well known; the fourth, the mimic glass lizard, was described in 1987 and is considered rare. Three of the four species occur over most of the state, whereas one, again the mimic glass lizard, seems restricted to the panhandle and extreme northeastern Florida.

Glass Lizards: Genus *Ophisaurus*

All of our glass lizards are oviparous. Females provide parental care throughout the incubation period.

The anguids are often referred to as lateral-fold lizards, a reference to the longitudinal expansion fold found from nape to vent on most species. The folds often harbor a number of ticks.

Despite the superficial similarity of glass lizards to snakes, there are some important differences. Glass lizards have functional eyelids and ear openings (snakes have neither), and the glass lizards do not have the enlarged belly scales so characteristic of most snakes. Because of the presence of osteoderms (bony plates beneath each epidermal scale), the glass lizards lack the sinuosity and suppleness of snakes.

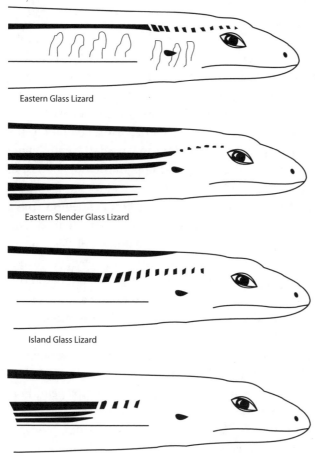

Eastern Glass Lizard

Eastern Slender Glass Lizard

Island Glass Lizard

Mimic Glass Lizard

Patterns and placement of stripes on four species of glass lizards

The glass lizards have very long tails, and three of the four species possess caudal fracture planes (a weakened area in a caudal vertebra to facilitate ready breakage). The island glass lizard lacks fracture planes. The tail of the three species with fracture planes regenerates well and almost fully. The tail of the island glass lizard does not.

All of the glass lizards are native species.

50. Eastern Slender Glass Lizard

Ophisaurus attenuatus longicaudus

Size: Adult eastern slender glass lizards range in size from 24 to 36 inches. The record size for this glass lizard is 42 inches (an even 3½ feet). The length of the tail is about 2½ times that of the SVL. Hatchlings are 8–9½ inches long and have proportionately larger heads and shorter tails than adults.

Identification: Similar to other Florida glass lizards in coloration, the slender glass lizard is the only one of the four to have dark ventrolateral stripes (stripes *below* the lateral groove). The uppermost and heaviest of the dorsolateral stripes may continue onto the back of the head without interruption. If a vertebral stripe is present, it is best defined on young specimens. The ventrolateral stripes may be more poorly defined than those above the groove, but they are present. The dorsal color is a warm sandy brown; the venter is lighter. Some degree of ontogenetic change occurs. With advancing age the longitudinal pattern often fades and is replaced by anterior crossbarring and stippling. There are a series of 7 to 9 dark-outlined light vertical bars beginning beneath the eye and continuing onto the neck and anterior body.

Habitat/Range: This is a species of sandy pine and oak scrub woodlands, uplands with yielding soils, field edges, and other similar habitats. It does not prefer perpetually wet habitats. Although it is fully capable of burrowing, it does so less persistently than other glass lizards. It is found throughout most of the state but is absent from the Everglades.

Abundance: Although the eastern slender glass lizard can be found nearly throughout the state of Florida, it is absent from wetlands, uncommon in some seemingly ideal habitats, but common to abundant in others.

Behavior: This is an alert lizard that allows close approach but will thrash wildly, often breaking its tail off (autotomizing), if actually restrained. It is often seen crossing sandy country roadways in the late afternoon or early evening, or during or following daytime showers.

Reproduction: Number of eggs ranges from 5 (small females) to 20 (large females). The nesting site chosen is often beneath clumps of field- or wiregrass or beneath manmade debris. The female attends to the clutch throughout the 48–65-day incubation.

Similar species: The four species of glass lizard are difficult to separate. Please see accounts 51, 52, and 53 for comparisons, and use the photographs and range maps. The scales of the Florida worm lizard are in whorls, and it lacks functional eyes.

Comments: Although once you have become familiar with the overall appearance of the different species of glass lizards you will probably become adept at separating them, initially a comparison of intensity, completeness, and positioning of the dark striping will be necessary.

51. Island Glass Lizard

Ophisaurus compressus

Size: This is one of the two small species of glass lizards in Florida. The island glass lizard is adult at 16 to 22 inches. Hatchlings are 6½ to 7½ inches long.

Identification: This species undergoes considerable age-related pattern change. Young specimens are prominently striped for their entire length. Anteriorly, older specimens become crossbarred and stippled. A vertebral stripe *may* be present. There is a single heavy lateral stripe. There are no stripes below the lateral groove. The unmarked venter is cream to white. Young specimens have a series of 7 to 10 prominent *dark* (not *dark-edged*) vertical markings posterior to the ear opening. These obscure with advancing age. This species lacks caudal fracture planes. Although the tail will break, it does not readily do so, and tail regeneration is comparatively imperfect.

Habitat/Range: This is a resident of sandy habitats. It shuns perpetually wet situations but may be present in some numbers in the drier pine-oak scrubland above ephemeral ponds. The island glass lizard occurs in suitable habitat throughout peninsular Florida. It is absent west of Franklin County on the panhandle.

Abundance: This glass lizard can be locally common; however, in overview, it is not a frequently seen species.

Behavior: This glass lizard may be seen in warm weather crossing roadways in sandy areas in the late afternoon or at dusk. It is very difficult to find at other times.

Reproduction: Up to 12 eggs may be laid in a moisture-retaining nesting site by a large female. The chosen site may be amid the roots of bunch grasses or beneath debris or ground litter. Females remain with the clutch through the 45–65-day incubation period.

Similar species: See species accounts 50, 52, and 53 for descriptions of the other three species of glass lizards. The legless Florida worm lizard has no functional eyes.

Comments: In one small area of inland Lee County, island glass lizards could be seen with regularity in the late spring and early summer between the evening hours of 7:30 and 8:30. Despite extensive searching in the area, they were not found at other times. Had we not accidentally learned the window of surface activity, we would not have suspected the presence of the lizards at this locale.

52. Mimic Glass Lizard

Ophisaurus mimicus

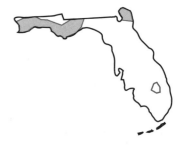

Size: Most specimens seen are in the 16–20-inch range, but mimic glass lizards are known to attain a length of 24½ inches. Hatchlings are 6½–8 inches long.

Identification: The mimic glass lizard is clad dorsally in earthen tones and ventrally in an immaculate off-white. It has a dark vertebral stripe of variable definition (usually best defined posteriorly) and a series of 3 or 4 dark side stripes, all above the lateral groove. The uppermost of these is the most prominent. There are no stripes below the lateral fold. About 7 vertical bars occur posterior to the ear opening. The bars are predominantly dark but may have narrow white centers. Indication of bars (or spots) between the eye and the ear opening may be visible. The tail vertebrae have fracture planes, and the tail autotomizes with comparative ease.

Habitat: This is another of the glass lizards that prefer sandy habitats. Although much about it remains conjectural, it is thought to be a species of sandy but seasonally wet pine flatwoods as well as of open mixed woodlands. It is known to range across much of Florida's panhandle and also occurs in Nassau County.

Abundance: This small glass lizard is seemingly uncommon.

Behavior: Mimic glass lizards may be seen crossing roads in the early morning and late afternoon hours. They seem particularly visible on dirt country roads and may be seen in some numbers on hot afternoons following a shower. They allow close approach but not actual restraint.

Reproduction: This is an oviparous species, but little else is known about its reproductive biology. It is probable that the clutch size does not exceed 12 and that the female remains in attendance throughout the incubation period.

Similar species: The slender glass lizard has stripes below the lateral groove. In addition to its vertebral stripe, the island glass lizard has only one stripe on each side. Eastern glass lizards of all ages lack a well-defined vertebral stripe. See accounts 50, 51, and 53 for comparisons of the three other species of glass lizards. The Florida worm lizard has no functional eyes.

Comments: Many questions remain about this species. Its existence was discovered in 1987 when museum specimens of the genus were being examined. This species was so similar to the slender glass lizard in appearance that it had been overlooked. Because of this similarity, when the lizard was described, it was given the specific name *mimicus*—the mimic glass lizard. The life history of this species is badly in need of research.

53. Eastern Glass Lizard

Ophisaurus ventralis

Size: Most examples seen are between 19 and 28 inches in length. Very occasional specimens near 36 inches, and the record size is 42⅝ inches. Hatchlings are about 8 inches long.

Identification: Striking ontogenetic changes occur. Young specimens are often an olive tan with two prominent dark dorsolateral lines. The venter is yellowish. At adulthood the stripes fade, a suffusion of turquoise or green appears dorsally, and the venter turns a rather bright yellow. Dark spots develop on the rear of the dorsal scales, and light spots on the lateral scales. At no stage in the life of this lizard are there dark lines below the lateral fold. The tail is very easily broken.

Habitat/Range: The eastern glass lizard may be found in both moist and dry habitats. It seems as abundant in grassy suburban yards as in the woodlands and wetlands with which it is often associated. It occurs throughout Florida.

Abundance: This is the most abundant and least habitat specific of the glass lizards.

Behavior: This big and pretty lizard is often seen poking its head up from beneath the recumbent stems of freshly watered lawn grasses or basking on sidewalks or road edges on cool mornings. It is the only one of the four glass lizards to be regularly associated with damp marsh, swamp, and canal edge situations. It also occurs in fairly dry, open woodlands but usually seeks moister habitats than those sought by its congeners.

Reproduction: Up to 18 eggs can be laid by large female eastern glass lizards. The incubation duration varies from 56 to 70 days, the longest occurring when temperatures are cool. The nesting site is beneath a log, trash, leaf mat, grass clump, or some other moisture-retaining debris. Females remain with the clutch until hatching.

Similar species: This is the only one of our glass lizards to appear turquoise or greenish when adult. Please also see accounts 50, 51, and 52 for species comparisons. The smaller Florida worm lizard lacks functional eyes.

Comments: This is the bulkiest and most commonly seen species of glass lizard in Florida. It may occasionally be seen in some numbers, late on summer afternoons, along the pavement edge of rural roadways.

OLD WORLD CHAMELEONS: FAMILY CHAMAELEONIDAE

These are lizards of remarkable and unmistakable appearance. The tail is strongly prehensile. The large turreted eyes have tiny openings and are capable of independent movement, and the toes are bundled into opposed clamps. A single species, the veiled chameleon, is now established in Florida, but reports of feral panther chameleons are increasingly common; however, the latter is not yet known to be established. A third species, the giant Jackson's chameleon, was known to breed in Hillsborough County in the 1960s and 1970s but is now thought to have been extirpated.

True Chameleons: Genera *Chamaeleo* and *Furcifer*

The veiled chameleon is indigenous to the Arabian Peninsula. The founder stock of the several populations was deliberately introduced.

54. Veiled Chameleon

Chamaeleo calyptratus calyptratus

Size: Males attain a length of nearly 24 inches; females are fully grown at only 14 inches. Hatchlings are about 2¼ inches long.

Identification: Turquoise and gold, turquoise and white, or green are all commonly assumed colors. Males have a huge (occasionally to 4 inches in height) cranial crest (casque). Females have a proportionately lower casque. The body is laterally flattened, and a vertebral crest is present. Hatchlings are green with a few white or purplish spots on the sides. Males of all ages have a spur (calcar) on each heel.

Habitat/Range: Adults are found in shade trees and large shrubs; neonates are usually closer to the ground. This chameleon occurs in Collier, Lee, Hendry, and Okeechobee counties.

Abundance/Range: Although local, where introduced this is a common chameleon.

Behavior: This is a fully arboreal and amazingly camouflaged chameleon. When coupled with frequent observation stops and swaying like a breeze-blown leaf, its methodical foot-over-foot method of progression prevents attention being drawn to this stealthy lizard.

Reproduction: This amazingly fecund chameleon can attain sexual matu-

Chameleons—Veils and Panthers; Two New Floridians

Most of the alien lizard species now established in Florida are quick, agile escape artists. The introduction of most can be attributed either to deliberate release or to accidental escape, but to think that the presence of the slow-moving, easy-to-cage chameleon—any species of chameleon—has been anything but deliberate, is ludicrous.

And yet, despite laws supposedly preventing the release of exotic taxa into the Florida wilds, several populations of the beautiful veiled chameleon are firmly established, and the equally pretty but very different-appearing panther chameleon is now gaining a foothold.

The best-known locale for the veiled chameleon is in Ft. Myers. When I visited this locale during the day in 2000, I saw no chameleons, but when I visited the same site at night, I quickly found several sleeping hatchlings in the beam of the flashlight. All were clinging to weeds and saplings 2 or 3 feet above the ground. One half-grown chameleon, also soundly sleeping, was on the low branch of a pinnate-leaved exotic tree.

Both before and since my visit, lizard enthusiasts have found and taken innumerable chameleons of all sizes from that site, including 2-foot adult males. I have been told that new owners of the site no longer allow nocturnal visits by herpers, but I have not attempted to check this out. Yet the Ft. Myers site is rather insignificant when compared with other locales, both known and incipient, in Florida.

It seems unlikely that the presence of chameleons in Florida will adversely impact a habitat already reeling with other, even more common, exotics such as the brown anole. Do chameleons belong here? The unequivocal answer is no—but it sure is exciting to find one of these unique, exotic saurians when searching habitats at night.

rity at 6 months of age, lay up to 70 eggs in a clutch, and produce several clutches annually.

Similar species: See comments below (account 54A, the panther chameleon).

Comments: The veiled chameleon is one of the few omnivorous species in this family. In addition to insects and other arthropods, it eats leaves, blossoms, and fruit.

54A. Panther Chameleon

Furcifer pardalis

Comments: Although not known to be established in Florida, feral examples of the panther chameleon have been found in Lee, Monroe, Broward, and Miami-Dade counties. It is indigenous to northern Madagascar (including many of the islands). The panther chameleon varies geographically in color. It is also dimorphic. The ground color of the males may be turquoise to green, tan, orange, or pink. Darker barring is present. There is a broad, irregularly edged, lateral stripe that may be either lighter or darker than the ground color. The panther chameleon is capable of undergoing extensive color and pattern changes. Females are often of varying shades of brown with orange highlights. Head crests and a very short rostral appendage are present. There is a low serrate vertebral crest. Large males may occasionally exceed 18 inches in total length. Females are smaller. A range map for this chameleon is not yet feasible.

GECKOS: FAMILY GEKKONIDAE

Of the 20 gecko species now found in Florida, 19 are of introduced status. The single exception is the Florida reef gecko, *Sphaerodactylus notatus notatus*, one of the least conspicuous of all gecko species.

Of the 19 introduced species, several have proven very adaptable and are now present over wide areas of the state; others have not spread much beyond their small area of actual introduction. Feral examples of other species, such as the smooth-backed flying gecko, *Ptychozoon lionotum*, are occasionally found on warehouses now or formerly housing reptile dealers in Alachua, Lee, St. Lucie, Miami-Dade, and Broward counties.

Because of their affiliation with dwellings, the most conspicuous geckos are the house geckos of the genus *Hemidactylus*, the wall geckos of the genus *Tarentola*, and, with increasing frequency, the gigantic tokay gecko, *Gekko gecko*. Although all of these are nocturnal, they are often seen basking in the warmth of porch lights or hunting insect prey in their glow.

Because of their nocturnal propensities (only three species are diurnal), the geckos of Florida have essentially filled a niche unexploited by our native lizards. The three diurnal taxa are the two species of large day geckos and the much smaller yellow-headed gecko.

Geckos—A Fading Presence

We stood before a venerable tamarind tree. More than a year earlier we had been told of its existence (but it seemed as if our vacations were always carrying us northward to the mountains rather than southward to the Keys), and we had only now found the time to seek out the tamarind. It wasn't just the tree we had wanted to see, although it, by itself, was a vision to behold.

Tall and bigger around at head height than three people could reach around with their arms, this old tamarind was a tree with a history. Not only was it a tree of record size, but it was also home to a gecko species I had not seen in Florida for many long years and had never seen in the Keys—*Gonatodes*—the yellow-headed gecko. I don't know who it was that first learned that this tamarind was populated by yellow-headed geckos, but someone had discovered it, and over time the story had been passed on to Patti and me.

The tiny yellow-headed gecko is known in one subspecies or another in the West Indies, Mexico, Central America, and northern South America. It was originally known in Florida in two discrete populations—one in Coconut Grove and the second from Keys south of the 7-mile bridge. In the late 1950s I lived in Coconut Grove, and it was there, after some very extensive searching, that I first found the species—just one example, and it was a female.

But finally, after a hiatus of more than 20 years, during which the mainland population faded quietly away, Patti and I had decided to try our luck on the tamarind. We succeeded. In the folds and crevices of that ancient trunk we actually found a pair of yellow-heads and a few Mediterranean geckos as well.

Interestingly, the yellow-heads and the Mediterraneans seemed to coexist with little if any strife, but in nature as elsewhere, things seldom remain static for long. Patti and I made another gecko-watching trip or two and found yellow-heads each time. But on one of our last trips we found that the relatively benign Mediterranean geckos had been replaced by the far more aggressive and predatory tropical house gecko, *Hemidactylus mabouia*, and on that trip we failed to find any yellow-heads on the tamarind.

A thriving population that Walt Meshaka and I had found on some gnarled, hollowed, but still stately Russian olive trees had also been rent asunder—trees and all—by a fierce hurricane. We never could find a yellow-headed gecko in any of their old haunts. Despite learning about other locales from hobbyists and researchers, we failed in those searches also. We continued to fail until a day in 2002 when I chanced on two female yellow-heads in a grove of palms, head-downward on the trunks. A couple of years later I found a single male. Researcher Joe Burgess also found one male on a Key far to the north of the location where the yellow-head had been known to exist. No females were found, and we have no explanation for this new range confirmation.

Despite these few finds, it is speculated that after surviving on the Florida Keys for more than 60 years, the population of yellow-headed geckos is now so diminished (or so scattered) that its continued existence is in jeopardy. Since it is an alien species, this should be of no consequence to me, but I must admit that I find joy in watching these elfin exotics in the wild, and I will miss them if they do succumb.

Of the Florida geckos, all but the yellow-headed gecko have distended toe pads that allow them to climb even smooth surfaces agilely. The toe pads are more complex than they might seem. The pads are transversely divided into a series of lamellae containing vast numbers of tiny bristle-like setae. The setae are tipped with an equally vast number of micro-scopic nonskid suction cups. To fully appreciate the complexity of these climbing devices, simply watch the way a slowly moving gecko curls its toes upward when disengaging a foot. After watching this action in slow motion, you will sit back and marvel at the speed with which geckos can dart along vertical and inverted surfaces.

All Florida geckos lack functional eyelids; instead, their eyes are protected by a clear spectacle (the brille).

All are cold sensitive. Most are restricted to the southern half of the peninsula, but two species of house geckos are now found throughout the state.

Typical geckos are among the few lizards with a voice (the ability to hiss doesn't count). Vocalizations range in volume from the barely audible squeaks of tiny house geckos to the loud two-syllabled advertisement calls of the 12-inch-long tokay. Sphaerodactyline geckos do not seem able to vocalize.

All geckos have an easily broken tail. Some species are capable of au-totomizing tails with little, if any, external help. A great many geckos seen in the field have a partially to fully regenerated tail. These always differ in scalation and appearance from the originals.

Male geckos are territorial at all times, but especially during the breeding season. Serious skirmishes can occur if two males meet and one does not quickly back down. A gecko's skin is thin and can be easily torn, but wounds also heal quickly.

Two species, the Indo-Pacific gecko and the mourning gecko, are parthenogenetic, all female species.

Many geckos are quite capable of undergoing strong color changes. They are darker and (often) more heavily patterned by day, lighter and less contrastingly patterned by night.

House, Day, and Wall Geckos: Genera *Gehyra, Gekko, Hemidactylus, Lepidodactylus, Pachydactylus, Phelsuma, Ptychozoon,* and *Tarentola*

A group of very variable yet very typical geckos appear in species accounts 55–68A. These are the geckos you are most apt to see on the walls of dwellings and warehouses and on the trees and power poles surrounding them. They vary in size from the 3-inch total length of the mourning gecko to the nearly 12-inch-long tokay and day geckos. All have well-developed toe pads and are agile climbers.

55. Stump-toed Gecko

Gehyra mutilata

Size: This heavy-bodied gecko is adult at 3½–4½ inches in total length. Hatchlings are just under 2 inches long.

Identification: The stump-toed gecko is capable of a great degree of metachrosis. While foraging at night it may be so light in color that it appears white. When inactive during the daytime it is usually of some shade of gray with paired small lighter spots dorsally. A light stripe runs from the tip of the snout to the tympanum. The belly is off-white to very light yellow. This gecko has 4 large chin shields, the medial pair the largest, divided subdigital (undertoe) lamellae, and broad subcaudal scales. The skin of this gecko tears very easily.

Voice: The stump-toed gecko voices territorial squeaks.

Habitat/Range: At present this gecko is known from only the walls of a few buildings in Pinellas and Broward counties.

Abundance/Range: Unknown, but at present probably uncommon in Florida.

Habitat: A very arboreal gecko; where it occurs in numbers, this is one of the "house geckos." It also seeks shelter in and on warehouses and docks and in piles of lumber, palm fronds, and other debris. It may also be found on trees and beneath rocks.

Reproduction: Little is known about the reproductive biology of this gecko in Florida. It is known that females are able to lay several pairs of hard-shelled eggs at 3 or 4-week intervals. It is suspected that in Florida the deposition season is restricted to late spring, summer, and early autumn.

Similar species: The stocky countenance and large chin shields should differentiate this gecko from other species. The Indo-Pacific gecko may be the most similar in appearance, but it is slim, lacks enlarged chin shields, and has a rather bright yellow or orange belly.

Comments: This gecko is a relatively new introduction to Florida.

56. Tokay Gecko

Gekko gecko

Size: One of the three largest gecko species in Florida; specimens nearing 12 inches in length are frequently encountered.

Identification: These predaceous lizards are unmistakably colored, with orange and white markings against a gray or blue gray ground color. The protuberant eyes may vary from yellow green to orange. The pupils are complex and vertically elliptical. The toe pads are large and easily visible.

Voice: The loud, sharp "geck-o, geck-o, geck-o-o-ooo" calls of the males of the Tokay gecko resound on warm spring and summer nights from secluded areas in and on buildings, shade trees, and other such locations. Their two-syllabled calls begin with a chuckle, evolve into a series of "geck-os" or "to-kays," and end in lengthened, slurred notes.

Habitat/Range: In southern Florida where the normally benign subtropical climate allows the species to survive in the wild year-round, tokays have expanded their ranges from original points of release to neighboring structures. In urban areas they may now be seen and heard in shade trees and palms, on power poles, and in other such habitats. Tokays have been found in Alachua, Lee, Hillsborough, Palm Beach, Broward, Collier, Dade, and Monroe counties.

Abundance: This rather firmly established species occurs in many areas of southern Florida. It is abundant near several warehouse complexes and on trees near Miami International Airport as well as on many of the Keys.

Behavior: These big geckos are primarily nocturnal, but they may thermoregulate in sunny areas on mornings following cool nights. Tokays are well able to overpower and consume other lizards, frogs, insects, and other arthropods but may also accept nestling birds and rodents as well. If threatened with capture, tokays open their mouths widely, "growl" with a drawn-out "geccccck," and, if hard pressed, jump toward the offending object and bite. They often retain their grip with a bulldog-like tenacity, tightening at intervals to convince you they're still there. Although the consequences of a tokay bite are not serious (hardly more than those of any prolonged pinch), it can be a frightening encounter for an unsuspecting person.

Reproduction: The hard-shelled, paired, adhesive-shelled eggs are deposited in secluded areas of buildings, tree hollows, and similar spots. With her hind feet the female manipulates the eggs into the spot she has chosen. Wet and pliable when laid, the calcareous, moderately adhesive eggshell soon dries, holding the eggs in the desired spot. Each female may lay several clutches annually. The young exceed 3 inches at hatching. Communal nestings occur.

Similar species: None.

Comments: For years tokays have been a mainstay of the pet industry. In the usually misguided assumption that they will rid dwellings of roaches, people have released the big geckos in residences and office complexes throughout much of the United States. Such free-ranging indoor tokays often succumb to lack of available water, but where weather conditions and escape routes allow, they may move outdoors and thrive.

56A. Golden Gecko

Gekko ulikovskii

Comments: Because it is common in the pet trade and an adept escape artist, feral examples of this robust 6–8-inch (with females the smaller sex) arboreal gecko may be found near animal dealer facilities in St. Lucie, Broward, and Miami-Dade counties. It is not yet known to be established in Florida. It is native to Vietnam. The ground color is olive brown to fawn. Cold temperatures and other stresses cause this gecko to darken in color. Males usually have a decidedly yellow back, which is lacking in females.

57. Common House Gecko

Hemidactylus frenatus

Size: Although most seen are in the range of 3–4 inches, this gecko is known to attain a length of 4½ inches.
Identification: Dorsally this species is ashy gray with an irregular pattern of obscure darker pigment. It becomes very light at night. Ventrally it is nearly white. A gray lateral line is usually visible. The scales of the body are mostly smooth, but there are 6 rows of rather pronounced spinous scales on its tail.
Voice: A barely audible squeak is voiced by restrained or combating males.
Habitat/Range: The walls of buildings. This gecko is restricted in distribution to a few spots on Key West and Stock Island in the Lower Florida Keys and on a few warehouse complexes in Broward and Lee counties.
Abundance: Unknown, but thought to be rare.
Behavior: This wary gecko is most active on hot, muggy nights. It may be seen hunting for insects in the halos produced by porch lights.

Reproduction: Little is known about the reproductive biology of this gecko in Florida. This is not a parthenogenetic species. Captive animals have revealed that the eggs are only weakly adhesive and usually placed in crevices or beneath loose ground debris. Several clutches are produced by a female annually. Communal nesting is known. The 2-inch hatchlings emerge after about 48 days of incubation.

Similar species: The ease with which the common house gecko may be confused with the more widely ranging Indo-Pacific gecko may partially account for the paucity of records. *Hemidactylus frenatus* has a white or whitish (sometimes just on the yellowish side of white) belly, whereas the venter of *H. garnotii*, the Indo-Pacific gecko, is always some shade of yellow (often lemon), and the underside of the tail is orange. Both the tropical and Mediterranean house geckos are strongly tuberculate. The flat-tailed gecko has more extensive webbing between the toes and is of more depressed body conformation.

Comments: Although known to exist and breed in Florida for more than 2 decades, this remains an uncommon gecko species. In other areas of the world, the common house gecko has proven prolific and aggressive toward other gecko species.

58. Indo-Pacific Gecko

Hemidactylus garnotii

Size: This interesting gecko is adult at 3¾–5 inches in total length. Hatchlings are 2 inches long.

Identification: Dorsally, this delicate appearing gecko varies from a rather dark grayish brown (day) to a translucent flesh white (night). There may or may not be indications of darker or lighter spotting. If present, the spotting is often strongest on the dorsal surface of the tail. The belly is yellowish, and the underside of the tail is often a rich orange. The body is covered with tiny nontuberculate scales. The sides of the tail appear vaguely flanged.

Voice: This is a vocal species, but the weak squeaking sounds it produces may easily be overlooked.

Habitat/Range: Buildings, trees, fences, and similar structures are all suitable habitat for the Indo-Pacific gecko. In the Florida Keys this species is abundant in mangrove forests, under bridge abutments, and on cement power poles. This species is widespread in many urban and suburban areas of Florida but spottily distributed. It continues to expand its range.

Abundance: Common.

Behavior: If you hope to see this gecko, choose a still, humid night on which to look. They will be most easily found on the walls of dwellings and warehouse complexes. On breezy or cool nights, they often remain near cover. Be keenly observant as you approach the outer perimeters of the halos surrounding lit porch lights or other sources of outdoor illumination. Indo-Pacific geckos are vigilant and often quick to seek cover.

Reproduction: *Hemidactylus garnotii* is a parthenogenetic (unisexual— all female) gecko. Even though unisexual, motions of courtship are indulged in and may, in fact, be necessary to stimulate egg development. Several sets of 2 eggs are produced annually by each breeding individual. In the warmest areas of Florida this species breeds year-round. The eggs are placed in crevices, on windowsills, or beneath ground debris. Incubation lasts about 7 weeks.

Similar species: No other gecko of Florida has a yellow belly and orange beneath the tail.

Comments: Of Florida lizards, only this species and the mourning gecko are known to be parthenogenetic. Despite its delicate appearance, this is a hardy and successful gecko.

59. Tropical House Gecko

Hemidactylus mabouia

Size: This is marginally the largest of our four introduced "hemis." It commonly attains a robust 4 inches in total length and may occasionally attain 5 inches. Hatchlings are about 2 inches in total length.

Identification: By day the dorsal color of this gecko is darker than by night. Day colors can vary from tan to gray or olive brown. Several darker, backward–pointing markings resembling chevrons are usually well defined. Tuberculate scales are liberally scattered over the dorsum and especially abundant laterally. The venter is light. At night, if on white walls, tropical house geckos often appear an unpatterned, ghostly white.

Voice: This is a garrulous species. Males squeak quite audibly if restrained or when involved in territorial disputes.

Habitat/Range: Of our five house gecko species, the tropical seems the most willing to expand its sphere of activity to tree trunks and debris piles well away from human habitation. It is rapidly expanding its range in Florida. It is now known to occur with regularity as far north as Volusia, Hillsborough, and Marion counties.

Abundance: This prolific gecko is aggressive toward other gecko species.

Behavior: These robust geckos can be seen at night clinging tightly to the trunks of trees or high on the walls of dwellings and other buildings. They often assume a head-down position. They are wary and quick to take fright.

Reproduction: Eggs and hatchlings have been found year-round in southern Florida. The tropical house gecko is a communal nester. Incubation varies from 45 to 55 days. Females produce several sets of 2 eggs each.

Similar species: Neither the Indo-Pacific nor the common house geckos have tuberculate scales. The Mediterranean gecko has tuberculate scales, but they are less numerous and proportionately larger. The dorsal markings of the Mediterranean gecko are less precisely defined and never chevron shaped.

Comments: This is an aggressive and predatory house gecko. Adults are fully able to overpower and consume hatchlings of small anole species, other small geckos, and the more usual invertebrate prey.

60. Asian Flat-tailed House Gecko

Hemidactylus platyurus

Size: The flat-tailed house gecko is adult at about 3½ inches in overall length.
Identification: *Hemidactylus* (formerly *Cosymbotus*) *platyurus* is a flattened (depressed) gecko. Its broad tail has serrate edges, and there are skin flanges on the sides of its body and rear legs. When the lateral flanges are spread outward, this little lizard casts little if any shadow; hence it is nearly invisible against many natural backgrounds. The toes are partially webbed, with digits greatly expanded distally. The pupils are vertically oriented. Like many geckos, the flat-tailed gecko is quite capable of changing its color. It is often lighter at night, at times appearing a unicolored, pasty cream; by day, however, it can be quite dark with numerous darker bands.
Voice: Males produce a series of clicks as "advertisement" calls or a weak high-pitched squeak if distressed.
Habitat/Range: In Florida, the flat-tailed house gecko seems restricted to buildings. This gecko is known to occur only on a few warehouses in Pinellas, Lee, and Alachua counties.
Abundance: Rare.
Behavior: The Asian flat-tailed house gecko is persistently nocturnal, quite wary, and arboreal.
Reproduction: Little is known about the reproductive biology of this gecko in Florida. Since eggs have not been found on the outer walls of the warehouse complexes these geckos populate, it is thought they might be deposited in protected areas inside the buildings. It is probable that adult females lay several clutches of 2 eggs each during the summer months. Extrapolating from other house geckos of the genus *Hemidactylus*, we can guess that the incubation duration for *Hemidactylus platyurus* is between 40 and 50 days.
Similar species: See the species accounts for the other four species of house geckos (accounts 57, 58, 59, and 61). The Indo-Pacific gecko has less extensive toe-webbing and a yellow venter.
Comments: Despite being established in Florida for at least two decades, this gecko's very limited distribution and failure to disperse prompt us to consider it a tenuous introduction at best.

61. Mediterranean Gecko

Hemidactylus turcicus

Size: Although most individuals are smaller, this species occasionally attains 5 inches in total length. Hatchlings are nearly 2 inches long.

Identification: The dorsal tubercles are prominently large and most abundant on the upper sides. Those on the tail are conical and sharp-pointed. Mediterranean geckos are darker by day (brownish to gray) than by night (light gray to pasty white). Somewhat darker, irregular dorsal markings are usually visible but may disappear at night. The venter is white.

Voice: The males of this species make weak squeaking sounds. They may vocalize during territorial scuffles or when captured by human or other predators.

Habitat/Range: This gecko is strongly tied to human habitations. It is seldom seen on trees or other such natural vantage points. This species is widespread but of patchy distribution in the Florida peninsula. It seems to be losing ground in south Florida where more aggressive congeners are now present.

Abundance: Extirpated in some areas where it was once abundant, this gecko remains common in other areas.

Reproduction: Unlike its congeners, which breed year-round (at least in southern Florida), the Mediterranean gecko breeds only during the warmer months of the year. Females lay several sets of 2 eggs each. Incubation takes about 48 days.

Similar species: Of the two warty gecko species in Florida, the Mediterranean gecko is the more strongly tuberculate. The dorsal markings of the tropical house gecko are in the shape of chevrons, while those of the Mediterranean gecko are less precisely defined and never chevron shaped.

Comments: Once the common house gecko of Florida, the Mediterranean (also called "warty" or "Turkish") gecko now seems to have been displaced over much of its south Florida range by one or more of three other (and newer) interloping species. Look for these geckos on still, humid nights near the outer perimeter of the halos produced by porch lights. They are less active and more difficult to approach on breezy or cool nights.

62. Mourning Gecko

Lepidodactylus lugubris

Size: This small gecko is fully grown at 2¾–3¼ inches in length. Hatchlings are a bit more than 1¼ inches in total length.

Identification: This is a tiny arboreal gecko with a ground color of tan, reddish brown, light brown, or gray. Dorsal markings consist of a series of darker "W"s with lighter trailing edges beginning on the nape and continuing onto the tail where they become light blotches. A dark bar crosses the snout from eye to eye. A dark ocular stripe runs from the tip of the snout to the rear of the jaw. There are 5 rows of moderately enlarged chin scales decreasing in size from front to back. Lamellae are divided at toe tip.

Voice: A vocal gecko, *Lepidodactylus* produces easily heard squeaky chirps while foraging, during courtship, and if restrained.

Habitat/Range: This gecko of Oceania is now known in Australia, Costa Rica, and the Hawaiian Islands. In Florida it may be occasionally seen on warehouse complexes in Broward, Lee, Hillsborough, and Pinellas counties.

Abundance: Unknown in Florida.

Behavior: While still a "house gecko" in Florida, elsewhere the mourning gecko may be found on trees, rocks, and tidal wrack, as well as on buildings. It is wary, agile, and fast.

Reproduction: This is a parthenogenetic, all-female species. Following a stylized courtship, two (rarely only one) sticky-shelled eggs are laid. Several clutches are laid during the summer. Incubation takes about 65 days.

Comments: This gecko has never been particularly popular in the pet trade. The origin of the Florida population is unknown.

63. Bibron's Gecko

Pachydactylus bibroni

Bibron's gecko
Turner's gecko

Size: Specimens in the Florida population seem to top out at about 5½ inches in total length. This species is known to attain 8 inches in Africa. Hatchlings are about 2½ inches in total length.

Identification: This robust gecko has a tuberculate, tan to buff or light brown dorsum. Transverse dark bars are usually present, and scattered tubercles are white. The venter is white. These geckos are lighter in color at night when they are active than when at rest during the day.

Voice: Squeaking clicks are produced by males both when restrained and during territorial combat. Vocalizations have been heard when there seem to be no other geckos in view, indicating that the calls may also be used as an advertisement mechanism.

Habitat/Range: In Florida, Bibron's gecko is usually seen on the outer walls of dwellings on hot, humid, windless nights. It occasionally moves from houses to nearby power poles and trees. This southern African species is known only from its small Manatee County introduction site.

Abundance: Relatively common but restricted in distribution.

Behavior: These hefty geckos are seldom seen before nightfall. They position themselves head down on walls near the eaves. This robust species is able to eat both small vertebrates and the more normal invertebrate prey.

Reproduction: Although this gecko is often bred in captivity, nothing is known of the reproductive biology of the wild population in Florida. Female captives in Florida produce several sets of 2 eggs each during the summer months. Incubation takes up to 74 days.

Similar species: Young Moorish geckos have a scalation and pattern very similar to that of Bibron's gecko; however, the ranges of the two in Florida are widely separated at present. The white-spotted wall gecko has smoother scales and four white spots on the shoulder.

Comments: Feral specimens of this gecko were first seen in Florida in the early 1970s. The continued existence of the colony was recently confirmed. This species was a popular item in Florida's pet trade. It seems likely that the Manatee County population is the result of a deliberate introduction.

Bibron's gecko has now been largely replaced in the pet trade by the genetically different but look-alike *P. turneri* (photo 63A). Feral examples of this latter species have been seen in some numbers on the warehouse of a Broward County pet dealer as well as on a dealer facility in Hernando County. It is not yet known whether they are established, dispersing, and breeding.

64. Giant Day Gecko

Phelsuma madagascariensis grandis

Size: Although the largest examples in certain populations may exceed a total length of 11 inches, most are fully adult at 8½–9 inches. This is one of the three largest geckos in Florida, the Standing's day gecko and tokay gecko being the others. Males are larger than females and have very prominent femoral pores. Hatchlings are 2½ inches long.

Identification: When healthy and unstressed, adults of this lizard are bright Kelly green both dorsally and laterally. Spots or blotches of brilliant orange (and more rarely of robin's egg blue) are often present dorsally. An orange stripe extends on each side of the snout from nostril to eye, and an anteriorly directed orange V may extend from above each eye to the top of the snout. An orange spot is usually present posterior to each eye, and several similarly colored spots are present on the rear of the head. Except for the stripes from the nostril to the eye, the amount of orange is very variable and may be lacking entirely. Bruises and tears in the skin will show dull green until fully healed. The belly is whitish. Fright or cold temperatures will cause the lizard to assume a much darker, less pleasant green coloration on the back and sides. The scales of the back and sides are granular. The large lidless eyes have round pupils. The toes are broadly expanded, and this gecko is an agile and persistent climber.

Hatchlings are a bit duller than the adults and have scattered orange dorsal spots.

Voice: Although the giant day gecko can vocalize, it does not seem as prone to do so as many other gecko species.

Habitat/Range: This gecko can be seen on palms and other trees in residential areas of Broward, Miami-Dade, and Monroe counties. It has also been reported from Lee County.

Abundance: This impressively beautiful lizard has been found on several occasions on the southern peninsula and is now abundant on some of the Florida Keys.

Behavior: This highly arboreal gecko darts with great ease over the walls of dwellings, on the trunks of palm trees, and on power poles. Many of those seen on palms were near the frond axils and quickly darted into the "boots" and living fronds when approached. Besides eating insects, day geckos lick pollen, exudate from overripe fruit, and fresh, sweet sap.

Males are strongly and aggressively territorial. Although females are less so, hierarchies (pecking orders) are often established. If stylized head-nodding and tail-wagging do not dissuade an encroaching male from additional overtures, fierce skirmishes will follow. As with many geckos, the tail of this species is easily autotomized, and the delicate skin may be torn even during gentle handling.

Reproduction: Adult, sexually active female giant day geckos have an endolymphatic (chalk) sac on each side of the neck. It is thought that the calcareous material it contains is important in the formation of egg shells. Nothing has been reported about the breeding biology of this species in Florida; however, in both its native Madagascar and captivity, adult females deposit several clutches of eggs during the warm months of the year. Duration between clutches varies from somewhat more than two weeks to more than a month. The sticky, hard-shelled eggs are laid in pairs in secluded, protected areas. Hatchlings emerge after a 50–70-day period of incubation.

Similar species: This is the only large bright green lizard with lidless eyes and expanded toes known to be established in Florida.

Comments: When temperatures are suitably warm and food is plentiful, this gecko can attain sexually maturity in considerably less than a year's time. The presence of this species in Florida can be traced to both escaped pet trade animals and deliberate releases.

65. Standing's Giant Day Gecko

Phelsuma standingi

Size: Another of the very large taxa, although most examples are adult at 8 to 10 inches, Standing's day gecko can attain 12 inches in length. Hatchlings are about 2¼ inches long.

Identification: Hatchlings are more brightly colored and strongly patterned than the adults. On hatchlings the top of the head from the tympani forward is lime green, the dorsum and legs are gray, and the tail is blue. All dorsal surfaces from snout to tail pit are busily banded with broad red bars.

Adults pale noticeably. Their head is lime green, the back and legs are gray, and the tail is grayish blue. The crossbands fragment into myriad reddish spots of irregular shape. The belly is white. Bruises and tears in the skin will show dull green until fully healed. Frightened or cold geckos are a darker, less pleasant color. The scales of the back and sides are granular. The large, lidless eyes have round pupils. The toe pads are prominent.

Voice: Although it has a loud and easily heard voice, unless involved in territorial disputes or restrained, this is a quiet gecko.

Although Standing's giant day gecko can vocalize, it does not seem as prone to do so as many other gecko species.

Habitat/Range: Known only from a few of the Florida Keys (Monroe County) and Broward and Palm Beach counties.

Abundance: This Madagascar native is still an uncommon form in Florida.

Behavior: Little is yet known about the behavior or habitat preferences of this gecko in Florida. Although they unhesitating take to nearby trees when frightened, most Standing's geckos have been seen on dwellings. Despite its large size it is agile and fast. Insects, pollen, exudate from over-ripe fruit, and fresh, sweet sap make up the diet.

Males are strongly and aggressively territorial. Although females are less so, hierarchies (pecking orders) are often established. The tail of this species is easily autotomized, and its delicate skin may be torn even during gentle handling.

Reproduction: Like other members of this large genus, adult, sexually active female Standing's giant day geckos have an endolymphatic (chalk) sac on each side of the neck. Nothing has been reported about the breeding biology of this species in Florida; however, both in their native Madagascar and in captivity, adult females deposit several clutches of eggs at 3–4-week intervals during the warm months of the year. The sticky, hard-shelled eggs are laid in pairs in secluded, protected areas. Hatchlings emerge after a 50–70-day period of incubation.

Similar species: None

Comments: A relative newcomer to Florida, feral Standing's giant day geckos have been present on the Florida Keys since the turn of the century.

66. Smooth-backed Flying Gecko

Ptychozoon lionotum

Comments: Although there are two very similar species of Southeast Asian/Malaysian flying geckos in the American pet trade, the smooth-backed flying gecko is the more commonly seen. The second species, *P. kuhli*, has scattered tuberculate scales on its back. Both are about 6 inches long. The smooth-backed flying gecko varies from warm tan to brown in ground color and has several darker wavy crossbars on the nape, back, and tail. The feet of this strongly flattened gecko are fully webbed, the edges of the tail are strongly scalloped, and skin flanges are present on the sides, limbs, and head. The tail can be extended or coiled at will. When resting quietly on a tree with flanges extended, these geckos produce almost no shadow and are almost invisible. They can be seen more readily on the walls of a building. Besides providing a wonderfully effective camouflage, the extended skin flaps allow a flying gecko, when jumping, to glide for relatively long distances. This interesting gecko is present in Broward County.

67. White-spotted Wall Gecko

Tarentola annularis

Size: Adults of this robust gecko attain a 6-inch total length. Hatchlings are about 2 inches long.

Identification: This grayish or sand-colored gecko has 4 discrete white tuberculate spots on its shoulders. Males are the larger sex. Although rough, the dorsal scales are not as rugose and tubercular as those of the related Moorish wall gecko. Belly scales are smoother than dorsal scales. Elongate toe pads are present.

Voice: An audible squeak is voiced when these geckos are restrained or indulging in territorial disputes. It is not known whether the voice is used as an advertisement call.

Habitat/Range: This species is known from several warehouse complexes where it is seen on the outside walls on warm evenings. It is now known to occur in both Lee and Dade counties.

Abundance: Locally distributed but reasonably common within its range.

Behavior: In Florida this species is seemingly restricted to the walls of warehouse complexes and nearby dwellings. Although it has now been known in South Florida for more than 20 years, its potential for further dispersal is not yet known.

Reproduction: Details are unknown in Florida. Hatchlings have not yet been reported. It is known that females of this northern African gecko produce several sets of 2 eggs in a season.

Similar species: Neither Bibron's nor Moorish wall geckos have white shoulder spots.

Comments: This is a heavy-jowled predaceous gecko that may well prey on other lizards as well as invertebrates. Pet trade escapees or releases are responsible for the presence of this gecko in Florida.

68. Moorish Wall Gecko

Tarentola mauritanica

Size: Adults attain a length of about 6 inches. Hatchlings are about 2 inches long.

Identification: Adults are uniformly sandy tan to olive tan dorsally, with both granular and tubercular scales. The overall appearance is that of a very rough-scaled gecko. The venter is smoother. Young specimens have dark transverse bands. At night these geckos pale considerably from their daytime color. Elongate toe pads are present.

Voice: Males emit audible squeaks during territorial disputes and as advertisement calls.

Habitat/Range: Moorish wall geckos may be seen on the outside walls of dwellings, warehouses, and stone garden walls. This is a locally distributed gecko. This gecko is now found in Lee, Sumter, Miami-Dade, and Broward counties.

Abundance: Unknown, but several small but apparently established populations are now known.

Behavior: This wary gecko is active on outside walls on sultry nights. This is a strong-jawed predatory gecko that is known to eat both invertebrate and small vertebrate prey.

Reproduction: Two semiadhesive eggs are laid in nooks and crannies in buildings, amid ground litter, or in hollows of trees. A female can produce several clutches annually. Incubation duration is about 50 days.

Similar species: Bibron's gecko has a scalation and pattern very similar to those of young Moorish geckos; however, Bibron's geckos are currently known only from Manatee County. The white-spotted wall gecko has smoother scales and 4 white spots on the shoulder.

Comments: The presence of this gecko in Florida can be traced to the pet trade. Hatchlings were first reported in 1996.

Yellow-headed, Ocellated, Ashy, and Reef Geckos: Genera *Gonatodes, Sphaerodactylus*

Florida's four sphaerodactyline geckos are discussed in species accounts 69 through 72. These are the smallest of our geckos—the smallest of our lizards, in fact. Some are adult at a mere 2 inches in total length. All are agile and adept at avoiding detection. The yellow-headed gecko is basically diurnal; the other three taxa are crepuscular to nocturnal.

69. Yellow-headed Gecko

Gonatodes albogularis fuscus

Size: Adults of this small gecko attain a length of only 3¼ inches in total length. Hatchlings are about 1¼ inches long.

Identification: The yellow-head has round pupils and lacks toe pads. Dimorphic, it is only the dark-bodied males (with a bluish sheen, especially at night) that have the yellow (or yellowish) head. A dark shoulder spot, sometimes outlined with blue, is also borne by males. The male's tail may also be yellow and if not regenerated will have a white tip. The colors are heightened during the breeding season or during territorial disputes or other times of stress. The grayish brown females often display a rather pronounced lighter collar. Hatchlings may have whitish spotting and dark mottling against a ground color of gray.

Voice: None.

Habitat/Range: These geckos hang from the underside of low, large-diameter, rough-barked horizontal limbs. They are also found in rock and rubble piles, on the trunks of palms, and behind exfoliating tree bark. A native of the West Indies and Latin America, the yellow-headed gecko was introduced both in and near Miami and on the Keys. Specimens were once quite common in both areas; however, they now seem extirpated from their mainland range and have become very rare on the Florida Keys.

Abundance: Rare.

Behavior: The yellow-headed gecko differs from other Florida geckos by being almost exclusively diurnal in its activity patterns.

Reproduction: Unlike most other geckos, which produce eggs in pairs, the yellow-head lays only a single egg at a time. Each reproductively active female can produce several eggs annually. Incubation duration is a few days more than 2 months.

Similar species: Its diurnal activity and lack of expanded toe tips will identify this gecko.

Comments: Although the yellow-headed gecko is known to have been present in Florida for nearly 60 years, it was once much more common than it now is. A major population in Coconut Grove (Miami-Dade County) seems extirpated. Although it is still present on Key West and on at least one other key, these populations, too, seem reduced. We no longer feel their continued presence in Florida is assured.

These little geckos are extremely wary and difficult to approach.

70. Ocellated Gecko

Sphaerodactylus argus argus

Size: This species is adult at between 2 and 2½ inches. Hatchling are about 1¼ inches long.

Identification: The ocellated gecko takes its name from the several pairs of dark-edged, light ocelli on the head, nape, and shoulders, usually on both sexes. Some specimens may have the ocelli rather indiscriminately arranged, or fused into longitudinal stripes. The tail is reddish, the body darker. Males are darker than females. Light lines are usually present on the head. The dorsal scales are smaller than the lateral scales, and both are keeled. A supraocular projection is present above each eye. Toe pads are present.

Voice: None

Habitat/Range: Although it is well able to climb and often found between the boots of palms or behind loosened bark, *S. argus* seems to prefer terrestrial situations where, like its congeners, it can take advantage of leaf litter and other ground debris. Ocellated geckos are apparently restricted in distribution to Key West and Stock Island.

Abundance: Thought only a few years ago to have been extirpated from Florida, this tiny gecko is now known actually to be quite common.

Behavior: Virtually nothing is known with certainty about the habits or behavior of this gecko in Florida.

Reproduction: Like other sphaerodactylines, the female ocellated gecko lays a single egg at intervals during the summer months. It is a communal nester.

Similar species: The ashy gecko has nonkeeled body scales, and the reef gecko has large, heavily keeled dorsal scales and only dark lines on the head. Female reef geckos usually have only a single pair of relatively large, light ocelli, on the posterior nape.

Comments: Until 2006, this was considered a rare gecko. Sightings had been at most once every 10 to 20 years. At one time the species was even declared extirpated from its stronghold on the Lower Keys; however, from 2006 through 2009 upward of 100 have been seen, and eggs and hatchlings have been documented. This gecko was probably accidentally introduced to Florida in commerce.

71. Ashy Gecko

Sphaerodactylus elegans elegans

Size: With a total length of 2¾ inches, the ashy gecko is the largest (by nearly half an inch) of the three Florida species of this genus. Males are the larger sex. Hatchlings are slightly more than 1 inch in total length.

Identification: Considerable ontogenetic color change occurs during the life of this species. Adults are dark with irregular light spots and dots and streaks. Hatchlings are pale green with dark crossbands and brilliant orange tails. The color change from juvenile to adult is gradual; however, even the darkest of adults is apt to be a pasty white at night. The body scales are nonkeeled. Toe pads are present.

Voice: None

Habitat/Range: The ashy gecko is the most arboreal of Florida's sphaerodactylines. Ashy geckos climb well and often ascend trees, buildings, and other structures in search of insects. On warm, humid summer evenings, ashy geckos are abundant on the walls of motels and other such structures as well as behind the loosened bark of Australian pines and other trees. They also seek shelter beneath moisture-holding ground debris. This Cuban native is restricted in distribution to the lower Keys.

Abundance: This is a common but secretive nocturnal gecko.

Behavior: Although they are reportedly diurnal and crepuscular, ashy geckos seem most active after darkness has fallen. They have been seen hunting insects under porch lights until long after midnight.

Reproduction: A single egg is laid at intervals throughout the summer months. Incubation (in captivity) lasts 55–70 days.

Similar species: Both the reef and ocellated geckos have keeled dorsal and lateral scales.

Comments: On the Lower Keys, ashy geckos were once commonly seen in the company of Mediterranean geckos on the walls of dwellings; however, with the now burgeoning population of the more predatory tropical house gecko, ashy geckos are less often seen. This gecko was probably introduced to Florida in commerce.

72. Reef Gecko

Sphaerodactylus notatus notatus

Brown [X]
Green [←G]

Size: The snout-vent length of this species is barely more than 1 inch. Total length is about 2 inches. Hatchlings are just over 1 inch in total length.

Identification: Both sexes of this dimorphic species are darker by day than by night. The males are a study of dark on dark—deep brown specks against a slightly lighter ground color. Very old males may be nearly or entirely deep brown. Females are also dark flecked but have dark stripes on the head and usually a pair of light ocelli in a dark shoulder spot. The tails of both sexes may be just on the orange side of brown. Both dorsal and lateral scales are large and keeled. This species has well-developed toe pads.

Voice: None.

Habitat/Range: Reef geckos are particularly abundant (or at least most easily found) beneath tidal wrack. On some of Florida's lower keys it is not uncommon to find three or four of these minuscule lizards beneath a board or bit of flotsam just above the high-tide line. Although a few individuals have been found in Broward and Palm Beach counties, they are most common in Miami-Dade and Monroe counties.

Abundance: This elfin gecko is abundant in leaf litter and beneath debris.

Behavior: Reef geckos are amazingly fast and adept at instantaneously disappearing into the tiniest of fissures or openings. Reef geckos are commonly found under human debris in the ubiquitous roadside dumping areas so prevalent in the keys. These lizards can climb but are principally terrestrial.

Reproduction: A single egg is laid at intervals during the hot summer months. Incubation takes somewhat more than 2 months.

Similar species: The ocellated gecko has small dorsal scales, usually several pairs of light ocelli on the head, nape, and shoulders, and an orangish tail. The ashy gecko has nonkeeled scales.

Comments: The discovery of one of these geckos does not necessarily equate with sufficient time for positive identification. When exposed, they are amazingly adept at instantly finding cover.

IGUANIAN LIZARDS: FAMILIES CORYTOPHANIDAE, IGUANIDAE, LEIOCEPHALIDAE, PHRYNOSOMATIDAE, POLYCHROTIDAE, AND TROPIDURIDAE

Of the six iguanian lizard families, five are represented in Florida (Leiocephalidae is the exception). All were formerly contained in the family Iguanidae. Some researchers continue to classify them as such.

BASILISKS: FAMILY CORYTOPHANIDAE

The impressive lizards in this small family were long considered members of the Iguanidae. Only one species is known with certainty to be established in south Florida, the northern brown basilisk. It lacks well-defined vertebral and caudal crests.

Over the years several dozen examples of the very beautiful green basilisk have been seen or collected along the canals in Miami. It is not yet known to be reproducing in the wild.

Male basilisks are much larger than the females. Males may exceed 24 inches in total length. The very long tail may be two or even three times longer than the lizard's head and body length.

Basilisks have fringed rear toes. Buoyed by surface tension and a great toe surface area, basilisks are able to run quickly across the surface of quiet water.

Basilisks—The Water Walkers

In the mid-1900s, when I first wanted to see a northern brown basilisk, I had to travel to central Mexico to accomplish the mission. To see a green basilisk, Patti and I headed to Costa Rica. (Of course, while in Costa Rica we also looked up the southern brown basilisk, so we sighted two taxa on one trip, effectively cutting our cost per species in half, a ploy familiar to birders.) When I wanted to see the fourth species in the genus, the red-headed basilisk, I headed to the country of Colombia. But now, to see at least one and possibly two of the species, a searcher in the United States need travel only as far south as Miami, which brings the cost per species down to almost the level of pocket change.

Despite the fact that it is nervous and difficult to cage and handle (adult males especially so), the northern brown basilisk has long been a mainstay of the pet trade. In very short order, unless specialized care and quarters are provided, most captive brown basilisks will severely injure their noses and declining health will begin.

Through the years many ailing basilisks have been turned loose by or escaped from Miami reptile importers; it seems that enough were present in the wild to reproduce and begin hearty new populations in most of the greater Miami region, extending northward into Broward County.

The basilisks seem to have taken hold in South Florida during one of my long hiatuses from the region. But when I returned in the 1980s, a person watching with interest as I searched for Jamaican giant anoles asked if I had seen the big gray lizards in Tropical Park? The answer was "no," and I queried him about their appearance. All I could learn was that they were big and gray and lived in the bushes.

So, of course, my next stop was Tropical Park. This is a fair-sized park with a playground (complete with green iguanas), extensive pathways (complete with green iguanas), a large parking lot and many additional amenities (all complete with green iguanas), and a sizable pond partially edged with shrubs (complete with yet more green iguanas).

Ignoring the iguanas, I looked around and did a double take. In the shrubbery were a fair number of little brownish (oh, okay, grayish brown) lizards with cream to yellow flash markings. Beyond the shrubs, at water's edge, was a big brownish lizard with very well-defined flash markings and a tall cranial crest. Those "gray" lizards were northern brown basilisks.

So, you ask, what's the possible second species I mentioned at the outset? Almost every summer since the early 1990s, one or two green basilisks, those beautiful lizards with three tall crests—on head, body, and tail—have been found and reported from green spaces in Miami. They're still not common; they may not even be breeding, but at least a few are present.

73. Northern Brown Basilisk

Basiliscus vittatus

Brown
G Green

Size: Males may slightly exceed 24 inches in total length; females are considerably smaller. Hatchlings are about 6 inches in total length.

Identification: This is an unmistakable, gangly (long-limbed, long-toed) yellow-striped brown lizard. Basilisks can both hop and run swiftly. When running, they usually assume a bipedal stance. They are capable of swift movement and able to run over the surface of quiet water when startled. If the running basilisk slows, it sinks. The males have a prominent crest on the back of the head, and the low, serrate vertebral crest extends onto the tail. Females have a folded "hood" outlining the back of the head and a lower vertebral crest than the males. Both sexes are dark barred dorsally and have variably distinct yellowish dorsolateral lines. The lips and venter are light. Young specimens are more prominently patterned than the adults.

Habitat/Range: In Florida, as elsewhere, basilisks are traditionally associated with water-edge situations. They now occur along many canal and pond edges in Miami-Dade and southern Broward counties. They are common and apparently increasing in numbers. This lizard is native to a vast region of Latin America. It is found from Central Mexico southward to northern Colombia.

Abundance: This lizard is now very common in South Florida.

Behavior: This is an alert, agile speed demon of a lizard. Brown basilisks are difficult to approach; they are capable of climbing, running, and swimming, all with equal facility. Adult males are particularly wary and may often be heard crashing to safety through the underbrush long before they can be seen by an observer.

Reproduction: This oviparous lizard lays from 3 to about 15 eggs. A secluded, moisture-retaining nesting site is chosen, often a hole along a canal bank. Eggs hatch in 55–65 days.

Similar species: No other lizard in Florida has the suite of characteristics that identifies the brown basilisk.

Comments: These are remarkable lizards that catch the attention of nearly everyone who sees them. They are prominent in the pet trade and were once imported from Colombia in large numbers; now, however, most northern brown basilisks seen in the pet trade are captured from the feral south Florida populations.

73A. Green Basilisk, *Basiliscus plumifrons*. Although still rare, this basilisk is found along Miami canals with increasing regularity. In habits, length, and reproductive biology, it is similar to the northern brown basilisk; however, in their green coloration both sexes of the green basilisk (also called the plumed basilisk) differ from its brown relative. Color, habits, and the 3 tall crests of the males (a double crest on the head, a full-length vertebral crest, and an anterior tail crest) positively identify this lizard.

IGUANAS: FAMILY IGUANIDAE

Iguanas—The Giant Green Cows of South Florida

What's big and green and grazes like a cow?

If you happen to live in Miami, you can answer that poser without even thinking about it.

The answer, of course, is an iguana—a big, green iguana.

Actually, three species of iguanas now dwell in southern Florida. The two species of spiny-tails exceed 4 feet by just a bit, but because of their heavy bodies and stout tails, they look bigger. The green iguana exceeds 6 feet, but the tail is comparatively slender, and individuals may look a bit smaller than they actually measure. Of the three, the giant green is the most visible and the most objectionable.

In the 1950s, 1960s, and early 1970s, huge numbers of wild collected green iguanas were imported from Colombia and Peru for the pet trade. Because we did not understand reptile nutrition back then, most died. Then, almost overnight, both these countries slammed shut the door of exportation, and for many years green iguanas were almost a rarity in the pet trade. But while those large numbers were being imported, the inevitable escapes and releases occurred, and because the now-free iguanas could dine at will on Miami's succulent vegetation, a few survived the Florida experience, living to and through their years of sexual maturity. Counts of survivors were too low to garner much attention.

Then, in the 1980s, green iguanas were again hot in popularity and a resurgence of trade in iguanas occurred. A few iguana importers set up iguana farms in South America, and almost overnight, the pet markets were literally flooded with bright green 8-inch hatchlings.

If the iguana sales of the 1960s and 1970s were considered huge, those of the late 1980s, '90s, and early 2000s were nothing short of stupendous. Marketing techniques were amazingly good, iguanas were inexpensive, and most people who saw the pretty little green hatchlings bought them without thinking ahead. Well, maybe the wholesalers and pet stores weren't altogether honest about all the details of housing, feeding, and caring for a 6- to 7-foot lizard that could become aggressive. New iguana owners discovered that following instructions for care meant their pet would live 15+ years, growing far too large for readily obtainable housing.

Now owners had to face the realities of maintaining a 6-foot lizard. Some lizards were sold, some were kept, but many accidentally escaped or were surreptitiously released. Those lucky enough to have been released in South Florida survived, bred, and became the very large green lizards seen feeding along canals and in cherished foliage trees and breeding enthusiastically along roadways and waterways.

No longer fussy eaters, iguanas seem to have become more cosmopolitan in their choices of food (Miami has this effect on humans, too). Hibiscus and mallows are special favorites, and many an ornamental garden has now been eaten and enjoyed.

To see feral iguanas in Florida, simply travel south of Palm Beach on the east coast and Naples on the Gulf coast and keep an eye on shrubbery and roadsides. Once you near Deerfield Beach, Ft. Lauderdale, Miami, Everglades National Park, or the Keys, the iguanas become even more common. They are especially numerous in parks and public gardens and along canals. Some of the green iguanas (especially the breeding males) are partially or completely fire orange. Local tolerance for these bad-tempered creatures has largely disappeared. Since they are not native, the lizards are not protected by any ordinance, so if you'd like to catch a few or a dozen, go ahead.

Just don't turn them loose, anywhere.

Under current taxonomic definitions, three species of iguanas are now established in Florida. All are large (to 48 inches or more), and all have long been mainstays of the pet trade.

While the green iguana is readily recognizable to most folks, the two species of spiny-tailed iguanas are very difficult to differentiate from each other. Of the three, the green iguana and the Central American spiny-tailed iguana are firmly established. The continued presence of the Mexican spiny-tail seems somewhat more tenuous.

Iguanas: Genera *Ctenosaura* and *Iguana*

The genus *Iguana* contains only two species: one endangered West Indian form and the widespread Neotropical species now resident in Florida. Both are large lizards. The genus *Ctenosaura* contains about a dozen Latin American species, some of which are large and robust, like the ones in Florida, while others are only 12 inches (or less) in length.

The iguanas are predominantly vegetarian and often wreak havoc on suburban gardens.

74. Mexican Spiny-tailed Iguana (also called Black Iguana)

Ctenosaura pectinata

Size: Hatchlings are about 7 inches in total length. Adult females commonly attain a total length of 36 inches; adult males may near or slightly exceed 48 inches.

Identification: Hatchlings are grayish but change to a pale green within just a few days. With growth they gradually assume the adult coloration of black bars on a tan ground. Although reproductively active males in some populations assume an overall intense fire orange coloration, those in Florida may be black or black and gray with orange highlights. After the breeding season is over, the orange fades to tan or buff. Females are usually less colorful than males. A prominent vertebral crest is present. The scales of the crest are longest in adult males. There are more than 2 rows of small scales between the whorls of spiny scales on the tail.

Habitat/Range: This species is native to the Pacific drainages and slopes of southern Mexico. Like the green iguana, this lizard is indiscriminate in its choice of habitats; however, it swims less readily than the green iguana. Excellent climbers, adults may occasionally be seen high in the trees.

Abundance: This is the rarer of the two species of spiny-tailed iguanas in Florida. It seems restricted to Miami-Dade County in distribution.

Behavior: This is an alert and wary lizard that knows its home territory well. Individuals are often seen basking, heads raised well away from the substrate, on piles of rubble and building materials. They retire to burrows at night and in inclement weather and may dart to the burrows or ascend a tree if frightened during the day.

Reproduction: From 12 to about 30 eggs are deposited in the late spring. Large healthy females deposit more and larger eggs than smaller specimens.

Similar species: In Florida, the two species of spiny-tailed iguanas, which can be identified by range alone in their natural habitats, are extremely difficult to differentiate. *Ctenosaura similis* may be darker but also becomes suffused with orange during the breeding season. The babies of *C. similis* tend to be a more brilliant green than those of *C. pectinata* and are more heavily marked with black. *C. similis* usually has only 2 rows of small scales separating the whorls of spiny scales on the tail.

Comments: As with the larger green iguana, the presence of this spiny-tail in Florida has resulted from pet trade escapees or discards. The lizard is not as frequently imported from the wild now as it once was. If carelessly restrained these lizards will scratch, bite, and swat with their spine-studded tail. Singly, any of these wounds can be painful. Together they will make anyone wonder why he or she chose to bother this lacertilian buzzsaw.

75. Central American Spiny-tailed Iguana

Ctenosaura similis

Size: Hatchlings are about 7 inches in overall length. Adult females attain 40 inches in total length, and adult males may near 55 inches.

Identification: The hatchlings of this species are a pale gray marked with a variable amount of darker gray to black. The gray ground color soon turns to a bright green then dulls again with age. When not in breeding color, the adults are quite dark both dorsally and laterally. Black, black and gray, and black and blue gray are all common colors. Breeding adults can be strongly suffused with orange. There are usually only 2 (rarely, 3) rows of small scales between the whorls of enlarged spiny ones on the tail. A prominent vertebral crest, best developed on adult males, is present.

Habitat/Range: Native to both drainages of southern Mexico, from the Isthmus of Tehuantepec and Vera Cruz southward throughout Central America, this lizard utilizes a wide variety of habitats but seldom enters water, even when hard pressed. It is an agile climber.

Abundance: This immense lizard is now abundant in Miami-Dade County as well as on Marco Island (Collier County) and Gasparilla Island (Charlotte County). It is also present on other Gulf coast islands.

Behavior: Even when comfortably basking, these wary lizards immediately notice a human intruder or other predator and quickly retreat to their burrows or climb a tree. They often bask while sitting alert, head well raised from the substrate. Be careful when handling large specimens. Scratches, bites, and tail-lashes are all painful.

Reproduction: From 10 to 28 eggs have been laid by captive females. Breeding biology of feral specimens in Florida remains unknown. Incubation duration is 75–95 days.

Similar species: Differentiating this species from the very similar Mexican spiny-tailed iguana, *C. pectinata*, can be difficult. Juveniles of the Mexican spiny-tailed iguana tend to be a paler green and have less black.

Adults of the Mexican spiny-tail tend to be less heavily suffused with black laterally than adults of the Central American spiny-tail, and there are usually three or more rows of small scales separating the whorls of spines on the tail. At best, these differences are all merely comparisons. Green iguanas have no enlarged spiny scales on the tail.

Comments: Because of the ease with which the two feral spiny-tails can be confused, the valid ranges of both species in Florida remain conjectural; however, there is little doubt that this species is by far the more common of the two.

76. Green Iguana

Iguana iguana

Size: Hatchlings are about 7 inches in total length. Adult females may attain 54 inches; adult males may attain more than 72 inches in total length.
Identification: Healthy babies are usually bright green but may be a rather bright reddish orange; ill ones may be brownish or yellow. Some (especially those from Peru) have dark bars across the back and sides. Adults tend to fade, retaining a green suffusion over grayish scales. Some individuals are suffused anteriorly with orange during the breeding season; others may turn an overall bright orange. A huge dewlap and vertebral crest are present and are larger on males than on females. A large rounded scale is present on the jowls. There are no enlarged, spiny scales on the tail.
Habitat/Range: In South Florida the green iguana utilizes every imaginable habitat except the air. Individuals can be found foraging in the tree canopy, basking beside or on canalside debris, or thermoregulating on downtown sidewalks and in urban backyards. Iguanas swim as well as they climb and run. This species is native to most of the Neotropics.
Abundance: The green iguana is now abundant throughout much of South Florida. Escapees and releases are also seen in other areas of the state during the warm months of the year.
Behavior: Both males and females are territorial and will indulge in push-

ups, tail-slapping, and actual skirmishing to rout interloping iguanas. If threatened with capture and not able to escape, adults will slap with the tail. If actually captured, their scratching and biting will quickly open wounds. Babies are very fast and dart quickly to safety when threatened. These lizards will drop considerable distances from the limbs of trees, hit the ground or water with a resounding thud, and either run or swim quickly away. The green iguana is an herbivorous species—a reptilian cow, if you will. Adults can wreak havoc on shrubs and gardens. They may often be seen grazing on roadside grasses in urban and suburban areas.

Reproduction: This is an oviparous species. Large, healthy green iguanas can lay 35 or more eggs. They usually dig an extensive nesting chamber, often angling downward from ground debris; however, some females merely scoop a sizable chamber directly beneath debris (such as a piece of discarded plywood, a large rock, or an old mattress, and lay their eggs almost in contact with this cover. This happens frequently where the soil is difficult to dig (such as in the surface limestone areas of Miami-Dade County).

Similar species: Both species of spiny-tailed iguanas have whorls of spines interspersed between rows of nonspinous scales on the tail. The knight anole, often referred to as an iguana, has no dorsal crest and a yellow(ish) jaw and shoulder stripe.

Comments: These magnificent lizards are usually able to tolerate the vagaries of South Florida winters, but they often succumb to cold temperatures farther north. Florida populations include a hodgepodge of genes from Peru, Suriname, Guatemala, Honduras, and Colombia. Pet trade escapees and unwanted releasees account for the presence of this species in Florida.

CURLY-TAILED LIZARDS: FAMILY LEIOCEPHALIDAE

Curly-Tails—Memories of a Childhood Pet

I was about 14 years old when I first heard of a Bahaman curly-tailed lizard. I had just received a price list from Quivira Specialties, and out of all the lizard listings, it was the curly-tail that caught my eye. What, I wondered, was a curly-tailed lizard? Well, I had the $1.25 cost saved up, postage was only another 30 cents, so off went my order.

About a week later I was looking at my first curly-tail—but it had a regen-erated tail that would never, ever curl again. I wrote to Charles Burt, owner of Quivira, and told him that, although I really liked this robust spiny lizard lookalike, I had spent my last dollar and a quarter in the whole world to see a lizard curl its tail, and I was disappointed that the one they had sent me couldn't do so.

A week later another box arrived, and in it was a smaller curly-tail, but this one had its original tail, and curl it, it did, time and time again! I got the lizards all set up in their new home, then wrote to thank the Burts for their kindness.

Flash-forward about ten years to 1962. I was living in Miami. Jerry Fine and I decided one day to hop aboard an old DC-3 flown by the Mackey line between Miami and Bimini. We wanted to see Bimini boas, dwarf boas, and Bimini racers. We saw all of those and, unexpectedly, curly-tailed lizards. The lizards were among the limestone boulders on the beach, and—voilà—my interest in leiocephaline lizards was stoked again. Without even suspecting that I was about to do so, I had landed literally on their home turf.

Now, of course, seeing two distinctly different species of curly-tails takes only a drive to Palm Beach, Broward, or Miami-Dade County. If you're lucky, you can sight a third species, but you usually have to be in restricted areas near Miami International Airport and work hard to do so.

Of the three species of curly-tails now in Florida, it is still the least colorful one, "my" Bahaman curly-tail (*Leiocephalus carinatus armouri*), that interests me the most. Perhaps this is just a lingering interest from those long-ago days when the Burts so kindly fulfilled the hope of a Yankee kid.

Now I know that on almost every trip I make through Palm Beach County, I can stop somewhere along the beach and watch the Bahaman curly-tails.

~~~~~~

Taxonomic note: Until recently these lizards were contained in the family Tropiduridae.

The three species of this family now found in Florida are introduced species. In general conformation these lizards look much like robust swifts. They can be immediately differentiated from swifts by the pres-ence of a low serrate vertebral crest and lack of femoral pores. Curly-tails may or may not have a fold of skin (a lateral fold) on their sides.

The common name is derived from the fact that some species curl the tip of their tail upwards or to the side when alerted or during resting periods while foraging. This serves males as both a sexual attractant and a territorial mechanism.

Curly-tailed Lizards: Genus *Leiocephalus*

Of the 25+ species of West Indian curly-tailed lizards, 3 now occur in Florida. One was introduced by agricultural entities in hopes of controlling the sugarcane beetle, and two are pet trade escapees. Wary in some areas, these lizards become emboldened in the vicinity of open-air restaurant patios and skitter around eating crumbs and insects.

77. Northern Curly-tailed Lizard

Leiocephalus carinatus armouri

Size: These robust lizards range from 7½ to 11 inches in total length. Females are the smaller sex. Hatchlings are about 3 inches in total length.
Identification: Dorsally this lizard is gray to tan. Light nape stripes may be present as may light dorsolateral stripes and a variable amount of light stippling and dark spotting. The tail is rather prominently dark banded, and the venter is light. The dorsal scales are strongly keeled, and a low but noticeable vertebral crest is present. Hatchlings are similarly colored but have an orangish throat. This species has no lateral fold.
Habitat/Range: This curly-tail has populated parks, agricultural lands, canal edges, and myriad equally diverse habitats and is abundant near areas of ground rubble. It may occasionally climb. This lizard occurs in Florida's east coast counties of Miami-Dade, Broward, and Palm Beach. It has also been found in Highlands County. It is native to the Bahama Islands.
Abundance: This is a common lizard.
Behavior: These are active and alert lizards that dart about in pursuit of their insect repast. At each stopping point the tail tip curls upward. They are at home in nearly any setting but most at home on the landside

of sandy dunes and in construction or other disturbed areas. Curbs and landscape boulders are frequently used vantage points. They can climb but are more at home in terrestrial situations.

Reproduction: This species is a spring breeder, and females have been known to double-clutch. From 7 to 12 eggs are laid, and incubation lasts for somewhat more than 2 months.

Similar species: Swifts (scrub and fence lizards) have prominent femoral pores and lack a vertebral crest.

Comments: Northern curly-tails were first introduced to Florida nearly 60 years ago in an attempt to rid sugarcane of insect pests. Since then, additional releases have ensured that the species is firmly established. It is a popular pet trade lizard.

78. Green-legged Curly-tailed Lizard

Leiocephalus personatus scalaris

Size: Although some males attain a length of 8 inches, most males and all females are smaller. Hatchlings are 2¾ inches long.

Identification: Males of this pretty red-sided curly-tail have a brownish dorsum and a greenish venter, green hind limbs, and a dark mask. A low medial crest is present. Females are less brilliantly colored and tend to retain the juvenile pattern of prominent dorsolateral stripes. Females have a speckled belly. Juveniles are strongly patterned with dorsolateral and lateral stripes, but bear no brilliant colors. The tail of this species curls but not as tightly as that of the northern curly-tail. This species has no lateral fold.

Habitat/Range: The green-legged curly-tail seems less able to tolerate our occasional freezes than many other introduced lizards. It prefers lightly wooded or brushy areas over open expanses of land. It is known from several areas in Miami-Dade County, but it is not known whether these populations are self-sustaining or continually replenished by pet trade escapees.

Abundance: Although it has been known to exist in Florida since the 1970s, the presence of this lizard remains tenuous.

Behavior: This is a predominantly terrestrial lizard. Although quite alert, it often allows rather close approach. It is frequently seen sitting on a sidewalk, curbstone, or pile of rubble.

Reproduction: Females of this oviparous species may lay two clutches of up to 6 eggs. Hatchlings emerge after some 9 weeks of incubation.

Similar species: The red-sided curly-tail is larger, has smoother scales, and has a lateral skin fold. The northern curly-tail bears no red or green colors.

Comments: This species, thought to have been established in southern Florida in the 1970s, seems to have disappeared during the 1980s when lizard imports from Haiti temporarily ceased. Imports began again in the mid-1990s, and once again this lizard is seen in fields and parks in the vicinity of reptile importers. Whether these current populations will actually become truly established is questionable. The green-legged curly-tail does not seem able to survive our occasional periods of very cold weather.

79. Red-sided Curly-tailed Lizard

Leiocephalus schreibersi schreibersi

Size: Adult males occasionally attain 10 inches in total length. Females top out at about 8½ inches. Hatchlings are about 3 inches long.

Identification: As the more brightly colored sex, males are pale brown dorsally with a low yellowish vertebral keel and yellowish dorsolateral stripes. Red vertical bars occur on the flanks. Between the bars are patches of the palest blue. Turquoise may be present over the fore and rear limbs. The dark-banded tail is brown dorsally but often flecked with red ventrally. Females and juveniles are paler and have about 8 dark transverse bars crossing the dorsum. This species does not curl its tail tightly. A prominent lateral fold is present.

Habitat/Range: This aridland curly-tail has colonized open fields, the edges of parking lots, and piles of building or other rubble. It is active even on the hottest days. It has been seen in Broward, Charlotte, Lee, Miami-Dade, and St. Lucie counties. It is a native of Hispaniola.

Abundance: The several populations are each represented by small numbers of this beautiful lizard.

Behavior: This is a wary lizard, but if it is approached slowly it will often allow an observer quite near. It is robust and not as prone to curl its tail as some other members of the genus.

Reproduction: From 2 to 7 eggs are laid in the early summer. More than a single clutch may be laid. Incubation lasts for about 65 days.

Similar species: Neither the northern nor the green-legged curly-tail has lateral skin folds.

Comments: This species has been present in Florida for more than 30 years. It is a favored pet trade species.

SPINY LIZARDS AND RELATIVES: FAMILY PHRYNOSOMATIDAE

The Most Popular of the Swifts

Although the spiny lizards (or swifts) are interesting lizards in their own right, one member of their family now in Florida outshines all the rest in the fascination factor. This is the Texas horned lizard. Yes, the Texas horned lizard. This iconic, spine-studded lizard, native to the Great Plains states, was introduced into Florida (and other coastal southeastern states) more than 60 years ago. Today you can find examples in many widely separated, low-density populations from Miami-Dade County to Duval County on the Caribbean coast to Okaloosa and Escambia counties on the Gulf coast.

The first time I saw a Texas horned lizard ("horny toad" to many folks), I was within sight of the ocean in Duval County. I don't recall whether I was looking for anything in particular, but, if so, it was probably some sort of shorebird. I do remember that it was a sunny, early autumn day, and as I neared the beach I saw several children poking at something in the dune sand. Always curious, I strolled closer and found they had cornered a small, flattened, spiky lizard—a Texas horned lizard. Beyond that, recollections become mostly muddled, but I feel quite certain that I would have moved the little ant-eating beast from harm's way, then probably continued bird watching.

Since that initial encounter in the mid-1950s, I have happened across Texas horned lizards in other areas of Florida. Often when I approached, the lizard would simply drop to the ground and flatten itself to become as inconspicuous as possible. A few, though, have drawn their ribs tightly against their bodies, raised their bodies well above the ground, and scuttled away with all the speed their stubby legs could muster.

Once I saw a defense mechanism new to me—Chrissie, my bumbling cocker spaniel, sniffed a wild horned lizard too closely and got a stream of blood straight in her face. Yep. A stream of blood!

The Texas horned lizard is one of at least 8 species capable of squirting a stream of blood from each eye. This defensive mechanism occurs when internal pressure ruptures the microthin walls of ocular sinuses. The forcefully expelled droplets can travel for more than 4 feet and are usually directed toward the face of a predator. Because predators show indications of distaste when the blood enters the mouth, it is surmised that it contains a distasteful chemical.

The ploy worked: Chrissie jumped, shook her head, and walked a large detour around the horned lizard before resuming her beach exploration.

Although represented by dozens of species in the American west, Mexico, and Central America, there are only two species of spiny lizards and a single species of horned lizard (the latter introduced) in Florida. The spiny lizards are often referred to as swifts or fence lizards. One of the spiny lizards, the appropriately named scrub lizard, is restricted in distribution to rapidly disappearing sandy scrub areas, now largely in the center of the state. The remaining species, the southern fence lizard, accepts a greater variety of habitats.

The third member of this family needs virtually no introduction. It is the ant-eating Texas horned lizard (the "horny toad"), a species introduced decades ago to several areas in Florida and that still, despite insecticides and other pressures, persists in low numbers in a few locales.

Horned Lizards: Genus *Phrynosoma*

Represented in Florida by a single introduced species; additional species occur in our central and western states and in Mexico. Carpenter and honeypot ants are major components in the diet of most horned lizards. These lizards are frequently referred to as horned toads or horny toads.

80. Texas Horned Lizard

Phrynosoma cornutum

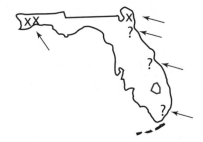

Size: Most specimens of the Texas horned lizard are between 3½ and 6 inches in total length. The 1¼-inch hatchlings emerge after some 45–55 days of incubation.

Identification: This is a reddish, tan, or buff lizard dorsally. The venter is white. From nape to hips there are 5 pairs of light-edged, irregular dark spots. When undisturbed the Texas horned lizard appears decidedly flattened. When frightened it may inflate itself prodigiously. The sides and rear of the head bear enlarged spines. The two center horns on the rear of the head are elongated. There are 2 rows of spines along each side.

Habitat/Range: In Florida, this remarkable little lizard has colonized sandy fields, dunes, and other such habitats. In Duval County, the Texas horned lizard seems now to be restricted to a few dune areas and seaside developments. It also occurs in littoral areas of Santa Rosa County and on parts of Eglin Air Force Base (Santa Rosa, Okaloosa, and Walton counties). Populations may still be present in St. Johns, Indian River, and Miami-Dade counties.

Abundance: Although rare in Florida, this lizard has persisted for decades in several different regions.

Behavior: If startled the Texas horned lizard can move with rather unexpected speed. Individuals often sun while sitting on open ground or in areas vegetated with low herbs and grasses. Very little is known about the life history of this species in Florida. This lizard is capable of squirting a few drops of blood from the corners of its eyes toward an enemy or captor.

Reproduction: This is an oviparous species. The 10–30 eggs are buried in the sand in moisture-retaining areas.

Similar species: None.

Comments: The Texas horned lizard is an ant-eating specialist. In its natural home on the Great Plains, it may often be found near the trails of harvester ants, where it picks off straggling ants, one by one. It often sidles beneath the surface of the sand, then sits quietly with only its eyes, horns, and nostrils visible. At night it may bury itself completely beneath the sand.

Fence Lizards, Scrub Lizards: Genus *Sceloporus*

As with the horned lizards, this genus is much better represented in our central and western states and in northern Latin America. Most species are primarily insectivorous.

81. Eastern Fence Lizard

Sceloporus undulatus

Size: Adults of this alert lizard vary from 5 to 6½ inches in total length. Both males and females are of similar length. Hatchlings are about 2 inches in total length.

Identification: Females of the southern fence lizard are colored differently than the males (dichromatism).

Females are the darker, with a gray to gray brown dorsum that contains about 8 dark, irregular transverse bars. There is usually at least an indication of a dark dorsolateral stripe on each side. Females have a dark flecked white venter that may have a little blue along each side.

Although males have a grayish dorsal ground color, both the dorsal markings and sides are brownish to terra-cotta. Males have a grayish midventral area and large bright blue ventrolateral patches bordered with black centrally. One or two black-edged blue spots are on the throat. The black edging from the throat spot broadens posteriorly and continues upward onto the shoulder as a black wedge.

Hatchlings are colored like the females.

Habitat/Range: Sandy pinewoods and mixed woodlands are preferred habitats, but these little lizards colonize oaks in yards and are often seen sunning on fallen trees, wooden fences, and porch railings, as well. They occur throughout the northern half of the state including the panhandle.

Abundance: This is a common lizard.

Behavior: These are alert lizards that skitter to the far side of a trunk or log when approached. When clinging to a tree, they usually do so oriented head up, ready to ascend if frightened. They may occasionally sun on the ground near the base of a tree but dart upward at the slightest disturbance.

Reproduction: Healthy adult females may lay several clutches of 5–12 eggs during the summer months. Incubation duration varies from 6 to 8 weeks.

Similar species: The Florida scrub lizard (account 82) is very similar in appearance but has broad, well-defined dorsolateral stripes.

Comments: These pretty lizards are often seen on old fences and buildings and fallen trees in much of rural northern Florida. Considerable populations persist in many state and federal parks and refuges.

82. Florida Scrub Lizard

Sceloporus woodi

Size: Florida scrub lizards attain 3½–5 inches in total length. Females are slightly the larger sex. Hatchlings are about 2 inches long.

Identification: Females and juveniles are gray dorsally with a broad, dark dorsolateral stripe and dark, wavy, transverse markings on the back. Males tend to lack the dorsal barring, are of a browner color dorsally than the females, and have brownish dorsolateral striping. The large turquoise ventrolateral patches are narrowly bordered by black. The chin is largely black but has a white median stripe and two small blue patches.

Habitat/Range: Although this lizard climbs agilely, it is often seen foraging on the ground some distance from the nearest tree. Its common name aptly describes this lizard's preferred habitat. Today (as of 2011) it occurs sparingly in Collier County on the southwest coast and in scrub along the sandy southeastern coastline. It is more abundant in suitable habitat on the Lake Wales Ridge and in the scrublands of Lake and Marion counties.

Abundance: This species is common but localized in distribution. It was once far more widespread in Florida's now largely developed sandy ridges.

Behavior: This lizard has well-defined terrestrial tendencies. If surprised while on the ground, the scrub lizard may either quickly dart across the sand to the safety of ground cover or ascend the nearest tree. It is adept at keeping a trunk or branch between it and its pursuer.

Reproduction: Healthy fully adult females may lay several (3–5) clutches of 2–6 eggs each summer. The babies hatch after 60–75 days of incubation.

Similar species: The southern fence lizard lacks well-defined dorsolateral stripes.

Comments: This is a beautiful lizard that is a joy to watch. If secure, it basks in abandon and when hungry either awaits the arrival of an arthropod at its resting spot or, more rarely, darts to and consumes nearby insects it sees. The continuing transformation of scrub habitats to golf courses and orange groves has accounted for the extirpation of many populations of this species.

ANOLES: FAMILY POLYCHROTIDAE

Anoles—Color Changing Lapel Pins: My Introduction to the Green Anole

When I (RDB) first met the green anole, the lizard was called an American chameleon and being sold as a living lapel pin at the New York Sportsman's Show (a tiny gold thread collar and leash threaded to a small safety pin held them securely to one's lapel). A half-dozen lines of text on each of the hundreds of boxes lined up on the table stated that the lizards should be kept warm and fed sugar water.

Money was tight in the late 1940s, and even though I wanted several of the lizards, I went home with only two, still in their boxes, in a little paper bag. I was one happy camper!

In those days herp care books were nonexistent, field guides hadn't yet been thought of, and computers? The Internet? What in the world were those? So if those care instructions were incorrect (which they were!) there was no way to find out.

Fortunately for those little anoles, even in those long-ago days I had an inquiring mind and was always looking for alternative ways to do everything.

My mother grew houseplants in almost every sunny window of the house. Despite her instructions to keep the lizards on their leashes and a shallow dish of fresh sugar water within their reach, one of the first things I did was to release the anoles on my mother's plants. Although it was already late autumn, there were still a few houseflies active, and one of them happened to land on a plant only a few inches from where the anole was quietly lying. It had just finished drinking droplets of water left after my mother watered the plants. That was lesson one—they drank droplets of water on plants.

Within seconds there were one happily gulping lizard, one fewer flies in the world, and one startled (but gratified) kid (me). That was lesson two— American chameleons eat flies. (Sugar water, eh? Yeah, sure.) Yet the largest lesson was not to blindly trust the written word—especially in the 1940s when it came to anole care.

I knew I needed insects of some type. Fortunately a neighbor raised mealworms for panfish bait. The anoles accepted small mealworms every bit as readily as the first had taken the housefly, but sadly, in those days we knew absolutely nothing about the vitamin and mineral needs of lizards deprived of natural sunlight. Neither lizard survived until the warming weather allowed us to open our windows again.

But at least I learned several lessons, and it seems probable that those anoles contributed to my lifelong interest in natural history in general and in reptiles and amphibians in particular.

Of the 11 species now established in Florida, only 2, the green anole and the Florida bark anole, are natives. The remaining 9 species of anoles have been deliberately introduced, have escaped from captivity, or have arrived as stowaways. Males of all are territorial and aggressive, especially during the spring and summer breeding season. Territorial and breeding displays are species specific. These displays include dewlap distension, lateral body flattening, push-ups, temporary erection of glandular nape and vertebral crests, and intimidating sidles.

Dewlap coloration is often species-diagnostic for human observers. It is, apparently, even more so for the lizards themselves, for they perceive and respond to ultraviolet reflections from the dewlaps.

Anoles are oviparous. Reproduction is stimulated by the increasing day lengths of spring and terminates in late summer when day lengths are again starting to diminish. After an initial annual breeding, sperm retention results in fertile eggs when the female is stimulated solely by courtship displays. From one (smaller anole species) to several (larger anole species) eggs may be laid at two-week or somewhat longer intervals. Many anoles prepare no actual nest, instead nudging their eggs into the protection of a grass clump or bromeliad leaf axil, or between fallen leaves, with their snout. Incubation varies between 35 and 65 days.

Anoles: Genus *Anolis*

The color-changing ability of many of the canopy species has led to the vernacular name of American Chameleon. The ability to change color is less well developed or largely lacking in many primarily terrestrial species. Those that change color do so in response to temperature and attitude rather than as camouflage.

Distended, elongate (teardrop-shaped) toe pads are characteristic.

83. Northern Green Anole

Anolis carolinensis carolinensis

northern
pale-throated

Size: Large males can attain a total length of 8 inches. The tail is nearly twice as long as the SVL. Females are noticeably the smaller sex. Hatchlings are about 2¼ inches long.

Identification: Green anoles have the ability to change color. Resting and content anoles tend to be of some shade of brown. They are darker when cold and turn a pasty gray when overly warm. Disturbed anoles may be patchy brown and green. Males involved in aggression are often bright green with a nearly black ear-patch. Breeding males are often green but lack the dark ear-patch. In South Florida indications of darker dorsal and dorsolateral streaking may be present. Female green anoles have a light vertebral line. Male northern green anoles have a decidedly pink dewlap.

Habitat/Range: This species is strongly arboreal. It favors tall native grasses, shrubs, and trees and was once abundant in cypress heads, in pine-palmetto scrublands, and even in shrubs along prairie edges. It often hangs head-down on trunks, wooden fence posts, and other such vantage points. Green anoles diminish in numbers in seriously disturbed habitats and where native plants are replaced by ornamentals. Green anoles continue to be a common backyard, canopy, and hammock species in undisturbed areas in the northern two-fifths of the state.

Abundance: Once one of the most common lizards throughout its range, habitat degradation and pressures from introduced anole species have now reduced its numbers in central and southern Florida.

Behavior: These are shy lizards that will sidle to the far side of a tree trunk or post or dart upward into the canopy if approached by day. They are more easily approached at night, when they sleep soundly.

Reproduction: A single egg is laid at 14–17-day intervals throughout the warm months of the year. Depending on temperature and moisture, incubation can vary from just over a month to nearly two months.

Similar species: Throughout most of its range, this is the only small color-changing anole. If in extreme south Florida, also see accounts 85 and 93 for discussions about the Haitian green anole and the Cuban green anole, respectively.

Comments: Research has disclosed that where the two are sympatric, the native green anole can be seriously outcompeted by the introduced brown anole. Adult male brown anoles are not only fully capable of eating hatchling green anoles, but the aggressiveness and high population density of the ground-hugging browns frequently drive the green anoles from low-level shrubs into the treetops, apparently eventually decimating the populations of the latter.

84. Pale-throated Green Anole, *Anolis carolinensis seminolus,* was described in 1991. This subspecies, restricted to southwest Florida, has a gray, white, or greenish dewlap. Except for dewlap color, it is identical to the northern form.

85. Haitian Green Anole

Anolis chlorocyanus

Size: Males can attain a total length of 8½ inches but are often smaller. Females are normally the smaller sex. The tail is about 190% of the SVL. Hatchlings are about 2¼ inches long.

Identification: In body color and color changes, this species closely parallels our native green anole, *A. carolinensis*; however, males have a large, and females a small *blue* to blue black dewlap. Whorls of enlarged scales are interspersed between several rows of small scales on the tail. The nose of the Haitian green anole is proportionately longer than that of the native green anole.

Habitat/Range: Primarily a canopy species, these wary anoles occasionally descend low on trunks to bask in the sun. This species is known from Broward and Miami-Dade counties.

Abundance: Although not uncommon, this pretty arboreal anole does not seem to be expanding its range.

Reproduction: Despite its presence in Florida for well over three decades, little is known about the reproductive biology of this anole. Captives have produced single eggs at 14–20-day intervals during the summer months, scattered in the leaf litter on the cage floor. Incubation duration varied, but averaged about 50 days.

Behavior: This is a wary canopy anole that quickly retreats high in the trees at the slightest disturbance.

Similar species: Similar-appearing green anoles have dewlaps of red, pink, gray, green, or white, never blue.

Comments: The presence of this species in Florida is directly attributable to pet trade escapees. It is a temperature-sensitive species that expands range slowly and fares poorly during Florida's occasional freezes.

86. Puerto Rican Crested Anole

Anolis cristatellus cristatellus

Size: Males occasionally attain 7½ inches. The tail is about 150% of SVL. Females are noticeably smaller. Hatchlings are about 2 inches long.

Identification: This olive tan to almost black anole reverses the anole-trend of being darkest when cold and lightest when warm. Even when seeming at peace with the world, warm, basking crested anoles are often nearly black in coloration. When the ground color of this anole is light enough, dark bars (often broken into spots), variable both in length and in contrast, may be present on both trunk and tail. The dewlap of the males may vary individually from olive green through various yellows to pale orange, usually with a darker orange border. Most males have a wavy crest on the tail. This may be nearly entirely absent or conspicuously high. A vertebral and nape crest can be raised by muscular contraction. Females and juveniles have a dark bordered light vertebral stripe and lack the tail-crest.

Habitat/Range: This anole is usually seen quite close to the ground on pilings, stone walls, abutments, fallen trees, and piles of rubble. It may also be seen clinging head downward low on the trunks of large trees or similar vantage points. If threatened, when possible it will move to a higher perch. This Puerto Rican species is now quite common in Miami-Dade County.

Abundance: This is a common anole in Miami-Dade County and in some parts of Broward County.

Behavior: If approached slowly this anole will allow close approach, but it darts quickly away when it feels its space is truly violated. It is more apt to seek safety by dashing upward than by descending. Males indulge in intricate sidling displays.

Reproduction: The reproductive biology of this anole has not been studied in Florida. Captive females produce an egg (one female routinely produced two) at roughly two-week intervals throughout the summer months. Incubation duration varied but averaged about 50 days.

Similar species: Puerto Rican crested anoles with low tail crests can be easily mistaken for the more common and widespread brown anole. When possible, compare dewlaps. The crested anole has an orange-bordered dewlap while the dewlap of the brown anole is edged in white.

Comments: It is not known whether the crested anole was introduced to Florida deliberately or accidentally in produce and ornamental plantings brought from Puerto Rico. Its presence seemed tenuous for the first decade, but it is now a commonly seen species. Although primarily insectivorous, crested anoles include blossoms and fruits from various fig trees in their diet.

87. Large-headed Anole

Anolis cybotes cybotes

Size: The large-headed anole is noticeably dimorphic, with males being much the larger sex. Males may attain 9 inches but are often smaller; tail more than 200% of SVL. Hatchlings are about 2 inches long.

Identification: The dorsal color is usually of some shade of brown (varies from pale reddish brown to nearly gray), and the flanks are lighter. A light (bluish, greenish, or cream) lateral stripe is often present. Adult males are heavy bodied and have a very large head. Females have a dark-bordered (often scalloped) light vertebral stripe, a light lateral stripe, and a light spot on each shoulder. The dewlap is huge and variably cream to yellow or yellow gray and may be pale orange yellow centrally. Through muscular contractions, males can erect both a vertebral and a nuchal crest.

Habitat/Range: This robust anole displays from low on tree trunks, fence posts, building walls, and concrete block fences. When frightened it is as apt to run downward and seek refuge in ground debris as upward. The crested anole seems most abundant in disturbed areas with well-separated trees. Small populations of this Hispaniolan anole are present in Miami-Dade, Broward, and Okeechobee counties.

Abundance: Although it has been present in Florida for more than 30 years, this is not a common or widespread anole.

Behavior: Males of this hefty anole display constantly during the warm hours of the day and are very territorial. Females are less confrontational.

Reproduction: Eggs have been found throughout the months of spring and summer among leaf litter and moisture-retaining debris. Captive females have produced one or two eggs at 2–3-week intervals. Incubation duration was not specifically noted, but was probably about 6 weeks.

Similar species: The enlarged head of adult males is diagnostic. Females have a rather well-defined light lateral stripe and a light spot on each shoulder. Please also see accounts 86 and 94 for discussions of the crested and brown anoles, respectively.

Comments: The questionably viable colony in eastern Broward County is the result of pet trade escapees. The populations in Miami-Dade and Okeechobee counties are the result of deliberate introductions. Besides insects and some small vertebrates, these lizards eat snails and ficus fruits.

88. Bark Anole

Anolis distichus

Size: This, Florida's smallest anole species, is adult at a total length of only 4½–5 inches. Sexes are about equally sized. Hatchlings are about 1¾ inches long.

Identification: Because of the intergradation of two subspecies, one green and the other brownish gray, the dorsal coloration of the bark anoles of south Florida is extremely variable. This can vary from brown through gray to pea green and is discussed further in Comments. Cold or frightened lizards are darker than warm or content ones. Sleeping lizards are lighter than active ones. There are often two small ocelli on the rear of the head, a dark interorbital bar, and a series of dark posteriorly directed chevrons on the back, and the limbs and tail are banded, the latter prominently so. This little spraddle-legged anole skitters more like a house gecko than like other anoles.

Habitat/Range: In South Florida the bark anole readily colonizes urban gardens and seems most common near dwellings and lushly planted office complexes. This West Indian anole is common to abundant in Miami-Dade, Monroe, and southern Broward counties.

Abundance: Within its South Florida range, this is now a common anole.

Behavior: Bark anoles seek their prey of ants and aphids while low on the trunks of ornamental trees, vines, and herbaceous plantings. They often sleep, with tail tightly coiled, on the upper surfaces of low, broad-leaved ornamental plants. This is a nervous and wary anole, usually skittering to the far side of a trunk and then ascending when approached.

Reproduction: A single egg is laid at approximately two-week intervals throughout the warm months of the year. Incubation duration is about two months.

Similar species: There is no other anole species in Florida with dorsal chevrons and a skittering gait.

Comments: The bark anoles of South Florida were long considered two subspecies; *A. d. floridanus* (thought by most researchers to be native to Florida) and the introduced *A. d. dominicensis*. The former was a grayish lizard with a pale yellow dewlap. The latter varied from greenish gray to pea green and had a very pale orange dewlap. Because the two races have now interbred throughout the greater portion of the Florida range, subspecific identifications are next to impossible. For this reason most researchers no longer attempt to designate a race; however, since *A. d. floridanus* is *never* green, when yellow green to pea green bark anoles are found, they can be rather reliably referred to as having characteristics of the Dominican subspecies.

The Bimini bark anole, *A. d. biminiensis*, was released 40 years ago in Lake Worth, but no current information is available on its status.

89. Western Knight Anole

Anolis equestris equestris

Size: Although usually somewhat smaller, male knight anoles occasionally slightly exceed a total length of 18 inches. The tail is about 150% of the SVL. Hatchlings are about 3 inches long.

Identification: As do most canopy species, the knight anole has the ability to change color extensively. Although its usual color is bright green with yellow flash marks below each eye and on each shoulder, cold or frightened knight anoles can darken their color to chocolate brown or almost black. The flash markings remain lighter and visible. Yellow bands may show on the tail, and light (cream to yellow) interstitial (between scales) skin may be visible. Through muscle contractions, the knight anole can raise a low vertebral and a much more prominent nuchal crest. The head is large and bony. Both sexes have pink dewlaps, but the dewlap of the male is proportionately immense. Both sexes display territoriality, but the displays of the males are more energetic and lengthy.

Some long-term captives turn blue. This is probably due to missing components (perhaps beta carotene) in the diet. It is not known whether with a corrected diet a blue knight anole will eventually turn green again.

Habitat/Range: Knight anoles utilize different habitats at different times of year. During the cool nights and short days of late autumn, winter, and early spring, knight anoles are primarily canopy denizens. As the weather warms and the hours of daylight lengthen, knight anoles descend from the canopy and station themselves, usually head-down, low on the trunks of ornamental trees. Conspicuous in this position, they become even more so when the males fan their pink dewlaps like semaphores. This Cuban anole, the largest of all anole species, is now a common denizen in much of Miami-Dade and Monroe counties. It has also been seen in Collier and Broward counties. Reports of this species in Lee County have not yet been verified.

Abundance: This very territorial anole is now abundant in southern Florida.

Behavior: This is an alert lizard that can be aggressive and bite painfully if restrained. It generally gapes widely, distends its dewlap, and turns its laterally flattened body toward a threat. The knight anole is slower than many other anoles and more prone to stand its ground if disturbed.

Reproduction: Other than the fact that this anole has become increasingly common through the years, little is known with certainty about its reproductive biology in Florida; however, captive females have produced 2–4 eggs several times each summer. Hatching took about 60 days.

Similar species: No other U.S. anole has as large and bony a head, nor do any attain as great a size as adult knight anoles. The yellow to white flash marks are diagnostic.

Comments: The knight anole was deliberately introduced to Florida more than 50 years ago. Additional accidental introductions have occurred. This immense lizard, often referred to as "iguana" or "iguanito" by the Miamians, is now a familiar sight in much of balmy Miami-Dade County. It is known to eat fruits (and is particularly partial to the various *Ficus* fruits) as well as insects and small vertebrates.

90. Barbados Anole

Anolis extremus

Comments: Once (and possibly still) present in Lee County, feral examples of this anole have apparently not been seen for several years. Since there is a chance that this lack of sightings is merely an oversight, we provide a description and photograph for identification purposes.

This is an olive brown to olive green, or bluish, anole, darker dorsally and patterned with dark blotches and light spots. It is greenest on the sides and posterior dorsum. The venter is a sunny yellow, and the head is gray to gray brown. Females are less colorful and smaller than the 7½-inch males.

91. Marie Galante Sail-tailed Anole

Anolis ferreus

Comments: Once (and possibly still) present in Lee County, feral examples of this remarkable anole have apparently not been seen for several years. Since there is a chance that this lack of sightings is merely an oversight, we provide a description and photograph for identification purposes.

This lizard is bluish gray to grayish brown with some yellowish to yellow green overtones dorsally and laterally. Some dark spots are occasionally seen. The eye turrets are cobalt. Females have a light lateral stripe, best defined anteriorly. The head is large but not distinctly bony, such as that of the knight anole. Males have a high caudal crest. The dewlap is gray at the throat and pale yellow distally. Males attain 12 inches or slightly more in total length. Females are smaller.

92. Jamaican Giant Anole

Anolis garmani

Size: Males may barely exceed 12 inches in total length but are usually an inch or two smaller. Females are smaller and less robust. The tail is about 200% of the SVL. Hatchlings are about 2¾ inches long.

Identification: This canopy species is able to change color quickly and completely. When content, individuals are often bright green but may be brown. When cold they are dark and very wary; when suitably warmed, they are lighter and may allow rather close approach. A well-defined crest of enlarged scales extends from the back of the head to about a third of the way down the tail. The crest is best defined anteriorly. Although male Jamaican giant anoles do display and spar, when compared to the very territorial knight anole, the former is a gentle giant. The large dewlap is pale to bright orange with a yellow border.

Habitat/Range: This species is much like the knight anole in its seasonal usage of varying habitats. During cooler weather (mid-autumn to mid-spring, inclusive), the Jamaican giant anole is a canopy species. It descends to the lower levels and is often seen only 3–5 feet above the ground on the trunks of shade trees in summer. It is most often seen in a head-down position. Hatchlings utilize ferns and such plants as heliconia, dracaena, and ginger as their preferred habitat.

Abundance: Common in Miami-Dade County, but the population formerly in Lee County now seems extirpated.

Behavior: Even where it is common, this is an unobtrusive anole seldom seen during the winter months. It becomes more conspicuous during warm weather when it hangs head-down low on the trunks of sizable trees. Besides insects, in the wild this anole eats *Ficus* fruit and the petals of blossoms.

Reproduction: This is a fecund anole. Females produce up to 4 eggs per clutch at intervals during the summer. Incubation duration nears 2 months.

Similar species: Only the knight anole equals or exceeds the Jamaican giant in size. The knight anole has an angular bony head and yellow flash markings. The Jamaican giant anole has a normal-appearing head and lacks flash marks. The very rare *A. ferreus* is never green, and males have a very high sail-like crest on the tail.

Comments: This anole has been established in Florida since the early 1980s. As with most large green lizards in southern Florida, *A. garmani* is often referred to by Miamians as either iguana or iguanito. It seems to be a hardy and tolerant anole.

93. Cuban Green Anole

Anolis porcatus

Size: Males attain 8½ inches, but females are smaller. Hatchlings are about 2¼ inches long.

Identification: Like most arboreal anoles, this species is capable of undergoing extensive color change. Content specimens are often a very intense green; disturbed examples may be brown or patchy brown and green. White(ish) spots may occur randomly on the body and neck. Ill-defined dark markings may be present on the dorsum. When bright green, males usually have some striping (interstitially) of robin's-egg blue on the nape and a dark-bordered light vertebral stripe, and they may have a dark spot on each shoulder. Females usually lack the dark dorsal markings. When clad in brown, males may have a series of darker brown lines laterally, and females, a cinnamon vertebral stripe. The dewlap of this species is red, and its nose is proportionately long and very pointed. Genetic differences most reliably differentiate this species from the northern green anole.

Habitat/Range: This anole frequents ornamental trees (including *Ficus* and palms), fences, yards, and the walls of houses. It is primarily arboreal, often ascending to the canopy, but also descends to rock piles and piles of rubble. This lizard is currently (2009) known from Broward and Miami-Dade counties. It is of Cuban origin.

Abundance: Because the Cuban green anole is so similar to the northern green anole, it is impossible to assess its population statistics in South Florida. The whereabouts of several populations are known, and within those populations it is common. It is probable that it is more widespread than currently realized. Apparently hobbyists have known of the presence of this lizard for years, but biologists did not learn of its existence until 1996.

Behavior: Little is known with certainty about this anole in Florida. Initial observations indicate that it is similar to the northern green anole in habits and actions but more readily accepts and colonizes disturbed habitats.

Reproduction: Nothing seems known about the reproductive biology of this species in Florida other than it is a spring and summer breeder and that females lay single eggs at intervals through the long days of summer.

Similar species: The Cuban green anole seems slightly bulkier and to have a more prominently ridged and longer snout than the native northern green anole. Male northern green anoles lack robin's-egg blue striping on the nape, but the lizard may need to be in hand to determine this.

Comments: The population of *A. porcatus* in Florida is badly in need of study. Other than the fact that it exists here in what seem to be increasing numbers, we know little about its life history in the Sunshine State.

94. Cuban Brown Anole

Anolis sagrei sagrei

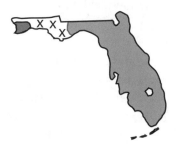

Size: Males attain a total length of about 8 inches. Females are substantially smaller. Hatchlings are about 2¼ inches long.

Identification: The brown anole is aptly named. Both males and females are of some shade of brown. The males often have bands of light (yellowish) spots and are darkest dorsally. Males can erect a nuchal, vertebral, and anterior caudal ridge. This is best developed on the nape and anterior trunk. The dewlap of the brown anole is usually a white-edged bright red orange; rarely the dewlap is pale yellow to yellowish red. When the dewlap is not distended, the white edging is visible as a white stripe on the throat. Female and juvenile brown anoles have a dark-edged, scalloped, light vertebral stripe.

Habitat/Range: This is a lizard that thrives in disturbed habitats and among ornamental plantings. It inhabits virtually every kind of inland and coastal habitat available in the state. Although often seen low in trees and shrubs, the brown anole is quite terrestrial and will often dart to cover on the ground when frightened.

It is abundant on the southern and central peninsula (including keys and islands) and is now known from most of Florida's larger North Florida and Panhandle cities. It forges a bit farther northward and westward each year.

Abundance: In the last four decades, this lizard has gone from comparative rarity to being one of the best-known lizards in Florida. It varies from common to abundant over the southern four-fifths of the peninsula but may still be considered rare in the more northerly portions of its range.

Behavior: These are feisty anoles that bluff and display throughout the warm days of the year. They are somewhat less aggressive (but far from benign) during the nonreproductive winter days. Brown anoles will even distend their dewlaps and indulge in agonistic behavior if a human makes eye contact and bobs his or her head at the lizard. These are now the most abundant anoles over the southern half of the Florida peninsula, and population densities are increasing all the way to the Georgia state line.

Reproduction: This is a prolific anole species. Males strut, bob, and display from mid-spring to late summer. Although only a single egg is laid at a given time, most eggs seem viable, and each adult female lays several each summer at roughly 14-day intervals. Incubation is rapid, taking only about one month. Although intraspecifically territorial, brown anole populations can be immensely dense.

Similar species: Of the several brown-colored anoles found in Florida, only the brown anole has a white-edged red dewlap and a white stripe on the throat when the dewlap is not distended.

Comments: Current taxonomic procedures have divulged that although intergrading between the Bahaman brown anole and the Cuban brown anole have occurred, brown anoles present in Florida today should be recognized as the Cuban race.

Although studies continue, it is thought that in combination with other factors, the brown anole continues to contribute to a reduction in numbers of the native northern green anole.

SOUTH AMERICAN COLLARED LIZARD: FAMILY TROPIDURIDAE

Tropidurines—A Lizard Alone

Besides the fact that at least one deliberately introduced population exists, almost nothing is known about this lizard in Florida. Although I have seen many of these gray to brown, prominently collared, swiftlike lizards in the Guianas, I have not seen this taxon in the Sunshine State. But it just might have become established here.

Even though the South American collared lizard was not very high on my "I wannasee" list in Guiana, I found them common to abundant in seasonally dry habitats. I saw them on and among walls, railings, boulders, and rocks. They were wary and not easily approached. They basked extensively on sunny mornings and, once warmed, foraged for insects (their predominant prey) or occasionally for blossoms.

The core examples of the population in Florida were turned loose by an animal dealer on and around his home property in Martin County in 2002–2003. The dealer has since moved from Florida, and it is not known whether the collared lizards are reproducing.

The South American collared lizard is a member of a genus of about 15 species that are predominantly arboreal and saxicolous. It is the only species of that genus to occur in Florida and is not yet thought to be an established species. It is known only from Martin County.

95.Guyana Collared Lizard

Tropidurus hispidus

Comments: This lizard is known from a small population in Martin County. It is native to much of South America, where it inhabits dry savannas and woodlands. This lizard climbs readily. It is not known whether this 7–12-inch lizard is established in Florida or whether its feral colony will soon succumb. This rather slender, tan, brownish, or gray egg-laying lizard looks most like a swift or fence lizard, but unlike the swifts it has an easily discernible vertebral crest of short serrate scales extending from the nape to well onto the tail. Well-separated darker dorsolateral and lateral blotches are present. It is from the prominent black collar, darkest on the sides and interrupted vertebrally, that the common name is derived.

SKINKS: FAMILY SCINCIDAE

The 10 species of skinks found in Florida are contained in 5 genera: *Chalcides* (1 species), *Mabuya* (1 species), *Plestiodon* (formerly *Eumeces* and *Neoseps*) (6 species) *Scincella*, with a single species, and *Trachylepis* with one species. Of the 10 species, three are adult at 6 inches or less in total length, five may push 8 inches, and two may near or slightly exceed 12 inches.

In general, skinks are elongate lizards with long, easily autotomized tails, short to diminutive legs, and shiny scales. Most have some degree of striping on either (or both) the dorsal and lateral surface(s). Many species undergo extensive ontogenetic (age-related) color and pattern changes, some (especially the males) develop brilliant orange heads or cheeks during the breeding season, and many of the species are sexually dimorphic (the sexes vary in appearance). Except for the live-bearing ocellated barrel skink, the skinks of Florida are oviparous (they lay eggs). The females of most oviparous species attend the eggs throughout the incubation period. All are wary and secretive. Two species are burrowers (one persistently so) in sandy scrub areas, one is rather arboreal, one is associated with stream-edge situations and readily dives into the water to escape threat, and the remaining three are habitat generalists.

The larger skinks often make a very audible rustling when darting away from danger.

The smooth scales make these lizards hard to grasp and even more difficult to noose. Most will bite if carelessly restrained; the bite of the large species can be painful.

One species, the specialized sand skink, *Plestiodon* (formerly *Neoseps*) *reynoldsi*, lacks ear openings. Two, the previously mentioned sand skink

Skinks—The Orange and the Brown

The orange and the brown.

Strange colors for someone who lives in Alachua County, the land of the orange and the blue, the colors of the University of Florida's football team, the Gators.

But since I'm not much of a football fan, for me it is the orange and the brown that count most, and I often don't have to do more than step outside my door to see them. These are the colors of our two backyard skinks, the big feisty broad-headed and the tiny skulking brown.

The orange, of course, is the fiery orange seen in spring and early summer on the head of dominant male breeding broad-heads. After the breeding season and especially during winter hibernation, the head may be dull orange to a brown, the same color as the body.

And the brown? Well, I might as easily be referring to the body color of the broad-head as to the dorsal color of the abundant but flighty little ground skink (formerly known as the brown-backed skink). Since I mentioned the prettily and distinctively contrasting color of the head of the broad-headed skink, it is probably only fair to mention that during breeding season, the head of the ground skink develops overtones of gold. At that time these elfin lizards become quite pretty.

Although both species are present, the broad-head is far less numerous (but far more conspicuous) than the ground skink. Except in late summer when the orange-striped, blue-tailed hatchlings skitter abundantly about on our deck, rails, and fences, we don't see many. There are probably no more than three or four dominant male broad-heads watching over the dozen or dozen-and-a-half nondominant males and adult females living on the front stoop, fallen trees, and pile of moldering limbs they all call home. On the other hand, although seldom seen, the ground skinks probably number in the many dozens, perhaps in the hundreds.

But few or many, big or small, whether in the flamboyance of seasonal hormonal splendor or the subdued colors of winter dormancy, these beautiful lizards add measurably to our outside enjoyment. At all seasons, all are welcome sights.

and the ground skink, *Scincella laterale,* have transparent scales (windows) in their lower eyelids.

Numerous examples of the Old World burrowing skink species, the ocellated barrel skink (*Chalcides ocellatus*), have been found in sandy regions of Florida's mid-Atlantic coastal region.

96. Ocellated Barrel Skink

Chalcides ocellatus

Comments: A few examples of *Chalcides ocellatus,* the ocellated barrel skink, have been found in Florida's Atlantic coast counties of Indian River, St. Lucie, Palm Beach, and Broward. This cylindrical, short-tailed skink is of North African origin and a pet trade staple. The ground color of this 9–11-inch burrower is silvery gray, and the back and sides are liberally adorned with black ocelli in a lineate pattern. It is a live-bearing species. Although it has not yet been confirmed as an established Florida species, sufficient adults have been found in sandy fields that we felt a photograph would be appropriate.

97. Brown Mabuya (also called Many-lined Grass Skink)

Mabuya multifasciata

Size: This southeast Asian skink is adult at between 8 and 10 inches. The tail is about two-thirds the total length. Neonates are about 3½ inches long.
Identification: The dorsum is olive brown to a bronzy brown. Dorsal scales are weakly multikeeled. A pale dorsolateral stripe separates the back from the darker brown of each upper side. The sides are flecked with

discrete light spots. The lower sides and belly are gray to cream. Females may be marginally lighter in color and contrast than the males. Breeding males acquire a suffusion of orange on the sides.

Habitat/Range: Known only from one locale (the Kampong Botanical Garden) in Miami (Miami-Dade County), where it is often seen along the walkways and in the mulch near and in plantings.

Abundance: Common in its small range.

Behavior: Primarily insectivorous, this skink also feeds on fruit and blossoms.

This secretive lizard is often seen amid the plantings (including tropical trees) and mulch in the gardens. It is alert and agile and quickly takes cover in the undergrowth when approached. It burrows avidly through loose mulch and leaf litter.

Reproduction: From 1 to 12 live young are produced in midsummer.

Similar species: Only the southeastern five-lined skink resembles the brown mabuya. Except for adult males that may lack stripes, the former bears 5–7 light stripes on the back and sides and a bright blue to gray blue tail. During the breeding season adult males have a suffusion of orange on the head.

Comments: This was once a very popular and inexpensive pet trade species. It seems probable that the origin of this population can be traced to escapees or a deliberate release.

Typical Skinks: Genus *Plestiodon*

In the United States, there are currently 11 species of skinks in this genus; of these, 6 occur in Florida. The 3 species of five-lined skink are all relatively conspicuous. Others such as the mole and sand skinks are more specialized and unless found by accident must be diligently sought.

98. Southern Coal Skink

Plestiodon anthracinus pluvialis

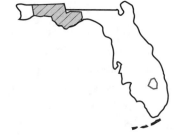

Size: Adult size is 6½–7½ inches. Males may be marginally larger than females. The tail is 180–200% of the SVL.

Identification: This is an attractive four-lined skink of moderately heavy build. The males are most brightly colored when in breeding condition. The dorsum is tan to olive tan, the sides are dark brown, and a well-defined off-white to yellow(ish) dorsolateral and ventrolateral line is present on each side. Counting toward the side from the middle of the back, the dorsolateral stripe is on scale rows 3 and 4. These light stripes, which extend well onto the tail, separate the dorsal and ventral colors from the side color. If a vertebral stripe is present, it is only weakly defined, often interrupted, but strongest anteriorly. Variably distinct light spots may be present on the supralabials from beneath the eye to the rear of the mouth. There are no stripes on the top of the head. Reproductively active males become suffused with pale orange on the face, chin, and throat. The mental scale (the anteriormost chin scale) is not divided.

Hatchlings of the southern coal skink in Florida are black with light anterior supralabials and prominent white spots on the posterior supralabials. The white spots often continue onto the sides of the neck.

Habitat/Range: In Florida the southern coal skink is associated with pine-woodland brooksides and cool, moist ravines that drain through sphagnaceous seepages and ultimately into brooks. Of all Florida skinks, the coal skink seems the most prone to take to the water to escape a threat. It readily hides beneath stream-bottom debris and in submerged vegetation. The southern coal skink is secretive and shelters in moisture-retaining areas such as beneath sphagnum mats and fallen trunks.

Abundance: Although little is known about the population statistics of this skink in its limited Florida range, it seems to be uncommon or is at least infrequently observed.

Behavior: The southern coal skink is secretive and more aquatic than other Florida members of this family. Adults can sometimes be found beneath logs or other forest litter, or may be surprised as they forage for arthropods. Behavioral studies of this skink in Florida are badly needed.

Reproduction: Other than the fact that it is oviparous, virtually nothing is known about the reproductive biology of the southern coal skink in Florida. It is supposed that the eggs number between 4 and 10, are deposited in mid-to late spring, and that the female southern coal skink remains in attendance of the clutch throughout the incubation period.

Similar species: The mole, ground, and sand skinks are tiny and proportionately slender. The three remaining species all have 5 (to 7) lines when young, but dull with age. These three have divided mental scales. **Comments:** This is the most poorly understood of Florida's native skinks.

99–103. Mole Skink

Plestiodon egregius ssp.

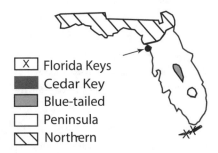

- ☒ Florida Keys
- ▓ Cedar Key
- ▓ Blue-tailed
- ☐ Peninsula
- ◪ Northern

Size: Although mole skinks up to 6½ inches in length have been found (the blue-tailed mole skink is marginally the largest of the five races), most specimens seen are in the 4–5-inch range. Males may be slightly larger than females. The tail is about 180% of the SVL.

Identification: Mole skinks of all races can be of variable body and tail color. They are attractive, shiny, agile, and fast. The intensity and length of the body stripes (if present) are also variable. Each dorsal and lateral scale (including scales on the top and sides of the tail) may be outlined with dark. The lighter scale centers give the appearance of light striping on the body, while the brighter tails appear dark striped. A light line is present above each eye, and the labial (lip) scales are often of a light color. The body color varies from tan to a rather deep brown that may or may not be darkest on the sides. The tail is heavy and particularly so when moisture and food are abundant. Tail color varies from pale cream or brownish red through red and purple to bright blue (see comments below). Hind limbs may be nearly as brightly hued as the tail. Regenerated tails are not distinctively colored. Sexually active males usually develop an orange blush ventrally. This may carry over to the sides of the face and fades after the breeding season. The legs are tiny but fully developed and entirely functional. Five toes are present on each foot. The hatchlings of all subspecies of the mole skink are paler diminutives of the adults but have more brightly colored tails. Although it has been consistently stated that the hatchlings of the Cedar Key mole skink are black (and, indeed, some are), the fact that this is not invariable was recently proven by hatchlings from two eggs of this subspecies that were brown with lighter body stripes and a bright orange tail.

Habitat/Range: All subspecies of the mole skink are persistent burrowers in sandy habitats. In such areas they may be found beneath surface debris (papers, boards, discarded appliances, fallen leaves, and lichens) and (if near the beach) may be most plentiful on the beach side of tidal wrack, near the base of shrubs and grasses. These lizards seem to dig more deeply when the weather is cold but are adept at thermoregulating. On cool but clear winter days, when the sand surface is sun warmed, mole skinks may be very near the surface and very agile. Mole skinks are occasionally found in the sandy mounds of the pocket gopher or in other exposed patches. All five subspecies occur in Florida. See individual subspecies accounts and range map for precise ranges.

Abundance: When the five subspecies are considered as a group, it may be said that mole skinks are fairly common where suitable habitat remains intact; however, these fossorial skinks dive so quickly beneath the sand when unearthed that an observer is often left wondering whether he or she has really seen a lizard. Some races of the mole skink are more abundant and widely distributed than others. Because of habitat loss and degradation, one subspecies, the blue-tailed mole skink of the central peninsula, is listed by both federal and state regulatory agencies as a threatened species.

Behavior: Mole skinks (called red-tailed skinks until discovery of the blue-tailed subspecies necessitated a change in common names) are agile and difficult to capture. Indeed, they are even difficult to see and are so secretive that considerable numbers may be present yet unsuspected. The mole skink's name rather graphically describes the propensities of this species; however, it implies nothing about its remarkable agility.

Reproduction: Although up to 11 eggs have been recorded, most clutches contain between 3 and 5, and a few contain only 2 eggs. In their quick-draining habitats, wild females must choose nesting sites that retain sufficient moisture to prevent egg desiccation. Nests have been reported from near surface level beneath debris to a depth of several feet. Females reportedly remain with their clutches. Captive females have chosen moisture-retaining areas of their terraria to nest (beneath water dishes or partially buried limbs, or against the stems of succulent plants) and remained curled around their clutch for the entire incubation period. We have not seen them eat during this period, but since termites and pinhead crickets often also congregate in moisture-retaining areas, it is possible that the lizards eat occasionally while never leaving their nests. **Similar species:** The ground skink is of very similar body shape but not a persistent burrower. It has a long, slender brown tail and a broad dark dorsolateral stripe on each side. It preferentially chooses more heavily wooded and damper habitats than those preferred by the mole skinks. The sand skink is very pale and has a sloping shovel-like snout and degenerate legs with only 1 (forefeet) or 2 (hind feet) toes. Hatchling five-lined skinks have a blue tail like that of the blue-tailed mole skink, but have 5–7 prominent yellow lines on the body. **Comments:** The five subspecies of mole skinks can be difficult to identify if geographic origin of the specimen(s) in question is not known. Tail color differs on some, striping differs on others, but both characteristics are variable and may overlap broadly. While counting the scales around the trunk at midbody and the number of labial (lip) scales is difficult, it may help to confirm a subspecific identification by comparing certain features, as follows:

- Usually 22 or more scale rows at midbody: *P. e. egregius*
- Usually fewer than 22 scale rows at midbody: All races except the above.
- Usually 6 supralabials: *P. e. similis*
- Usually 7 supralabials: All races but the above.

99. Florida Keys Mole Skink, *P. e. egregius,* occurs only on the Florida Keys and is the *only* race on the Florida Keys. The tail is dull to bright red. Young of this race have 8 light lines on the body, but adults may lack all vestiges of striping. When present the striping is of uniform width, and the lateral stripes are often longer than the dorsal stripes.

100. Cedar Key Mole Skink, *P. e. insularis,* skink is restricted in distribution to Cedar Key and surrounding keys (including, among others, Seahorse, North, and Atsena Otie keys) in Florida's Gulf Hammock area. The body stripes, if present, are inconspicuous; the tail is orange to orange red, brightest on moderately large adults.

101. Blue-tailed Mole Skink, *P. e. lividus,* is the only one of the five races that ever has a blue tail (it may be blue only on the distal half), but not

all specimens actually have a tail of the namesake color. Thus, tail color alone may not be diagnostic. Juvenile and young adult specimens have the bluest tails, while the tails of aging adults may be red and those of very old adults, brown. The range of this imperiled race follows the yielding white-sand habitat of the Lake Wales Ridge northward from southern Highlands County to northern Polk County.

102. Peninsula Mole Skink, *P. e. onocrepis*. Although it is still found over much of the Florida peninsula, the peninsula mole skink is no longer as common as it once was because of habitat loss and degradation. Despite areas of suitable habitat, this skink may be uncommon or absent from many areas of central and southwest Florida. The tail of this race can vary from whitish to nearly red, rarely to lavender or purplish red. The tail color usually loses brilliance with advancing age.

103. Northern Mole Skink, *P. e. similis*, is another race with red or red orange tail. It is the only one of the five races to occur beyond the Florida state line (it ranges eastward from central Alabama through much of southern Georgia). In Florida the northern mole skink ranges as far south as Dixie, Union, and Clay counties.

104–106. Florida's Three Five-lined Skinks

Comments: Although differentiating the three species of five-lined skinks (*Plestiodon fasciatus, P. inexpectatus* and *P. laticeps*) may seem intimidating at first, once you have become familiar with each, the task is not overly difficult. Please read the "Similar species" sections carefully and refer to the range maps for all three of these striped skinks.

All three species undergo similar age-related (ontogenetic) changes. At hatching they are black lizards with 5 (sometimes 7) white to yellow stripes and electric-blue tails. With advancing age, the tail and body colors fade, and the lines become more obscure. Males may lose all vestiges of the lines. Reproductively active males develop widened temporal areas and an orange(ish) head. Females often retain at least some indications of juvenile striping but develop neither the widened temporal area nor the orange head coloration.

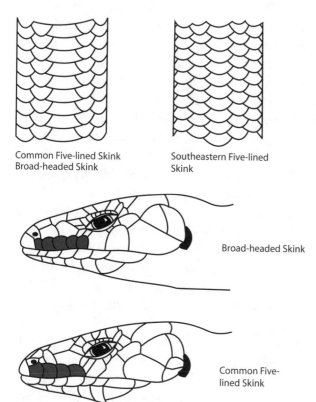

Common Five-lined Skink
Broad-headed Skink

Southeastern Five-lined
Skink

Broad-headed Skink

Common Five-
lined Skink

Subcaudal and supralabial patterns of three species of skinks

104. Common Five-lined Skink

Plestiodon fasciatus

Size: This moderately robust skink attains a length of slightly more than 8 inches. Males may be marginally larger than females. The tail is about 150% of the SVL. Hatchlings are about 2¼ inches long.

Identification: Ontogenetic changes are marked. The black juveniles have

5 broad off-white to orange lines and an electric-blue tail. Females fade to brown or olive brown but usually retain at least a vestige of striping. A dark lateral color is separated from the lighter dorsum and venter by a light dorsolateral and light ventrolateral lines. The vertebral stripe is usually the narrowest and palest but well defined. Males are like the females but have a somewhat broader head with an orangish blush on the jaws. The jaws, sides of the face, and temporal areas become more intensely orange during the spring and early summer breeding period. There are usually only 4 upper labial scales, and 2 enlarged postlabial scales contact the ear opening. The center subcaudal scale row is widened.

Habitat/Range: Although a basically terrestrial species, the five-lined skink swims, climbs, and burrows well. An uncommon species throughout most of its Florida range, it is most often encountered at the edges of damp woodland openings, in logged areas where decomposing stumps and fallen trunks remain, and amid debris at the yard peripheries of rural dwellings. In Florida it is found from Volusia and Citrus counties northward and throughout the panhandle.

Abundance: Although present in the northern one-third of the state, this seems the least common of the three species of five-lined skinks in Florida. Accurate population statistics are badly needed.

Behavior: This is an alert and wary lizard that quickly hides when approached. It may either choose ground cover or climb a tree to escape. Five-lined skinks thermoregulate in patches of sun but usually remain quite close to cover. Males tend to move about more openly in the spring when seeking mates.

Reproduction: Females create a nesting chamber beneath ground litter and remain with the 3 to more than a dozen eggs throughout the 55–65 day incubation period.

Similar species: The southern coal skink has 4 light lines. The broad-headed skink lacks any enlarged postlabial scales, usually has 5 upper labial scales, and has 5–7 well-defined but thin light lines. The median row of scales beneath the tail of the southeastern five-lined skink is of about the same width as those that border it. Its light stripes are narrow, and the vertebral stripe can be particularly vague.

Comments: Unless actually in hand, females of the five-lined skink can be very difficult to differentiate from immature females of the broad-headed skink.

105. Southeastern Five-lined Skink

Plestiodon inexpectatus

Size: This common skink is adult at from 5½ to 8 inches (rarely to 8½ inches) in total length. The tail is somewhat more than 150% of the SVL. Hatchlings are about 2¼ inches long.

Identification: The 5 (rarely 7) yellow to orange lines of the juveniles are brightest anteriorly and narrow, with the vertebral line particularly so. The tails of young skinks are bright blue, but all contrasting patterns and colors fade with advancing age. Breeding males develop an extensive orange wash on the sides of the face, chin, and throat. The medial row of subcaudal scales (beneath the tail) is not noticeably widened.

Habitat/Range: This species is rather a habitat generalist, being found in pinewoods, humid hammocks, and most habitats between these extremes. This is the most terrestrial of the three five-lined skinks, but it often basks atop inclined and fallen trees, cement walls, or piles of rubble. It is often a common lizard in tidal wrack, dumps, and trash piles. It can swim and climb but usually seeks cover beneath logs, rocks, leaf litter, or debris. This species occurs throughout the state of Florida.

Abundance: Although found over most of the southeastern United States, this skink seems most common on the southern two-thirds of the Florida peninsula.

Behavior: Like most skinks, the southeastern five-line is alert, wary, and difficult to approach closely. If on an inclined or fallen tree, it will often seek cover beneath exfoliating bark or by moving to the far side of the trunk. This species readily darts beneath logs, rocks, and debris. Some may climb trees to escape a threat.

Reproduction: Females produce between 3 and 7 eggs (rarely to a dozen). Females construct a suitable nesting chamber and remain with the eggs during the two-month incubation period.

Similar species: Both the common five-lined and broad-headed skinks have a row of noticeably widened scales under the tail. The southern coal skink has only 4 body lines.

Comments: This slender-lined skink is the most abundant of the five-lined skink species in Florida. It may be encountered in habitats ranging from backyards to open woodlands far from human habitation.

106. Broad-headed Skink

Plestiodon laticeps

Size: With the occasional male reaching 12½ inches in length, this is our most spectacular skink. The tail of an adult is about 120% of the SVL; tails of younger individuals are proportionately longer. Hatchlings are about 3 inches long.

Identification: This is the largest of our southeastern skinks. The yellow to orange lines of the juveniles are usually better defined and more precise than those of the southeastern five-lined skink but narrower than those of the common five-lined skink. Juvenile broad-headed skinks often have a rather prominent ventrolateral stripe on each side, giving them 7 rather than 5 lines. Adult broad-headed skinks of both sexes lose most of their striping. During the spring breeding season, the head of the male widens posteriorly and becomes an intense fiery orange. There are usually 5 supralabial scales. The center subcaudal scale row is widened.

Habitat/Range: This is one of the most frequently seen lizards on university campuses, a common resident of the many altered habitats of yards and most city and state parks as well as the wilds of moist deciduous and mixed hammocks and woodlands. The broad-headed skink is the most arboreal of our southeastern skinks. If frightened it often scampers up a tree, or it may be seen just sunning or foraging on high limbs amid resurrection ferns and poison ivy vines. It is found in woodlands and wooded suburban areas in the northern one-half of the state and throughout the panhandle.

Abundance: This skink is common to abundant.

Behavior: This is a strongly arboreal skink. In urban settings and busy parks, this normally alert and wary lizard can become rather accustomed to humans. If approached slowly, obliquely, and not too closely, many examples will remain watchfully in place. To escape, some retreat to ground cover while many will rapidly ascend a nearby tree.

Reproduction: The 5–15 eggs can be laid in moisture-retaining piles of ground debris, under fallen logs, or in secure, damp, leaf-filled crotches or hollows of large trees. The female usually remains in attendance on the clutch throughout the 55–65-day incubation period. Communal nesting has been documented.

Similar species: Size alone will identify the adults of this skink. There is no other five-lined species even approaching it in size. The southern coal skink is smaller and has only 4 body stripes. The southeastern five-lined skink lacks a row of widened scales beneath its tail. The common five-lined skink has 2 enlarged postlabial scales touching the anterior of the ear opening and only 4 supralabial scales on each side.

Comments: Broad-headed skinks are occasionally collected from the wild for the pet trade. They are favored terrarium lizards and live for a decade or more if properly cared for.

107. Florida Sand Skink

Plestiodon reynoldsi
(formerly *Neoseps reynoldsi*)

Size: At 3½–5 inches, this skink is one of the smallest skinks of the southeast. The rather thick tail is 90–100% of the SVL. Hatchlings are about 2½ inches long.

Identification: This is a silvery to buff-colored skink. Tiny darker dots are present on most scales, imparting a vague lineate pattern that may be strongest laterally. A dark mask runs from the snout, through the eye, to the back of the face. There are no ear openings. All legs are greatly reduced and are folded back into grooves when the lizard is moving forward. The forelegs are especially small. Each forefoot bears only one toe, each hind foot, two. The eyes are small, the lower lid has a transparent window, the snout is wedge shaped, and the lower jaw is countersunk.

Habitat/Range: This remarkably adapted "sand-swimming" skink is endemic to white-sand habitats in several central Florida counties. It continues to occur in some numbers on the Lake Wales and Winter Haven ridges but seems only rarely found on the Mt. Dora Ridge. Sand skinks are most common in the low, rolling, sparsely vegetated scrubs that host plant communities of lichens, rosemary, turkey oak, saw palmetto, and sand pine. In such habitats, the sand surface dries quickly into the yielding consistency needed by this specialized skink, but moisture might be encountered from one to several inches below the surface. Sand skinks can be found by raking through surface sand with the fingers; they are most common near the base of plants, beneath fallen leaves, and under patches of lichens or manmade debris. On the hottest days they are seldom seen, apparently burrowing more deeply.

Abundance: Although both a federally and state threatened species, the sand skink can be locally common in suitable habitat.

Behavior: This is a persistent burrower usually seen only when it is dug up or when surface debris is moved. Even then, it again squirms beneath the sand surface so quickly that one is left wondering, what exactly he or she has just seen. Tiny insects and other arthropods often abound in the protection of fallen palm fronds or other moisture-retaining plant material, and it is thought that the sand skink preys extensively on these.

Reproduction: The reproductive strategies of the sand skink are poorly known. Female sand skinks are known to deposit clutches of 2 eggs in the late spring or early summer. Hatchlings have been found in July and August. Incubation is thought to take approximately 45 days. The deposition sites are unknown, but it seems reasonable to assume that the female chooses moisture-retentive sites such as beneath logs, fallen palmetto fronds, or other such ground debris.

Similar species: There are no other skinks in Florida with such reduced limbs or a dark mask.

Comments: It is illegal to take or restrain this protected species without a permit.

Ground Skink: Genus *Scincella*

This genus contains about 25 species, most of Asian distribution. All are small, slender skinks that are alert and fast moving and secretive. Only a single species is indigenous to the United States.

108. Ground Skink

Scincella laterale

Size: This skink occasionally attains a slender 5½ inches in total length (of which two-thirds is tail) but is usually about an inch shorter. Hatchlings are about 1¾ inches long.

Identification: This active little lizard, once called the brown-backed skink, is of an overall dark coloration. The broad, dark brown dorsolateral stripes, extending from the snout well onto the tail, separate the light brown dorsum from the even lighter sides. There is no light striping. The top of the head may be coppery colored, and this can be especially noticeable on juveniles or on adults in breeding condition. The tail is not contrastingly colored. The legs are tiny but fully functional and bear 5 toes each. Although it is not easily seen, there is a transparent area (a window) in the lower eyelid.

Habitat/Range: This secretive little skink may be seen in woodlands darting from the cover of one leaf to another, gliding in a serpentine manner amid the grasses of a well-manicured lawn, or hunting tiny insects in relatively dry scrub. It occurs in dry upland woodlands as well as along stream and pond edges. The ground skink may take to the water if threatened and often hides beneath logs, boards, and other manmade and natural ground litter. It can be seen in urban, suburban, and open woodland habitats throughout the state, including the Florida Keys, but not in the Everglades.

Abundance: This is one of Florida's most common lizard species.

Behavior: Although this tiny skink is often seen on top of or next to leaves, it is seldom more than one quick squirm from cover. It is alert and rarely allows close approach. Quiescent individuals may be startled into movement by the approach of motorized lawn equipment.

Reproduction: This little terrestrial skink does not remain with its eggs through incubation. It is the only one of Florida's skinks known to regularly multiclutch. Although up to 7 eggs are reported, most clutches contain 2–5. A healthy female can lay several clutches of eggs at 4–5-week intervals throughout the late spring and summer. Incubation duration is in the 50–60-day range.

Similar species: The sand skink is light colored and black masked with a reduced number of toes. The various mole skinks usually have a contrasting tail color as well as light dorsal stripes.

Comments: Although the legs are fully functional and used when the ground skink is moving slowly, the legs are folded against its body and the lizard relies on serpentine squirming when haste is required. Juveniles are especially pretty, gleaming in the sunshine like burnished copper.

108A. African Five-lined Skink (also called African Rainbow Skink)

Trachylepis quinquetaeniata

Size: Adult at 7–10 inches, with the tail about two-thirds of total length. Neonates are about 3¼ inches long.

Identification: This is a strongly dimorphic species, and males undergo extensive ontogenetic changes. Throughout their lives, females are dark brown with 5 straw-yellow stripes. The vertebral stripe begins at the back of the head and terminates about one-third of the way down the tail. The lateral stripes begin on the tip of the snout and terminate about one-third of the way down the tail. The dorsolateral stripes begin above each eye and extend a third of the way down the tail. The tail is cobalt blue (juveniles) to vaguely bluish (adults). Juvenile males resemble the females.

As they near adulthood, the males pale to brownish tan. The vertebral and dorsolateral stripes fade. The lateral stripes pale posteriorly but are quite visible anteriorly. Two to three lightly outlined dark spots are present posterior to each tympanum.

Fully adult males are tan to bluish gray dorsally, grayish laterally, and yellowish ventrally. The lateral stripe may remain visible from tympanum to the forelimb but fades posteriorly. Limbs are tan to bluish; tail is bluish.

Habitat/Range: Although widely distributed in Africa, where it is native, this skink is known in Florida only from a small locale in St. Lucie County, where it occurs near buildings formerly occupied by an animal dealer. There it may be seen along the walkways and in plantings.

Abundance: Common in its small Florida range.

Behavior: This skink is primarily insectivorous but may also eat smaller lizards as well as some fruit and blossoms.

An alert and agile lizard, the African five-lined skink quickly takes cover in the undergrowth and beneath landscape boulders when approached. It is capable of burrowing through loose soil, mulch, and leaf litter.

Reproduction: From 1 to 12 eggs are produced in a clutch. Two clutches may be laid in a season.

Similar species: The southeastern five-lined skink (account 105) and the six-lined racerunner (account 111) might be confused with the African five-lined skink.

Comments: The African five-lined skink is a very popular and inexpensive pet trade species. Its presence in Florida may be traced to escapees or deliberate releases.

RACERUNNERS, WHIPTAILS, AND TEGUS: FAMILY TEIIDAE

Native teiids are far better represented in our western states than in Florida. In fact, of the five teiid species that occur in Florida, only one, the six-lined racerunner, is native. The others, all of prominent importance in the pet industry, are of Neotropical origin.

All teiids are fast, nervous lizards. They routinely move about in the open in short bursts of speed. Most either construct burrows or utilize burrows made by other animals.

All teiids are active foragers that scratch through ground litter and loose sand to find their insect repast. Some readily eat plant materials. The lizards are confirmed heliotherms, basking between bouts of foraging. They tend to be most active from 9:00 in the morning to noontime but may forage well into the afternoon. All Florida species are terrestrial, and all are capable of bipedal locomotion.

The dorsal and lateral scales of all racerunners and whiptails are small and evenly granular. The ventral scales are large and platelike and arranged in 8 (*Aspidoscelis* and *Cnemidophorus*), 12 (*Ameiva*), or more than 30 (*Tupinambis*) parallel rows.

Teiids—The Big and the Small: Whiptails, Racerunners, and Tegus in Florida

Despite the fact that at least seven species of teiids now live in Florida, in all of Florida—the entire state—there is but a single native form, the 8-inch (most of the length is tail) six-lined racerunner.

The other six species are escapees or deliberate releases from the pet trade or bored pet owners—and although it doesn't say much for my ecological perspicacity, I really like one of these introduced species, the beautiful, many-hued rainbow whiptail.

From the late 1950s though the mid-1970s, tens of thousands of rainbow whiptails were imported from Colombia for the pet trade. Even though they did not withstand shipping as well as some other taxa, the lizards were beautiful and very, very cheap. Many died in transit, many arriving in suboptimal health were released rather than killed, and the healthy ones were sold far and wide.

During the 1960s I spent almost as much time in the field in Colombia as in the United States. I soon learned how abundant rainbow whiptails were in their home range. The lizards seemed to be everywhere. If I stepped quickly into a scrub-edged clearing on a sunny morning, these lizards bearing streaks of yellow, green, and blue darted everywhere. How could you not learn to love these abundant and active lizards?

By the 1970s it was apparent that in Miami-Dade County (back then simply Dade County) several populations of rainbow lizards had become established. Most of these were in close proximity to warehouses rented by animal importers. In years with warm winters the populations had prospered; in years with cold winters they had noticeably dwindled. Then, in 1977, Miami experienced not only subfreezing temperatures, but also a bit of snow, adding to the residents' woes.

The populations of rainbow lizards dwindled further, but in several vacant lots sheltered by massive warehouses, the rainbow lizards survived. Today (2009), some 50+ years later, they are still there. As wary as ever, the little seven-striped greenish females and big spangled blue, green, and yellow males dart along railroad tracks or into burrows dug beneath the introduced puncture weed.

And yes, politically correct or not, I still enjoy making an occasional visit to assess the stability of the population and marvel at the beauty of what I consider one of the most beautiful of the teiids.

Ameivas: Genus *Ameiva*

This large genus is best represented in the West Indies but occurs in Latin America as well. The single introduced species in Florida is not only the largest of the genus but one of the most variably colored as well. This pet trade species ranges widely through northern South America.

109. Giant Ameiva

Ameiva ameiva

Size: There are two very different-appearing populations of this lizard. The dusky populations, once designated *A. a. ameiva*, contain the larger lizards. These can attain a length of 24 inches in overall length.

The populations of green-rumped lizards, once designated *A. a. petersi*, contain lizards seldom exceeding 18 inches in total length.

Hatchlings of both color phases are nearly 5 inches in total length.

Identification: The hatchlings of both phases are prominently striped with green against a body color of light gray, tan, or brown.

109A. Green-rumped phase: Some have a dorsum of warm tan anteriorly, shading to brilliant green posteriorly. Others are entirely green dorsally. In both cases, the sides are darker and liberally peppered with prominent dark-edged white spots. The belly has brilliant blue spots on the outermost rows of ventral scales.

109B. Dusky phase: The color of this phase changes dramatically with the age of the lizard, and males are always the darker sex. Adult females are dusky olive gray anteriorly but usually retain some evidence of striping posteriorly. The dorsum of adult males is charcoal to bluish gray with rather regular crossrows of pale blue to yellowish or whitish spots. The belly has numerous blue spots on the outer several rows of scales. Blue to whitish blue spots also appear on the limbs.

There are 12 rows of large belly scales.

Habitat/Range: The giant ameiva prefers open areas such as fields, parklands, weedy canal banks, and manicured lawns, as well as the cover of low shrubs at the edges of office complexes. This lizard can be found in several sections of Miami-Dade County and is of Neotropical origin.

Abundance: This variable species is locally common.

Behavior: Remarkably pretty and remarkably fast are the terms that most concisely describe these lizards. Ameivas are alert lizards that nervously move between patches of cover. If hard pressed, they quickly dart for their burrows.

Reproduction: Despite the fact that the giant ameiva has been established in Florida for nearly half a century, little is known with certainty about its breeding biology in the state. They are thought to lay single (rarely two) clutches of up to four eggs in the early summer. The eggs hatch in somewhat more than two months.

Similar species: Only the giant whiptail approaches these lizards in size. It has blue or bluish spangled sides and lacks any green coloration (see account 107).

Comments: In some areas of their tropical American range, the characteristics of the dusky and the green-rumped phases meld and overlap greatly. Escapees from the pet industry account for the presence of this lizard in Florida.

Whiptails and Racerunners: Genera *Aspidoscelis* and *Cnemidophorus*

The lizards of these closely allied genera are more diverse in our central and western states (*Aspidoscelis*) and in Latin America (*Cnemidophorus*) than in the east. Among their ranks are many parthenogenetic species, none of which occur in Florida. The two genera have only recently been separated. All species were considered to be in the genus *Cnemidophorus* in older texts.

110. Giant Whiptail

Aspidoscelis motaguae

Size: Males of this rather large lizard grow to 13 inches in total length. Females are smaller. Hatchlings are 4¼ inches in total length.

Identification: This whiptail has a golden brown vertebral area shading gently into tan or golden-spangled deeper brown sides. The lower sides are the darkest and spangled with white spots. The venter is gray with bright blue spangles ventrolaterally. Females are somewhat paler than the males. The tail is brown anteriorly, shading to reddish brown terminally.

Habitat/Range: Open fields, canal banks, grassy parking lot edges, and road shoulders are all favored habitats. In Florida, this northern Central American lizard is known only from Miami-Dade County.

Abundance: Construction has driven these lizards further from the epicenter of their Miami-Dade County introduction site, but population statistics there are scant. A second, seemingly well-established colony has been found.

Behavior: Like all whiptails, this is an alert and active species, adept at evading enemies, including human captors.

Reproduction: Nothing is yet known about the breeding biology of this species in its Florida habitat, and precious little is known about it in its natural range. A captive female had 4 eggs that hatched after 54 days of incubation.

Similar species: Giant ameivas have a dorsum that is either darker blue black or partially green.

Comments: Little is known about the life history of this whiptail in Florida. Comprehensive studies are needed on feral populations of this pet trade species in Florida.

111. Six-lined Racerunner

Aspidoscelis sexlineatus sexlineatus

Size: Adult males of this small teiid attain 7–8 inches in total length; females are an inch or so smaller. Hatchlings are nearly 3 inches long.

Identification: Males, females, and juveniles of this beautiful lizard have 6 (occasionally 7) yellow lines against a ground color of variable brown. The ground color is lighter middorsally and darkest low on the sides. Males have a suffusion of light blue over their entire bellies. Females have almost white bellies. Juveniles have light bellies and bluish tails.

Habitat/Range: The six-lined racerunner is adapted to areas such as well-drained sandy fields, rosemary scrub, sandy parking lot edges, and myriad other equally well-drained, sun-drenched habitats. It can be found throughout Florida except for the Everglades region.

Abundance: This is a common lizard throughout its range.

Behavior: The adjectives alert, agile, and remarkably fast can be well applied to this lizard. It is active in the morning and early afternoon, often resting during the hottest part of the day and resuming activity in the late afternoon. On cool days the lizards bask more extensively but remain surface-active longer. They may construct a burrow but more often utilize one already created or hide beneath surface debris.

Reproduction: Females lay two clutches of 1–6 eggs. Incubation takes about 48 days. The growth of the hatchlings is rapid.

Similar species: Female rainbow whiptails have orangish faces, more than 6 lines, and greenish tails. Immature skinks have shiny mirrorlike scales.

Comments: This is the only native teiid found in Florida. It remains common in sparsely developed and undeveloped areas where the soils are sandy and sharply drained.

112. Rainbow Whiptail

Cnemidophorus lemniscatus

Size: Usually in the range of 9–10 inches, some large males may attain or even exceed 12 inches in total length. Females are the smaller sex. Hatchlings are about 3½ inches long.

Identification: This is one of the most beautiful lizards now in Florida. The warm brown dorsum of the males is bordered by a thin yellow stripe with a lime green stripe beneath it. Another thin yellow stripe separates the green stripe from a broad, yellow-spangled golden lateral area. The face, throat, and anterior surface of all limbs is turquoise or robin's-egg blue. The tail is green. A white-spangled purplish shoulder spot is often present. Venter is grayish. Females lack much of the pattern complexity, having instead 7 to 9 yellow stripes on a field of greenish brown. The head is orange(ish); the hind limbs and tail are greenish. The venter is white.

Habitat/Range: Rainbow whiptails are found in heavily pebbled expanses of sandy soil with a sparse cover of low, mostly exotic, weeds. In Florida this northern South American lizard is known only from Miami-Dade County, where it can be encountered behind two or three warehouse complexes.

Abundance: These are common lizards within their very circumscribed range.

Behavior: These lizards probe the sand and pebbles of the fields over which they skitter. When sufficiently hot they retire either to their burrows or to the shade of a plant or building. Rainbow lizards feed not only on insects and other arthropods, but also on the leaves and flowers of European punctureweed, a diet toxic to endotherms.

Reproduction: Although some Neotropical populations are known to be parthenogenetic, the population of rainbow whiptails in Florida comprises both sexes. Captive females have laid two clutches of up to 4 eggs (usually 2 or 3) during the summer months. These have hatched after some 47–55 days of incubation.

Similar species: No other lizard in Florida has the combination of colors of the male rainbow lizard. Six-lined racerunners superficially resemble female rainbow lizards but have only 6 yellow lines instead of 7–9 and lack a suffusion of orange on the face.

Comments: The Florida population of this pet trade favorite is badly in need of comprehensive study. It has been established here for more than 40 years but, despite being locally abundant, virtually nothing is known of its life history. It is probable that the Florida population is of Colombian origin.

Tegus: Genus *Tupinambis*

This is a small genus of large South American lizards. Of the 6 species, 3 or 4 are important in the American pet trade. The introduced black-and-white tegu, indigenous to sub-Amazonian Brazil, northern Argentina, and Uruguay, is one of the largest and hardiest of this genus. By hibernating in secure burrows it survives mid-Florida winters. The status and behavior of the golden tegu in South Florida remains unknown.

113. Black-and-White Tegu (also called Argentine Giant Tegu)

Tupinambis merianae

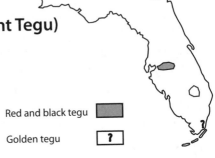

Red and black tegu

Golden tegu   [?]

Size: Males may attain or slightly exceed a heavy-bodied 54 inches in length. Females are smaller. Hatchlings are about 8 inches long.

Identification: Adults are an immense, stocky, (usually) black-and-white lizard that carries its body well away from the ground on sturdy legs. Some adults may become suffused with reddish pigment. The amount of light pigment is variable. Some tegus may be predominantly light while others are very dark. The white pigment is usually in the form of dense spots that form regular crossbars along the back and posterior sides and rings on the tail. Two black markings, a thin one from the eye to above the forelimb and a wider one below it extending from the level of the ear opening, over the shoulder, to midside, are usually present. All limbs are spotted with white. The chin and belly are light with dark spots. The scales are glossy, and the tail is round in cross section.

Hatchlings have a varying amount of bright green suffusing both the white and the black. The green is most intense on the head, neck, and shoulders.

Habitat/Range: In Florida this lizard now ranges from eastern Hillsborough County to central Polk County.

Abundance: This lizard is increasingly common and seems very well established.

Behavior: Although perfectly capable of constructing its own home burrow, the black-and-white tegu is just as apt to utilize and modify an existing armadillo or gopher tortoise burrow. Adults are well able to overpower and consume small rodents, other reptiles (including baby gopher tortoises and burrowing owls), amphibians, and eggs. They also eat nuts, fruits, and vegetation. This tegu hibernates during the several months of cold weather.

Reproduction: Females dig a two-tiered nesting burrow up to 48 inches

long. Vegetation is dragged by the female into the lower chamber, where up to 55 eggs are then deposited. The female remains in attendance in the upper chamber. Hatchlings emerge after 65–72 days of incubation.
Similar species: None within the current range of this species.
Comments: It is thought the Florida population of this lizard was due to deliberate releases. Whether the founder stock simply and literally outgrew its welcome or was released in the hopes individuals would breed and the babies could be captured for the pet trade is not known. Eradication efforts were initially attempted but have been largely discontinued because of lack of funding.

113A. Golden Tegu (also Colombian Tegu)
Tupinambis teguixin

Comments: Feral examples of this pretty gold (or more rarely, white) on black tegu are being seen in Broward and Miami-Dade counties with increasing regularity. The coloration of the gold and black individuals is distinctive. Those banded with white are generally slimmer, smaller, and less precisely banded than the larger black–and-white tegu. The golden tegu is not yet known to be breeding in Florida. It is native to much of the Amazon Basin. An adult length of 36–42 inches is attained. Despite its nervousness and propensity to bite and scratch, the golden tegu is a popular pet trade species.

MONITORS: FAMILY VARANIDAE

This family of Old World lizards contains species that vary in size from the 8 inches of the Australian short-tailed monitor to the bulky 9 feet of the Komodo dragon to the 12 feet of the comparatively slender crocodile monitor. Between the extremes are some 70 species and subspecies of intermediate size.

With two notable vegetarian exceptions, both of Philippine distribution, all monitors are voracious predators. Small species eat insects, and all others eat carrion and whatever creatures they can catch and overpower. When you are of the size of the Komodo dragon or the crocodile monitor, there are not many creatures of moderate size you cannot overpower.

Monitors—Comments on an Agile Predator

It seemed as if the state regulatory agencies weren't all that concerned about the introduction and establishment of alien species in Florida—there were, after all, so many of them.

It seemed that way, at least until the media hopped on the bandwagon and featured a hulking and very predatory lizard—the Nile monitor—originally from Africa, now of Lee County. Anecdotal reports of lizard sightings had been heard as early as the late 1980s, and by 1990 it was obvious the lizard had become established in Cape Coral.

If this sub-Saharan lizard actually became common, it could bode ill for some of our native wildlife, and the cute and cuddly-looking little burrowing owl could well be among them. How do you catch and eliminate a 6-foot lithe lizard that pops down any available burrowing owl burrow when danger looms? Eradication plans are in effect, traps are set, and studies and discussions continue. Despite all this, Nile monitors seem at least to be holding their own.

If you wish to see a Nile monitor, situate yourself in a coastal mangrove region, a tidal marsh, or along a canal in southwest Cape Coral. The monitors are in sparsely populated expanses as well as in residential areas.

Besides the population in Lee County, Nile monitors are now rather regularly sighted in the vicinity of Homestead and Card Sound, and they have also been reported from Sanibel, Pine Island, near Orlando, and numerous other locales. Although the Nile monitor is the only varanid reportedly breeding in Florida, two additional species—the African savanna monitor and the Asian water monitor—are mentioned anecdotally by field observers.

Although feral monitors of several species have been found in Florida, only the Nile monitor is known to have become established. It is a nervous species with sharp claws and sharp teeth. Despite its popularity in the pet trade, most Nile monitors remain untrustworthy, and many are intractable.

Numerous feral examples of both the Asian water monitor and the savanna monitor have been seen and documented in the Sunshine State. The savanna monitor, *Varanus exanthematicus*, is a heavy-bodied terrestrial species native to southern Africa. The massive Asian water monitor, *Varanus salvator*, is quite aquatic in habitats. All three—Nile, savanna, and water monitors—are popular in the American pet trade.

A single example of a fourth species, the gigantic and very rare crocodile monitor, *Varanus salvadorii*, was found in a Miami air-shipping facility in September 2009. Not only is this species uncommon and very costly, at an adult length of 8–10 feet (possibly longer) it is the longest known monitor (it is exceeded in weight by the Komodo dragon). It is native to New Guinea.

114. Nile Monitor

Varanus niloticus

N Nile

W Water

Size: Adult males attain a length of a bit more than 6 feet. Females are somewhat smaller. Hatchlings are about 8 inches long.

Identification: This is a long-legged, long-tailed, long-necked, and long-tongued lizard. While hatchlings are a study in black and yellow, the colors and patterns of adults dull and become indistinct.

Hatchlings and juveniles are darkest dorsally and have an intricate pattern of yellow spots and ocelli. The yellow head markings are in the form of bars, the neck markings are yellow chevrons, and on the back and the tail, bands of yellow ocelli alternate with bands of yellow spots. All limbs are yellow spotted. The colors and pattern on the lower sides and belly are essentially the mirror opposite of the dorsal color. On the sides and belly the color is yellow and the markings are dusky. The tail is laterally flattened and propels the monitor through the water.

The tongue is long and protrusible and used to gather scents.

Adults may be an overall gray or bluish gray on the head, back, upper sides, and tail.

Habitat/Range: The principal population of this huge sub-Saharan lizard is in Cape Coral, Lee County, where it has been regularly seen along canals. Mangrove swamps, marshes, and lake edges also provide suitable habitat. Over the years numerous sightings have also been made in Miami-Dade, Monroe, Charlotte, and Collier counties. It is not known whether this lizard occurs in breeding populations in these latter four counties.

Abundance: Although still considered uncommon, sightings of Nile monitors seem to be increasing.

Behavior: Hatchlings and juveniles are primarily arboreal. Subadults and adults are terrestrial and semiaquatic. This lizard readily enters fresh, brackish, and salt water. It is a strong swimmer and can easily travel to many of the barrier islands from either the mainland or other islands. Hatchlings feed on insects and small rodents and have sharp, grasping teeth. With growth these dull and become the crushing teeth of the adult monitors that feed on shellfish and crustaceans as well as other small animals.

Reproduction: Although rather well researched in Africa and in captivity, the breeding biology of the Nile monitor in Florida is not yet ascertained. Captive females construct nests in which up to 60 eggs are laid. Depending on nest temperature and moisture, incubation has reportedly taken as long as 10 months.

Similar species: None within the range of this species in Florida.

Comments: Much concern exists about the potential of this predatory lizard to adversely impact populations of numerous species of concern by marauding nests and eggs. Among the species mentioned are burrowing owls, sea turtles, American crocodiles, diamond-backed terrapins, and gopher tortoises. Methods of eradicating the Nile monitor are being explored, but none attempted have proven effective. The current breeding populations are probably the result of released "pets."

114A. Savanna Monitor

Varanus exanthematicus

Comments: This is a gray to sand-colored dryland monitor. It attains a length of about 5 feet. Although not yet known to be established in Florida, feral individuals have been seen on innumerable occasions.

114B. Asian Water Monitor

Varanus salvator

Comments: Rather similar to, but darker and of heavier build than the firmly established Nile monitor, the water monitor attains a length of 8 feet. It is a semiaquatic species that has been seen on numerous occasions in Florida but is not yet known to be established.

5

Peripheral Reptile Species

Reports of sightings of the southern painted turtle in Florida exist but lack verification.

BASKING TURTLES: FAMILY EMYDIDAE

---

115. Southern Painted Turtle

Chrysemys picta dorsalis

Size: While specimens of 4–5 inches are commonly seen, occasional adults of this turtle attain a 6-inch carapace length. Hatchlings are 1 inch long.

Identification: This turtle has a smooth black to brown carapace with a well-defined orange vertebral line. The plastron is usually an unrelieved yellow. Yellow lines are apparent on the brown head. Both sexes and all sizes are colored similarly. Duckweed often covers the carapace of basking southern painted turtles, obscuring the true colors of this chelonian.

Habitat/Range: The southern painted turtle can be found in ponds, marshes, lakes, canals, and slowly flowing rivers. It is known to occur just a few miles west of the Florida state line in the lower Alabama River.

Abundance: This turtle is abundant north and west of Florida.

Behavior: In the southernmost part of their range, southern painted turtles are active almost year-round. They bask persistently on sunny days, climbing out of the water onto snags and exposed banks to do so.

Reproduction: Clutches of 4–9 (occasionally more) eggs are known. Most females lay 2–4 clutches annually. The hatchlings emerge following a 55–70-day incubation.

Similar species: No other turtle in Florida has an orange vertebral line.

Comments: This pretty little turtle is the southeasternmost of the painted turtle group. Some researchers have elevated it to full species level, but this designation remains very controversial.

Glossary

Aestivation—A period of warm weather inactivity, often triggered by excessive heat or drought.

Allopatric—Occupying separate ranges; not occurring together.

Alveolar ridge (or **plate**)—A broad crushing plate posterior to the mandibles.

Ambient temperature—The temperature of the surrounding environment.

Anterior—Toward the front.

Annuli—Growth rings on the carapace of some turtle species.

Arboreal—Tree-dwelling.

Autotomize—Spontaneously or reflexively break free, with little or no external assistance, as in the case of the tails of some lizards.

Bridge—The "bridge of shell" between fore and rear limbs connecting a turtle's carapace and plastron.

Brille—The clear spectacle that protects the eyes of lidless-eyed geckos.

Carapace—The upper shell of a chelonian.

Caudal—Pertaining to the tail.

Chelonian—A turtle or tortoise.

Cloaca—The common chamber into which digestive, urinary, and reproductive systems empty and which itself opens exteriorly through the vent.

Congeneric—Grouped in the same genus.

Conspecific—The same species.

Costals—The row of carapacial scutes on each side between the vertebrals and the marginals.

Crepuscular—Active at dusk and/or dawn.

Cusp—Downward-projecting points on the upper mandible of a turtle.

Deposition—As used here, the laying of eggs or birthing of young.

Deposition site—Nesting site.

Dichromatic—Exhibiting two color phases; often sex-linked.

Dimorphic—A difference in length, form, build, or coloration involving the same species; often sex-linked.

Diurnal—Active in the daytime.

Dorsal—Pertaining to the back; upper surface.

Dorsolateral—Pertaining to the upper side.

Dorsolateral ridge—A glandular longitudinal ridge on the upper sides of some frogs.

Dorsum—The upper surface.

Ecological niche—The precise habitat utilized by a species.

Ectothermic—See **poikilothermic**.

Endemic—Confined to a specific region.

Endothermic—"Warm-blooded," pertaining to an organism that produces its own body heat.

Extralimital—Occurring beyond the scope of coverage.

Femoral pores—Openings in the scales on the underside of the hind legs of some lizards.

Femur—The part of the leg between the hip and the knee.

Form—An identifiable species or subspecies.

Fracture plane—A naturally weakened area in the tail vertebrae of some lizards; a natural breaking point.

Frugivore—An eater of fruit.

Genus (pl. **genera**)—A taxonomic classification of a group of species having similar characteristics. The genus falls between the next higher designation of "family" and the next lower designation of "species." Genus names are always capitalized when written.

Gravid—The reptilian equivalent of mammalian pregnancy.

Gular—Pertaining to the throat.

Heliothermic—Pertaining to a species that basks in the sun to thermoregulate.

Herpetologist—One who studies reptiles and amphibians.

Herpetology—The study (often scientifically oriented) of reptiles and amphibians.

Hybrid—Offspring resulting from the breeding of two species.

Intergrade—Offspring resulting from the breeding of two adjacent subspecies.

Interstitial—Between the scales.

Juvenile—A young or immature specimen.

Keel—A carapacial or plastral ridge (or ridges) or a longitudinal ridge on the scales of some lizards.

Labials—"Lip" scales; **supralabials** are the scales along the upper lip, and **infralabials** are the scales edging the lower lip.

Lamellae—The transverse divisions that extend across the bottom surfaces of the toes of anoles and geckos.

Lateral—Pertaining to the side.

Lateral fold—A longitudinal fold on the sides of curly-tailed lizards.

Lateral groove—A longitudinal expandable fold on the lower sides of anguid lizards.

Mandibles—Jaws.

Mandibular—Pertaining to the jaws.

Melanism—A profusion of black pigment.

Metachrosis—The ability to change color either at will or involuntarily, in response to external stimuli.

Middorsal—Pertaining to the middle of the back.

Midventral—Pertaining to the center of the belly.

Monotypic—Containing but one type.

Nocturnal—Active at night.

Nominate—The first named form.

Nuchal—Foremost unpaired scute separating the left and right marginals on a turtle's shell.

Ocelli—Dark- or light-edged circular spots.

Ontogenetic—Age-related (color) changes.

Osteoderm—A bony deposit in the scales of some reptiles.

Oviparous—Reproducing by means of eggs that hatch after laying.

Papillae—Small, fleshy, nipplelike protuberances.

Parthenogenesis—Reproduction without fertilization.

Phalanges—The bones of the toes.

Photoperiod—The daily/seasonally variable length of the hours of daylight.

Plastron—The bottom shell of a turtle.

Poikilothermic (also **ectothermic**)—Pertaining to an organism with no internal body temperature regulation. The old term was "cold-blooded."

Postocular—To the rear of the eye.

Preocular—Positioned in front of the eye.

Race—A subspecies.

Rostral—An enlarged plate on the tip of the snout.

Rugose—Wrinkled, warty, or rough.

Saxicolous—Dwelling on or among rocks.

Scute—Scale, especially the large scales on a turtle's shell or a snake's venter.

Septal ridge—A horizontal ridge on each side of the septum dividing a softshell turtle's nostrils

Setae—Hairlike bristles in the lamellae on the toes of anoles and geckos.

Sibling species—Two or more similar-appearing species supposedly derived from the same parental stock. Sibling species are often unidentifiable in the field.

Species—A group of similar creatures that produce viable young when breeding. The taxonomic designation below genus and above subspecies. Abbreviation, sp., plural spp.

Subcaudal—Beneath the tail.

Subdigital—Beneath the toes.

Submarginal—The underside of a marginal scute.

Subocular—Below the eye.

Subspecies—The subdivision of a species. A race that may differ slightly in color, size, scalation, or other criteria. Abbreviation, ssp.

Subsurface—Below the surface.

Supraocular—Above the eye.

Supramarginals—The row of small scutes between the costal scutes and the marginals on the carapace of an alligator snapper.

SVL—snout-vent length.

Sympatric—Occurring together.

Taxon (plural, **taxa**)—Taxonomic category or group, as species, genus, family, etc.

Taxonomy—The science of classification of plants and animals.

Terrestrial—Land-dwelling.

Thermoregulate—To regulate (body) temperature by choosing a warmer or cooler environment.

Vent—The external opening of the cloaca.

Venter—The underside of a creature; the belly.

Ventral—Pertaining to the undersurface or belly.

Ventrolateral—Pertaining to the sides of the belly.

Acknowledgments

The successful completion of a publication such as this one is due to the efforts and generosity of colleagues and friends. With this in mind, we gratefully acknowledge the comments and concerns of biologists C. Kenneth Dodd, Kevin Enge, Richard Franz, James H. Harding, Thomas Tyning, and R. Wayne VanDevender.

Karin Burns, Dennis Cathcart, Travis Cossette, Robert Ferran, Chris Gillette, Billy Griswold, Pierson Hill, Scott Cushnir, Steven Johnson, John Lewis, Barry Mansell Brian Mealey, Flavio Morrissey, Greta Parks, Nicole Pinder, Mark Robertson, Dan Scolaro, Jake Scott, Dave Strasser, Mike Stuhlman, Maria Camarrilla Wray, and Kenny Wray either joined us, or allowed us to join them, in the field and made certain that we noticed specimens that would otherwise have gone unseen.

Bill Love, Rob MacInnes, Robby Keszey, Chris McQuade, and Eric Thiss allowed us great latitude in photographing Florida reptiles and amphibians they felt would be of interest to us.

Walter Meshaka shared his encyclopedic knowledge of the introduced reptiles and amphibians of Florida, and induced us into the field that we might photograph many alien species in the wild.

To Paul E. Moler we owe more than just a word of thanks. Paul unstintingly shared his knowledge of the herpetofauna of Florida, offered comments and criticisms on the text, and steered us to habitats where we could photograph some of Florida's more elusive amphibians and reptiles. We are truly indebted.

Thank you all.

And thanks also to Dale Johnson who prepared much of the line art.

To the memory of E. Gordon (Gordy) Johnston who, more than 50 years ago, introduced me (RDB) to Florida and its incredible array of herpetofauna, I owe a never-ending debt of gratitude.

Bibliography and
Additional Reading

The following listings are only a few of the publications pertaining to Florida herpetology; they are, however, among the more important contributions.

Ashton, R. E., Jr., S. R. Edwards, and G. R. Pisani. 1976. *Endangered and Threatened Amphibians and Reptiles of the United States*. Herp. Circ. no. 5. Lawrence, Kans.: Society for the Study of Amphibians and Reptiles.

Ashton, R. E., Jr., and P. S Ashton. 1985. *Handbook of Reptiles and Amphibians of Florida*. Part II, *Lizards, Turtles and Crocodilians*. Miami: Windward Publishing.

Bartlett, R. D. 1988. *In Search of Reptiles and Amphibians*. New York: E. J. Brill.

Bartlett, R. D., and Patricia P. Bartlett. 1995. *Iguanas, A Complete Pet Owner's Manual*. Hauppauge, N.Y.: Barron's Educ. Series.

———. 1997. *Anoles, Basilisks and Water Dragons, A Complete Pet Owner's Manual*. Hauppauge, N.Y.: Barron's Educ. Series.

———. 1998. *A Field Guide to Florida Reptiles and Amphibians*. Houston: Gulf Publishing.

———. 2006. *Guide and Reference to the Crocodilians, Turtles, and Lizards of Eastern and Central North America (North of Mexico)*. Gainesville: University Press of Florida.

Behler, John L., and F. Wayne King. 1979. *The Audubon Society Field Guide to North American Reptiles and Amphibians*. New York: Alfred Knopf.

Buhlmann, Kurt, Tracey Tuberville, and Whit Gibbons. 2008. *Turtles of the Southeast*. Athens: University of Georgia Press.

Carr, Archie. 1952. *Handbook of Turtles*. Ithaca, N.Y.: Cornell University Press.

Conant, Roger, and Joseph T. Collins. 1991. *A Field Guide to the Reptiles and Amphibians of Eastern and Central North America*. 3rd ed. Boston: Houghton Mifflin.

Crother, Brian I., ed. 2008. *Scientific and Standard English Names of Amphibians and Reptiles of North America North of Mexico, with Comments Regarding Confidence in our Understanding*. Hammond, La.: SSAR

Duellman, William E., and Albert Schwartz. 1958. *Amphibians and Reptiles of Southern Florida*. Gainesville: Bulletin of the Florida State Museum, no. 3.

Enge, Kevin M., et al. 2004. Status of the Nile Monitor (*Varanus niloticus*) in Southwestern Florida. *Southeastern Naturalist* 3(4): 571–82.

Enge, Kevin M., and Kenneth L. Krysko. 2004. A New Exotic Species in Florida, the

Bloodsucker Lizard, *Calotes versicolor* (Daudin 1802)(Sauria: Agamidae). *Florida Scientist* 67(3): 226–30.

Enge, Kevin M., Kenneth L. Krysko, and Brooke L. Talley. 2004. Distribution and Ecology of the Introduced African Rainbow Lizard, *Agama agama africana* (Sauria: Agamidae), in Florida. *Florida Scientist* 67(4): 303–10.

Ernst, Carl H., and Jeffrey E. Lovich. 1994. *Turtles of the United States and Canada*, Second Edition. Baltimore: Johns Hopkins University Press.

Gibbons, Whit, Judy Greene, and Tony Mills. 2009. *Lizards and Crocodilians of the Southeast*. Athens: University of Georgia Press.

Krysko, Kenneth L., et al. 2010. The African Five-lined Skink, *Trachylepis quinquetaeniata* (Lichtenstein 1823): A New Established Species in Florida. *IRCF Reptiles and Amphibians* 17(3): 183–84.

Krysko, Kenneth L., and Kevin M. Enge. 2005. A New Non-Native Lizard in Florida, the Butterfly Lizard, *Leiolepis belliana* (Sauria: Agamidae). *Florida Scientist* 68(4): 247–49.

Halliday, Tim, and Kraig Adler, eds. 1986. *The Encyclopedia of Reptiles and Amphibians*. New York: Facts on File.

Iverson, J. B., and P. E. Moler. 1997. The Female Reproductive Cycle of the Florida Softshell Turtle (*Apalone ferox*). *Journal of Herpetology* 31(3): 399–409.

Meshaka, W. E., Jr. 1999. The Herpetofauna of the Kampong. *Florida Scientist* 62: 153–57.

Meshaka, Walter E., Brian P. Butterfield, and J. Brian Hauge. 2004. *Exotic Amphibians and Reptiles of Florida*. Malabar, Fla.: Krieger.

Meylan, Peter A., ed. 2006. *Biology and Conservation of Florida Turtles*. Chelonian Research Monographs 3, Chelonian Research Foundation.

Moler, Paul E. 1990. *A Checklist of Florida's Amphibians and Reptiles (Revised)*. Tallahassee: Florida Game and Fresh Water Fish Commission.

Moler, Paul E., ed. 1992. *Rare and Endangered Biota of Florida*. Vol. III, *Amphibians and Reptiles*. Gainesville: University Press of Florida.

Neill, Wilfred T. 1971. *The Last of the Ruling Reptiles*. New York: Columbia University Press.

Mount, Robert H. 1975. *The Reptiles and Amphibians of Alabama*. Auburn, Ala.: Auburn University.

Schwartz, Albert, and Robert W. Henderson. *Amphibians and Reptiles of the West Indies*. 1991. Gainesville: University of Florida Press.

Smith, Hobart M. 1946. *Handbook of Lizards*. Ithaca, N.Y.: Comstock.

Tyning, Thomas F. 1990. *A Guide to Amphibians and Reptiles*. Boston: Little, Brown.

Webb, Robert G. 1962. *North American Recent Soft-Shelled Turtles (Family Trionychidae)*. University of Kansas Publications of the Museum of Natural History 13(10): 429–611.

———. 1990. Trionyx. *Catalogue of American Amphibians and Reptiles*, 487.1–487.7.

Whitney, Elliue, D. Bruce Means, and Anne Rudloe. 2004. *Priceless Florida*. Sarasota, Fla.: Pineapple Press.

Wilson, Larry David, and Louis Porras. 1983. *The Ecological Impact of Man on the South Florida Herpetofauna*. Lawrence: University of Kansas.

Useful Websites

The Comprehensive Florida Hawksbill Research and Conservation Program
http://www.floridahawksbills.com

The Gopher Tortoise Council
http://www.gophertortoisecouncil.org/about.php

Index

Agama 140
  agama africana 140–41
  agama agama 141
  hispida 138
Agama
  Asian Tree 141
  Bloodsucker (*see* Agama, Variable)
  Butterfly 143
  Red-Headed 140–41
    East African 141
    West African 140–41
  Spiny 138
  Variable 142
Agamidae 138–43
Alligator 126–27
  American 126–27
Alligator mississippiensis 126–27
Alligatoridae 126–29
Ameiva ameiva 231–32
Ameiva 231–32
  Giant 231–32
    Dusky 231
    Green-Rumped 231
Amphisbaenidae 132–35
Anguidae 144–50
Anole 196–210
  Barbados 6, 206
  Bark 203–4
    Bimini 204
    Florida 204
    Green 204

Brown, Cuban 209–10
Crested, Puerto Rican 200–201
Giant, Jamaican 207–8
Green 198–99, 199–200, 208–9
  Cuban 208–9
  Haitian 199–200
  Northern 198–99
  Pale-throated 199
Knight, Western 204–5
Large-headed 202–3
Sail-tailed, Marie Galante 206
White-lipped, Hispaniolan 6
Anolis 198–210
  carolinensis 198–99
    carolinensis 198–99
    seminolus 199
  chlorocyanus 199–200
  coelestinus 6
  cristatellus cristatellus 200–201
  cybotes cybotes 202–3
  distichus 203–4
    biminiensis 204
    distichus 204
    dominicensis 204
  equestris equestris 204–5
  extremus 6, 206
  ferreus 206–7
  garmani 207–8
  porcatus 208–9
  sagrei sagrei 209–10
Apalone 112–18

ferox 114–16
mutica calvata 116–17
spinifera aspera 117–18
Aspidoscelis 232–34
  motaguae 232–33
  sexlineatus sexlineatus 233–34

Basiliscus 177–80
  plumifrons 180
  vittatus 179–80
Basilisk 177–80
  Green 180
  Northern Brown 179–80
Bipes biporus 135
Bronchocela mystaceus 141

Caiman crocodilus crocodilus 128–29
Caiman, Spectacled 128–29
Calotes 141–42
  versicolor 142
Caretta caretta 69–70
Chalcides ocellatus 214
Chamaeleo calyptratus calyptratus
  151–52
Chamaeleonidae 150–53
Chameleon 150–53
  Panther 153
  Veiled 151–52
Chelonia mydas mydas 70–71
Cheloniidae 68–73
Chelydra 77–78
  serpentine 77–78
  osceola 78
  serpentina 77–78
Chelydridae 75–79
Chrysemys picta dorsalis 242–43
Clemmys guttata 87–90
Cnemidophorus 234 (see also *Aspidos-
celis*)
  lemniscatus 234–35
Cooter 98–103
  Florida 100–101
  Florida Red-bellied 102–3
  Peninsula 101–2

River, Eastern 98–100
Suwannee 100
Corytophanidae 177–80
Cosymbotus platyurus (see *Hemidactylus
platyurus*)
Crocodile 126, 129
  American 5, 37, 123, 130
Crocodilians 123–31
Crocodylia 123–31
Crocodylidae 129–31
Crocodylus 129–31
  acutus 130–31
  species 129
Ctenosaura 182–85
  pectinata 182–83
  similis 184–85

Dermochelys coriacea 73–74
Deirochelys 90–92
  reticularia 90–92
  chrysea 92
  reticularia 91–92

Emydidae 87–109, 242–43
Eretmochelys imbricata imbricata
  71–72
Eumeces (see *Plestiodon*)

Furcifer pardalis 153

Gecko 153–77
  Ashy 175–76
  Bibron's 165–66
  Day 167–70
    Giant 167–68
    Standing's 168–70
  Flying, Common 170
  Golden 159
  House 159–60, 161–63
    Asian flat-tailed 162–63
    Common 159–60
    Tropical 161–62
    Indopacific 160–61
    Mediterranean 163–64

Mourning 164–65
Ocellated 174–75
Reef 176–77
Stump-toed 156–57
Tokay 157–59
Turner's 166
Wall 170–72
　Moorish 171–72
　White-spotted 170–71
　Yellow-headed 172–73
Gehyra mutilata 156–57
Gekko 157–59
　gecko 157–59
　ulikovskii 159
Gekkonidae 153–77
Geochelone sulcata 119
Gonatodes albogularis fuscus
　172–73
Gopherus spolyphemus 120–22
Graptemys 92–95
　barbouri 93–94
　ernsti 94–95

Hemidactylus 159–64
　frenatus 159–60
　garnotii 160–61
　mabouia 161–62
　platyurus 162–63
　turcicus 163–64

Iguana 180–86
　Green 185–86
　Spiny-tailed 182–85
　　Mexican 182–83
　　Central American 184–85
Iguana iguana 185–86
Iguanidae 180–86

Kinosternidae 79–87
Kinosternon 82–85
　baurii 82–83
　subrubrum 83–85
　　steindachneri 84
　　subrubrum 83–84

Lacertilia (see Sauria)
Leatherback, Atlantic 73–74
Leiocephalidae 186–91
Leiocephalus 186–91
　carinatus armouri 188–89
　personatus scalaris 189–90
　schreibersi schreibersi 190–91
Leiolepis belliana 143
Lepidochelys kempii 72–73
Lepidodactylus lugubris 164–65
Lizard
　Collared, Guyana 211–12
　Curly-tailed 186–91
　　Green-legged 189–90
　　Northern 188–89
　　Red-Sided 190–91
　Fence, Eastern 194–95
　Glass 144–50
　　Eastern 149–50
　　Island 147–48
　　Mimic 148–49
　　Slender, Eastern 146–47
　Horned, Texas 193–94
　Iguanian 177–212
　Rainbow, African (see Agama, Red-
　　headed)
　Scrub, Florida 195–96
　Worm 132–35
　　Florida 134–35
　　Baja Two-legged

Mabuya (see *Trachylepis*)
Mabuya, Brown 214–15
Mabuya multifasciata 214–15
Macrochelys temminckii 78–79
Malaclemys 95–97
　terrapin 95–97
　　centrata 95–96
　　macrospilota 96–97
　　pileata 97
　　rhizophorarum 97
　　tequesta 97
Monitor 237–41
　Asian water 240

Crocodile 239
Nile 239–40
Savanna 241

Neoseps (see Plestiodon reynoldsi)

Ophisaurus 145–50
  attentatus longicaudus 146–47
  compressus 147–48
  mimicus 148–49
  ventralis 149–50

Pachydactylus 165–66
  Bibroni 165–66
  turneri 166
Phelsuma 167–70
  madagascariensis grandis 167–68
  standingi 168–70
Phrynosoma cornutum 192–94
Phrynosomatidae 191–96
Plestiodon 215–26
  anthracinus pluvialis 215–17
  egregius 217–20
    egregius 219
    insularis 219
    lividus 219–20
    onocrepis 220
    similis 220
  fasciatus 221–22
  inexpectatus 223–24
  laticeps 224–25
  reynoldsi 225–26
Podocnemidae 110–12
Podocnemis unifilis 111–12
Polychrotidae 196–210
Pseudemys 98–103
  concinna 98–101
    concinna 98–100
    suwanniensis 100
  floridana 100–102
    floridana 100–101
    peninsularis 101–2
  nelson 102–3
Ptychozoon lionotum 179

Racerunner, Six-Lined 233–34
Rhineura floridana 134–35
Rhinoclemmys punctularia 108–9

Sauria 136–41
Sceloporus 194–96
  undulates 194–95
  woodi 195–96
Scincella laterale 226–28
Scincidae 212–29
Skink 212–29
  Broad-headed 224–25
  Coal, Southern 215–17
  Five-lined 220–25
    African (see Skink, Rainbow, African)
    Common 221–22
    Southeastern 223–24
  Ground 226–28
  Mole 217–20
    Blue-Tailed 219–20
    Cedar Key 219
    Florida Keys 219
    Northern 220
    Peninsula 220
  Ocellated Barrel 214
  Rainbow, African 228–29
  Sand, Florida 225–26
Slider 98, 103–5
  Red-eared 104–5
  Yellow-bellied 103–4
Sphaerodactylus 174–77
  argus argus 174–75
  elegans elegans 175–76
  notatus notatus 176–77
Squamata 132–41
Sternotherus 85–87
  minor 85–86
    minor 85–86
    peltifer 86
  odoratus 86–87

Tarentola 170–72
  annularis 170–71

mauritanicus 171–72
Tegu 235–37
  Black and White 236–37
  Golden 237
Teiidae 229–37
Terrapene 105–8
  carolina 105–8
    bauri 107–8
    carolina 106–7
    major 108
    triunguis 108
Terrapin 95–97
  Diamond-backed 95–97
  Carolina 95–96
  Florida East-Coast 97
  Mangrove 97
  Mississippi 97
  Ornate 96–97
Testudinidae 118–22
Tortoise 118–22
  African spur-thighed 119
  Gopher 120–22
Trachemys 98, 103–5
  scripta 103–5
    elegans 104–5
    scripta 103–4
Trachylepis quinquetaeniata 228–29
Trionychidae 112–18
Trionyx (see *Apalone*)
Tropiduridae 211–12
Tropidurus hispidus 211–12
Tupinambis 235–37
  merianae 236–37
  teguixin 237
Turtle
  Basking 87–109
  Box 105–8
    Eastern 106–7
    Florida 107–8
    Gulf Coast 108
    Three-toed 108
  Chicken 90–92

Eastern 91–92
Florida 92
Map 92–95
  Barbour's 93–94
  Escambia 94–95
Marine 67–74
Mud 79–87
  Eastern 83–84
  Florida 84
  Keys (see Striped)
  Striped 82–83
Musk 85–87
  Common 86–87
  Loggerhead 85–86
  Striped-necked 86
Painted, Southern 242–43
Ridley, Atlantic 72–73
River, Yellow-spotted Amazon 111–12
Sea 68–73
  Green 70–71
  Hawksbill, Atlantic 71–72
  Loggerhead 69–70
Snapping 75–79
  Alligator 78–79
  Common 77–78
  Florida 78
Soft-shelled 112–18
  Florida 114–16
  Smooth, Gulf Coast 116–17
  Spiny, Gulf Coast 117–18
Spotted 87–90
Wood, South American 108–9

Varanus 237–41
  exanthematicus 241
  niloticus 239–40
  salvadorii 239
  salvator 240

Whiptail 232–33, 234–35
  Giant 232–33
  Rainbow 234–35

R. D. Bartlett is a veteran herpetologist/herpetoculturist with more than 40 years' experience in writing, photographing, and educating people about reptiles and amphibians. He is the author of numerous books on the subject, including *Florida's Snakes: A Guide to Their Identification and Habits, Guide and Reference to the Amphibians of Eastern and Central North America (North of Mexico)*, and *Guide and Reference to the Amphibians of Western North America (North of Mexico) and Hawaii.*

Patricia P. Bartlett has coauthored many books with R. D. Bartlett, as well as writing *Dictionary of Sharks.* She was born in Atlanta, Georgia, but grew up chasing lizards in Albuquerque, New Mexico. She graduated from Colorado State University and moved to Florida to look for turtles and work for Ross Allen in Silver Springs. Pat has worked for Great Outdoors Publishing Company, for *Springfield* magazine, and for the Springfield Science Museum and was the first director of the Ft. Myers Historical Museum. Since moving to Gainesville she has worked as a science writer and as an Asian Studies coordinator. She maintains an avid interest in herpetology, entomology, and scientific illustration.